Moon Gate
DREAMS

A quest for Romance and Adventure
beyond the Moon Gate

by

George A. Barker, Jr.

ISBN 0-9657414-0-0

Library of Congress Catalog Card Number: 97-93223

Printed by • Maverick Publications, Inc.
P.O. Box 5007 • Bend, Oregon, 97708

Contents

Introduction

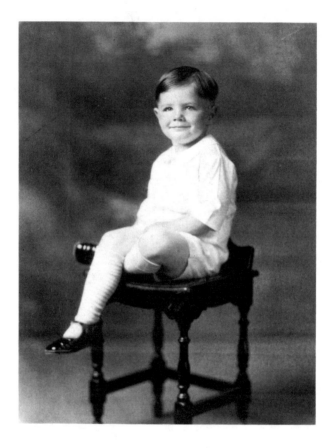

*"What a wee little part of a person's life are his acts and words.
His real life is led in his head, and is known to none but himself."*

- Mark Twain

This is an account of my seventy-one years, fifty-eight of them
with Spastic quadriplegia. It is how I recall events. Others may
recall them differently. Photos help tell my story.

This book is dedicated to Mary, my best friend

Thanks go to Peter Burchard, Jr. for proofreading and helping clarify the writing in parts of my story; to Ellen Pfeiffer for asking questions that made me realize I had missed important things; to Helga and Alfonso Medina for their encouragement and her computer skills; to Mike Frush who kept pushing me to call it done and get it published; to the myriads whose acts of selfless kindness have added much joy to my life; and to Whoever is in Charge for giving me a life long enough to let me finish it, with time left for more adventures.

Time changes names. Thus, Stanford Lane Hospital long ago moved out of San Francisco to the big campus at Stanford, and Pacific Medical Center built on its former site. Colorado State College of Education became University of Northern Colorado. San Francisco College for Women became Lone Mountain College, and then was absorbed by University of San Francisco. I have left them as they were at the time of my first encounter.

I have changed the names and appearances of a few minor actors in my life when I felt they might be embarrassed. I have tried to be fair.

I warn all readers of this book that desecrating it by using my experience as a standard for anyone else will cause their brains to rot and their teeth to fall out. Each of us is unique. No one benefits from stereotyping, including spastic quad-raplegics.

At left, me with Papa in Greeley; at right, Mama

Colorado, 1938-46

Chapter 1

Life is a series of little deaths out of which life always returns.

- Charles Feidelson, Jr.

A warm, green Sunday morning in August 1938, a month past my thirteenth birthday, I rode my new Iver-Johnson bicycle across the Colorado State College of Education campus to get a *Denver Post*. The beauty of the red sandstone buildings, the carefully tended grass and large trees usually made me feel euphoric, proud to be connected to the college. At Taylor's College Store I jumped off the bike, leaned it against the wall and bounded up the half-dozen steps into the homelike shop. Coyd Taylor turned and smiled to see me dart in.

Just before I reached out to pay him, a huge electric shock seemed to explode in my head and surge through my body. An intense feeling of dreadful sickness overwhelmed me, more terrible than anything I had ever experienced. I felt dazed, weak, and could barely keep from falling. I didn't even consider asking Coyd for help. All I could think of was concentrate, keep myself together, get home and lie down. Hands shaking uncontrollably, I threw the money on the counter, grabbed the paper and tore down the steps.

I managed somehow to get back on my bike. I made it back to our yard, leaned my bike against the house, called to Papa for help and collapsed on the lawn unconscious, in convulsions. The last thing I remember was Papa yelling "Stop it!" He thought I was kidding because I often acted as though I had some dreaded illness to tease him about his incessant concern about my health. I regained consciousness and found myself in my parents' bedroom, with its starched white curtains and fragrant carved brown camphor chest Mama bought in Shanghai. Papa, Mama, Uncle Kim and Dr. Barber, my pediatrician, stood gazing anxiously by the side of the bed. I recall being told I would have to go to the hospital and being carried to the car, but the rest of that day is a blank. I lapsed into a coma. When I emerged six weeks later, the leaves on the trees outside my window at Greeley General Hospital had turned bright autumn colors and were starting to fall.

That summer of 1938, I had savored the wild joy and immense sense of freedom of being on the threshold of adolescence and owning a bike. The euphoria of bike ownership was especially sweet to me because Papa had delayed it until my thirteenth birthday. He deemed it dangerous for children to be on the same roads with automobiles and was always fearful that some accident might befall me.

When I turned twelve, I wrote a contract stating I could purchase a bike on my next birthday, and Papa signed it. Before my thirteenth birthday, the Fourth of July, we went shopping. I took my savings of nineteen dollars from First National Bank of Greeley and Papa paid the rest.

Papa was a little above average height, heavyset, with a large head. My earliest memories are of him pulling me, in my little red wagon, around the campus of Colorado State College of Education campus with its red sandstone buildings, big shade trees and fish pond loaded with large golden carp. He would stop here and there to answer my myriad questions.

Papa served thirty-four years at the College as Professor of Geography and loved teaching with a passion. Before I was old enough to go to first grade, he often let me sit in the back of his classes, with the proviso that I be quiet. I loved his booming lecture voice, the roars of laughter from his huge classes, and felt proud of the respect everyone showed him.

When I was eight, Papa married a fellow teacher at the college, Ella Frances Hackman. My natural mother, Sybil McLean Barker, had died when I was only five months old. For eight years, a housekeeper Papa hired was my surrogate mother. Mrs. Gerwig, an older woman from the Ozarks, was hard-faced and rustic but kind-hearted. She imparted to me a kind of internal toughness that stood me in good stead in later years.

My step-mother had delicate features, blue eyes and soft brown hair, and trailed a faint fragrance of lavender or Devon violet. She became my mother in every sense of the word. I felt a need for more direction and this was the void she filled. She could be firm, almost unyielding, but was usually fair and thoughtful. She never raised her hand or voice but her tone could become steely, along with her posture, facial expression and eyes. If she said she would do something, she meant it, and she expected the same from me. I adored her. We were close friends for fifty-two years until she died.

Duty and Honor were deeply ingrained in her psyche. She agreed with her fellow Virginian, Robert E. Lee, who said, "Duty is the sublimest word in our language. You cannot do more, you should never wish to do less." Two of her brothers were West Point graduates and when I was ten, I had set my course to follow in their footsteps.

She coaxed fragrant roses, lilacs, iris, and peonies from the alkaline soil. I learned to water, mow and trim our extensive lawn, and keep it free of dandelions and crab grass, and that was my job. I also helped her clean house

Saturday mornings, dusting and running the vacuum cleaner. She was never satisfied unless I was doing the best work of which I was capable, and she tried to instill in me a sense of work pride.

For their honeymoon, Papa took her around the world on freight steamers. Every year until I was stricken they went to some exotic place—Bali, Turkey, the Peruvian Andes, Egypt, Japan and China. Before the advent of air travel, such places were beyond the ken of most.

Papa's special calling was to fascinate the largely rural students at the College with the peoples and ways of life of the rest of the world, which he did with a dramatic flair. He read and retained an enormous store of information. Mama said if she told him the house was burning down when he was totally immersed in a book or magazine, he would say, "That's interesting, Dear," and continue reading.

Local rumor held that he had sold his brain for a large sum to a rich foundation for research after he died. If he wasn't at home or in class, chances were he was at the College Library updating his lecture notes, which he usually scribbled in pencil on the back of a used envelope.

I stayed with the parents of my natural mother when Papa and Mama were on their wedding trip. To me, Grandma and Grandpa McLean's old farm on the outskirts of Greeley was an enchanted place—the big red brick house, the barn, the field mint under the long handled water pump, the flavor of the goats' milk, gathering eggs in the hen house, Grandpa in hip boots regulating the irrigation from the big ditch to the fields of tomatoes, squash and melons, Grandma's root cellar brimming with home-canned fruits and vegetables, root crops and sauer-kraut in huge crocks. Greeley was an irrigated oasis on the dry prairie of eastern Colorado.

When Papa and Mama were traveling, I often stayed with a school friend whose parents rented a cabin in the Rockies, about forty miles west of Greeley, on Fox Creek, upstream from Glen Haven village. I enjoyed horseback riding and hiking on mountain trails. We moved back in time to kerosene lamps, a wood stove, an outhouse and carrying buckets of icy, melted-snow, creek water for drinking, washing and cooking. At night, the stars twinkled brightly in the vast unsullied blackness. The rushing waters of the icy creek throwing itself on countless rocks and boulders and the sighing of the pines and aspens in the gentle breeze lulled us to sleep in an otherwise unbroken silence. We awoke each morning to the fragrance of yellow pine and smoke from the wood stove mingling with the smell of frying bacon, buckwheat pancakes and fresh-brewed coffee.

One of Mama's brothers, a tall, long-nosed man in his late twenties, lived with us for a while and attended the college to get his Masters Degree to become a high school history teacher. Uncle Kim did many of the things with me that Papa never had the time or inclination to do. He taught me how catch a ball, play chess, poker, solitaire, bridge, croquet and tennis, and toss horse-shoes. He played softball and kick-the-can with us neighborhood kids in the vacant lot behind our house.

I had a friend whose father managed a big seed company and we picked vegetables and melons fresh from the company's seed trial grounds in late summer and took them around door-to-door in big baskets on my friend's wagon. They were the cream of the crop and people were delighted to buy them. At Christmas, I sold evergreen wreaths door to door on commission for Mr. Sato, the Japanese florist, whose greenhouse was a humid heaven of fragrant flowers.

Greeley was surrounded with cattle ranches and feed lots. The cowboy mystique lived in our thoughts and dreams. Saturday afternoons I would go with one or two friends to a cowboy double-feature at the movies. The ideal of the solitary, self-contained cowhand by his campfire under the stars became one facet of my character by Saturday-afternoon osmosis.

Love of travel was another part of my character. I had it in my genes. When I was twelve, Mama and Papa took a freighter from New York through the Panama Canal to Columbia, Ecuador and Peru. They took me with them on the train as far as New York and left me with my Uncle Dave, a chemical engineer at Bell Laboratories, and my Aunt Emily. Uncle Dave was the elder brother of my natural mother. While Uncle Dave worked, Aunt Emily showed me about New York. She took me to all the big museums, and several times to my favorite, The American Museum of Natural History. At night, Uncle Dave joined us, and we went to the planetarium and Coney Island. We ate at the Automat and Caruso's Italian Restaurant, among many. A solid muscular man with a sly smile, Uncle Dave pioneered the touch tone phone and silicone chip miniaturization. He taught me how to fish and canoe in a private lake in New Jersey where he had a place. In his darkroom, he taught me the art of photography.

———

Another experience was going to Mexico City that Christmas. Mama and Papa and Kim and I drove in Kim's old car to Juarez and boarded the dusty, beat-up old steam train across the barren plain of Northern Mexico. Adobe and wood shacks, clothes drying in the dusty wind, serape-clad tortilla vendors and ragged children selling Chiclet gum seemed to be part of another world.

———

All the weeks I remained in the coma, Mama stayed by my side sleeping on a cot in my austere hospital room and going home only to eat and wash up.

Papa's first wife had died of bronchietasis, then my mother of tuberculosis. My situation was more than he could handle. When he wasn't teaching, he stayed home and drank scotch and water until he was numb. On weekends, Uncle Kim would come from Denver and try to get his mind off my plight.

Finally, one morning Dr. Barber told Mama he had asked Harry, the patient in the next room, what he had to eat for breakfast.

Harry hesitated, then shouted, "Bird seed!"

I had returned to consciousness and was listening to the doctor's story. I erupted in laughter. Mama and a couple of nurses turned in shocked surprise. The doctor gave a little choked cough, turned abruptly and left the room.

I had Western Equine Encephalitis, a mosquito-borne virus disease of the brain. Big, voracious genus Culex mosquitoes buzzed everywhere in the evening and were the vector of my disease. Mosquito bites during the summers were as unavoidable as dandelions and crabgrass in the lawn or icy sidewalks in winter. Citronella oil, the most popular repellent, seemed only to stimulate their appetites like a zesty barbecue sauce. A small epidemic of encephalitis erupted in northern Colorado that wet summer. I think of it as Destiny's Mosquito Bite because it changed the course of my life.

The virus ravaged my cerebral motor cortex, the switchboard that directs impulses from thought to individual muscles. Mine let the impulses flood through undirected. All my muscles moved when I wanted to move only one or two. At first, when I was still weak, I had a shaking palsy, but that soon changed to tension and muscle overflow.

I could not swallow, speak a word nor control a muscle, except to smile and frown. I became aware of my wasted body and protruding ribs. It reminded me of photos of starving people in National Geographic. Intermittently, I screamed and cried in pain, rage and utter frustration.

Communicating with me became an elaborate guessing game. Mama would ask me a question. I would smile for "Yes" and frown for "No." It was difficult and took a lot of time, but with practice we grew more adept and I was able to communicate without speech.

When the doctor allowed me to sit in a chair for a few minutes, I drooped limp as a rag doll. My head slumped forward until my chin rested on my chest. Strings of saliva drooled from my mouth.

Mama placed her hand on my shoulder, kissed my forehead and said with determination, "We're going to beat this thing." Papa looked like he had something in his eye and cleared his throat before he took the cue. "Yes, yes.

Don't worry. We'll beat this damn thing!" Papa wanted everyone not to worry, though he worried a lot himself.

I heard I had post-encephalitic Parkinson's. Then a Denver neurologist said I had spastic paralysis. The names meant nothing to me. No one told me how much I would be able to recover. I don't think anybody knew. The doctors told me I would have to relearn everything, like a baby, and it wouldn't be easy. Being an optimist and not afraid of hard work, I thought that in a month or two I'd be back to my old self.

I began physical therapy during my convalescence on the Boy's Ward atop Children's Hospital in Denver, an immaculately clean glass and brick Solarium. It took several months just to relearn swallowing and longer still to learn to chew. I was so ravenous in making up for time without solid food that an in-house physician told Mama I had a cast iron stomach that was a bottomless pit.

Nurses and orderlies helped me move about the ward in a heavy metal and wood wheelchair. My fellow patients were guys about my age with a wide range of serious disabilities, helped by a team of marvelously sensitive, upbeat nurses.

We boys chipped in together and persuaded a nurse to buy two dozen hot dogs, one for each of us, as a bedtime diversion from the nutritious but monotonous hospital fare. In the midst of our party the dreaded Night Supervisor marched onto the ward. Two dozen hot dogs swiftly and silently disappeared beneath the sheets. Not one boy smiled or acted as though anything was going on. As the elevator door closed behind the nurse, the ward erupted in a volcano of laughter.

In all the time before I had encephalitis, I had never met anyone severely disabled. Despite the seeming camaraderie, I did not quite know what to make of all these guys with wheelchairs, crutches and braces. I really liked only four or five. With arrogance born of ignorance, I thought I had an abundance of will power and that this was something I was passing through while most of them were locked into being crippled. Denial gave me time to avoid the trauma of truth until my mind could accept reality.

A few days before Christmas, the hospital released me. As Uncle Kim's car drew up in front of our home, eight of my friends, waiting in the December cold with band instruments in hand, broke into a spirited, if off-key, rendition of "Hail, Hail, the Gang's All Here." I felt gut-wrenchingly embarrassed being unable to talk, but managed to smile and lift one arm in an attempted wave before Uncle Kim carried me into the house.

Familiar surroundings, the warmth of family, the festive table, made all past Christmases pale. Presents were piled under the tree, on a card table and chairs, all over our large living room. Many were from people who knew me from my selling vegetables and melons and evergreen wreaths.

I quickly regained strength, but due to poor coordination and involuntary muscle movements could not walk without help. I was unable to dress or feed myself anything that could not be firmly stuck on a fork. I learned to drink through straws and to get up and down out of chairs and walk on my knees. I privately began to wonder if I would ever completely be my old self again.

Opposing sets of my muscles pulled against one another, making them very strong, but this was not helpful. My hands were powerful, but it was an embarrassment, because I could not shake hands without a vise-like grip. Like a baby, I had the reflex of forced grasping. I couldn't let go. I broke a couple of tea glasses, once cutting myself, and several times grabbed the tablecloth and wound up with a lap full of dishes and food. More than once, an old typewriter I tried to use came crashing into my lap.

Mama assisted me in walking, pulling me up by an arm and walking beside me like soldiers marching abreast. She had practiced a bit at Children's Hospital. My body would pitch and reel, but she was strong. It was good exercise.

A neighbor loaned us a wheelchair. We kept it on the back porch because moving it around among the antique heirloom furniture was awkward in a small house. The wheelchair became a symbol of giving up, so we never used it. We told each other that before long I would be walking again.

A friend of Mama's had given her a Ouija board, a game that had the letters of the alphabet written large and was supposed to put players in direct communication with departed spirits. I used it instead to communicate with my parents and friends.

I was desperately self-conscious. My speech was strained, I couldn't enunciate, and it was impossible for most people to understand me. I learned to talk using my eyes and facial expressions. The greater the emotional content of what I was trying to say, the more difficult it became. My whole body started moving, my facial muscles contorted, my tongue got stiff and my throat tightened as I squeezed the words out in a harsh, strained voice. On rare occasions, I exploded in an adrenaline rush, my face turned vivid red, I shook with palsy and anger, and bellowed inarticulately.

One of Papa's colleagues gave me training in phonics, lip movement and tongue placement. He tried to help me lengthen my breath span by having me count as far as I could in one breath. I quickly learned to make sounds but when struggling to make words tended to tighten and squeeze them out like toothpaste. The results were and still are difficult to understand.

He was the first of many therapists to tell me to relax and not try so hard. It was easy for people to say that. But I had been raised to give things my best effort. So I worked at relaxing when I talked, and tried very hard not to try so hard. The harder I worked, the more squeezed my speech was and the more tense and frustrated I became.

Before long, my friends were coming to see me every day. The gang was mostly sons of college personnel. Jack West was the son of Papa's assistant professor, Deane Carson of the Registrar, and Bud Williams of the heating engineer. Jimmy Newlon's dad was the maker of the local potato chip, Spud Chips. They all grew to be six-footers, except for me at five three.

They called themselves the "PB Boys," for "Probation Boys." By today's standards, their misdeeds were minor. The worst was to throw a rock through the window of a passing train. It landed in the lap of a Union Pacific detective, who surmised the perpetrators would return to the scene of their crime the next day. He was waiting for them.

Only my cerebral palsy kept me from trouble with the law. The local judge tried to break up our group on the grounds that we had "the gang spirit." For a time he laid down the law that only one of the PB Boys could visit me at a time, and they were not to be together at any time outside of school.

My speech improved enough for the guys to understand most of what I said without the Ouija board. When my folks changed our heating system from coal to natural gas, I persuaded them to convert the old basement furnace area to a large recreation room with asphalt tile floors and Celotex walls and ceiling. This became the hangout for the Barker's Basement Gang.

Before I had encephalitis, I felt I was a leader, that greatness dwelt within. Every year my peers elected me class president and I just naturally expected to get top grades. When you grow up thinking that way, it becomes part of your subconscious. I still received respect.

The guys came directly from school, went home for dinner, and returned to stay till bedtime. On weekends, three or four usually came after dinner and stayed all night, using an army cot and making makeshift beds with canvas director's chairs. I stayed down there with them, giving Mama a little rest, and letting me continue growing up with my pals.

The loyalty of these friends helped keep me on an even keel mentally. We made a darkroom out of the old coal room and developed, printed and enlarged numerous photographs. We made wine from cherries swiped from a neighbor's tree and got drunk unbeknownst to our elders. We wrestled and roughhoused on gym mats, and I was an active participant. We practiced hypnotism, which I had studied. We groomed and trained my purebred buff-colored cocker spaniel, Dudley, entered him in the Colorado Kennel Club's show in Denver and won a second prize red ribbon in the Novice class.

Bud found a Model T Ford in a vacant lot overgrown with weeds and negotiated to buy it for twenty bucks. Five of us chipped in and we found someone to tow it over to our driveway, since my folks didn't have a car. Bud got a manual and the guys took the motor apart, ground the valves, put in new piston rings, oiled it, greased it and did whatever else needed doing. We enameled the body royal blue and the fenders Chinese scarlet.

The day arrived when the guys cranked it up and it exploded in a symphony of loud regular bangs and the brightly colored body actually jumped up and down on the axles with each bang. The engine ran, even if noisily. We doubled up with laughter and soon the whole neighborhood was laughing and applauding at the spectacle of the bouncing, endlessly exploding little car.

We took it out to the vacant lot in back of my folks' place after the guys had tuned it down a little and they took turns driving it around. But the car had no license and they were too young to get driver's licenses, so we sold it.

A year after I recovered from the encephalitis, Papa decided it was time for us to take a trip. He offered a student an all-expense-paid adventure to drive Mama, me and him as far north in Alberta, Canada, as the road went. Papa was a walking encyclopedia of geology, botany, history and poetry which he shared with contagious enthusiasm.

He handed me the maps, put me in the front seat and told me, "You are the navigator." I think this expedition was designed in part to get me out of my painful self-consciousness about requiring help with practically everything. People along the way were generally quite thoughtful and understanding and made no fuss over me. Afterwards, I was still uneasy with strangers but better than before.

After two years trying to improve without much success, a local surgeon who had a daughter with what was then called "spastic paralysis" told my parents of a renowned specialist in Baltimore, Maryland. Uncle Kim drove us cross-country to consult with him. Papa made an expedition of it, taking us to Chicago, where he had been a student at the University, to Quebec, around the Gaspe Peninsula, through the Maritime Provinces and south to New England and New York, to Baltimore.

Doctor Winthrop M. Phelps, a tall, lean, soft spoken man with an aristocratic air, had been Head of Orthopedic Surgery at Yale Medical School, but quit to devote his life to the study of cerebral palsy. He taught at Johns Hopkins, had a private practice and directed a live-in school for cerebral palsied children and young adults.

He lived in a house like many of the old houses in Baltimore, red brick with white front steps. His office, lined with natural wood, was downstairs. Occasionally I would see his daughter, a gorgeous slender blonde in her early teens, coming through to the upstairs where they lived, and I would admire her from very far away.

The doctor explained that I still had some of my old reflexes. To demonstrate, he suddenly tossed me a baseball and I caught it. After reading my medical records, examining my muscles and reflexes, and talking to my parents and me together and separately, he told us I was doing as well as could be expected.

"George has the kind of cerebral palsy known as tension athetosis, slightly different from spastic palsy and shaking athetosis. There is no cure, but the condition is treatable and can be modified. George is not an invalid and should never be treated like one."

He was the first doctor to tell me directly that I couldn't expect to recover fully. I had begun to suspect as much after the first year went by and my progress slowed. I had started to have a life of my own and, while not ideal, it was good. He also told me that encephalitis had probably caused me to be three or four inches shorter than I would have been otherwise. Five foot three and 125 pounds suited me fine, and that's about where I have stayed. When I stood up, I seemed taller because I had to walk on both toes to compensate for my shortened left Achilles tendon which had contracted while I was in the coma.

He said my progress would have to be measured by small accomplishments. He approved of letting me do everything I could without help. This meant feeding myself everything I could, however messily, walking with assistance or crawling on my knees, rather than depending on a wheelchair. I rarely used a wheelchair until I was thirty-five and was fifty-eight before I used one inside the house.

Doctor Phelps wanted me to stay on and learn relaxation exercises to practice daily. He said we must devise a schedule for most of the hours in my waking day and live by it, and was insistent that I continue with my education without delay. My folks hired tutors for me. Since the college was basically a teacher training school, Papa had no problem finding three bright, young, enthusiastic male graduate students to tutor me in their chosen fields. I loved being tutored and did three years' school work in one, which put me even with my old class.

The guys in the gang wanted me back in school, although I could not walk three feet or even stand alone or talk so most people could understand. I couldn't write either. My folks talked to the Principal of College High and he said I could come back, especially since I had scored well on the standardized tests my tutors had given me, hitting the 99.7th percentile in algebra.

Papa hired a college student to drive me back and forth to school. For the next two years, one or two of the guys would come to my house in the morning, help me into the car and ride with me. With one of them on each arm, half lifting, half balancing, we tore the length of Kepner Hall and up and down several flights of stairs. Most of the time they just grabbed me and ran. By the time we reached class I was panting and perspiring, my feet kicking several steps behind.

As my friends grew into young manhood, they began the selection and pairing process. I found myself a loner in a going-steady world. Girls had an almost mystic aura, heartbreakingly lovely and exciting. Some in my class became close friends. Several confided in me details of their sex lives, perhaps because they felt I was non-threatening. Fear of losing them as buddies made me timid about trying to kiss, much less go farther.

One sweet blond friend asked me if I could "do it." With great bravado I said, "Sure," and let the matter drop. I wasn't sure what "doing it" required in terms of physical ability. My spastic speech with its strange, strained quality, my grasping hands, and uncontrollable facial contortions made approaching a girl seem almost impossible. Yet, I felt a lover lived inside, begging to be released. I sought solace in romantic daydreams. If I received a grain of sand for every sexual fantasy, my life would be a small Sahara.

In high school, some of my friends drove to the edge of town to Doris Bly's Tavern on Friday nights and took me along. Doris's daughter, Barbara Bly, was our classmate and, although we were under age, Doris thought we were responsible enough not to get into trouble. Usually we drank beer. I found that I had a good capacity for alcohol and could drink double shots of straight bar whiskey through a straw. Alcohol relaxed me physically and made me less inhibited around the girls.

The evening of our high school commencement in 1943, I was surprised and elated when the College President, Dr. George W. Fraiser, after handing out the diplomas, came down into the audience where I was sitting in the front row, to present me with a four-year scholarship to the Colorado State College of Education for "brilliant scholarship despite many handicaps." The applause seemed to go on and on, while my friends slapped my shoulders and I sat there dazed with a happy grin.

Afterward, some of my buddies drove their girlfriends and me up the narrow road between the steep red sandstone walls of the Big Thompson Canyon to a rendezvous near Estes Park. In a grove of yellow pines by the rushing waters of the Big Thompson River, they built a small fire under the stars and we roasted hot dogs on sticks and drank whiskey mixed with the icy snow melt of the river. Flickering light from the fire licked the loose-skirted thighs of the girls as they squatted close to its warmth. It was a bittersweet night for me. I was happy about the scholarship, but at that moment I would have sold my soul or done any desperate thing to have a warm, cuddly lovely with whom I could share the pleasures and mutual affection my friends were enjoying.

The U.S. was in the midst of World War II. The guys left immediately for their service assignments. I was sorry to see them go, but everyone was caught up in winning the war.

Mr. Ley, a family friend and the local Chevrolet dealer, found a low mileage 1923 Chevy in excellent running condition. I named it Vodka because it had the power to go ninety miles an hour, which we found out when the police pulled my buddy and me over. Thankfully, we were on a road out in the middle of nowhere, and the officer was more amused than offended and let us go with a warning to have our speedometer checked. Charles Hambrick drove me to the campus and "dragged" me around from class to class for the next three years. Charlie was a charming guy with a soft Oklahoma drawl, the son of our greatly beloved sixth grade teacher and brother of the beautiful, demure and gifted artist, Jo Ann, whom all the boys had a crush on. He had a punctured eardrum and was ineligible for military service. A year younger and a year behind me in school, he was tall and strong enough to take me anywhere on his arm without help, even up six long flights of steep stairs to the natural science classes on the third floor of Cranford Hall. My legs turned to jelly on those staircases and I would collapse into the nearest empty desk, as winded and sweating as an average person who had run a mile.

Several times Charlie and I invited girls to go with us to Denver to see big-time stage productions like *Winged Victory*, *Gaslight* and *Porgy and Bess*. On our way back to Greeley in Vodka one night, we and the girls got caught in a blinding late spring blizzard. At one a.m. we gave up and sought sanctuary at the jail in the small hamlet of Brighton. We spent the night trying to sleep on two hard tables in the jail office till snowplows arrived in the morning.

Charlie came back from a summer working at a munitions factory in Baraboo, Wisconsin, with a gift for me—a chunk of hard, black, greasy solid rocket fuel. We decided it would be most spectacular if we set it off in the Big Thompson Canyon where we would be surrounded on all sides by steep rock cliffs. Charlie lit the smooth, cylindrical chunk of fuel with a cigarette lighter. It took off in a roaring whoosh and a giant ball of incandescent fire, bouncing back and forth off the sides of the canyon, a display lasting not more than fifteen seconds. We watched in awed silence.

To me, science represented gemlike purity of thought and logic and I made it my college major. I felt that a strong grasp of science was probably the best preparation for life. Thinking in terms of light years, geologic eons and the slow pace of evolutionary change tends to make our trifling daily dramas pale into insignificance.

I had not yet decided what I wanted to do. Writing was something I thought I could learn and enjoy. I got my only college "C" in Intermediate Composition, but thought it was due to my skipping Beginning Composition out of deference to Papa, who had a low opinion of its teacher. I figured the main thing required to be a writer was practice, practice and more practice. I was beginning to type a little on a factory rebuilt IBM Electromatic typewriter my parents had bought for me.

I grew up fascinated by China. As a small boy I was befriended by a Mr. Yuen, a student from provincial China. He had been chosen to come to America and learn our ways of teaching. He was a small, delicate looking man with exquisite manners who sometimes wore the old style, high-collared gown of a Chinese gentleman. He liked my Dad and often visited, and brought little gifts, such as jasmine tea and dried lychee fruit. He returned to China before the Japanese bombed Shanghai. Greeley people tried to get in touch with him after the war but with no success.

I made several friends among the new students at the college. One of them, Edith Kwong, was the daughter of the Chinese consul in San Francisco and had grown up in Shanghai. She usually wore the traditional Mandarin collar and slit skirt dresses exposing a bit of thigh, which I thought exquisite. She told me many stories about Shanghai and life there. I was fascinated by China, the people and their culture, and loved Edi for her beautiful long-lashed almond eyes and her delicate bone structure and the graceful way she moved and did everything. She was always a welcome visitor at our house, and we frequently studied together. Sometimes she mentioned the San Francisco College for Women where she had studied before coming to Greeley.

For three years I had to study hard and race to get my Bachelor's degree. At the end of that time, Papa would be sixty-seven, the mandatory retirement age at the college, and Mama would have to return to teaching. I wanted to get away from Greeley where half the people had known me as a youngster. If we stayed, they would remember me as a promising lad. I didn't wish to be a "has been" at twenty-one. I wanted a clean break with my past and to make a fresh start.

In 1945, a week after Japan surrendered and gasoline rationing was lifted, my friend Jimmy Newlon, his two brothers and I, drove to Los Angeles in their father's old Plymouth. Then we drove north to San Francisco and over the

Golden Gate Bridge to the little village of Larkspur in Marin County where we spent several days visiting my Aunt Martha and driving around. I fell in love with the redwoods and abundance of plant life and the village atmosphere of Marin County. I felt this was the place I wanted to live someday. While we were there, I phoned Edith Kwong and she invited us to a Chinese meal in San Francisco.

When my parents were first married, a serious young man named James Michener had been hired to replace Mama as Supervisor of Student Teachers in the College Secondary School. By the time I graduated from the College, he was an editor for Macmillan Company in New York and was writing his Pulitzer Prize winning *Tales of the South Pacific*.

In the spring of 1946, Mama wrote Jim and received a contract from Macmillan Company to write a sixth-grade geography reader about the countries of Southeast Asia, from Afghanistan through India, Burma, Thailand, Malaysia and Indonesia. Mama was so busy preparing to teach, cooking family meals, doing everything my physically inept father was unable to help with, it became my job to take on the major part of the geography reader.

Papa tried to help but his mind wasn't organized for it. The spoken word was his forte. In his late sixties, the first signs of the arteriosclerosis that would lead to his death were beginning to give him difficulty writing a detailed, logical paragraph. He took impending retirement with sorrow and disbelief.

Edith had spoken so highly of San Francisco College for Women, I suggested Mama apply there for a teaching position. It sounded like the kind of genteel, academically sound school she would like. After she had applied for the job, several people told her the Sacred Heart nuns rarely hired teachers outside the Catholic faith and we had almost resigned ourselves to a college in rural Kansas. Then one glorious morning in May, a telegram came with a job offer from San Francisco. My parents took the train to California to investigate the offer and look for a place to live. Mama accepted the job at San Francisco College for Women and they bought an old house in Kentfield, Marin County, two miles from where my aunt had lived in Larkspur.

I stayed home with one of my high school buddies and started typing the book. I began with Burma. The preeminent religion in Burma is Buddhism. In the course of my research I became engrossed in the teachings of the Enlightened One. Buddhist philosophy seemed so neat, so logical, and so perfectly fitted to my situation. All life is suffering. The source of suffering is craving and attachment. By taking a detached view of life, one can achieve freedom from suffering. I embraced the philosophy for a time.

Occupational therapy, Stanford Hospital, 1952.

Me and Bud, early 1950's.

Above: Barker Manor from the road.

Below left: Papa in the 30's. Below right: My passport photo, 1954.

Wino in the Woods

Chapter 2

A Book of Verses underneath the Bough,
A Jug of Wine, a Loaf of Bread—and Thou
Beside me, singing in the Wilderness—
Oh, Wilderness were Paradise enow!

- The Rubaiyat of Omar Khayyam
Edward Fitzgerald version

After the war, Bud, my closest friend from the old gang, was discharged from the Navy Seabees after serving most of his time in the Admiralty Islands off New Guinea. He spent two months on his uncle's turkey ranch near San Diego, then came back to Greeley. I asked him how he would like to drive to California with Mama and me, stay with us for a year and go to college in Marin County. Mama would be busy teaching school, working on the book and taking care of the house. Bud could relieve her of most of the job of taking care of me. And we could enjoy each other's company.

The idea sounded good to Bud. He found Colorado harsh and barren after the South Pacific. The first of August, 1946, we piled into our new black Chevrolet sedan with Dudley, my cocker spaniel, and headed over the Rockies, across Utah and Nevada, over the Sierra and across California to Marin County. Papa followed by train after summer school was finished.

As we drove our new little Chevy up the driveway in Kentfield, I was stunned to see the house my parents had bought. Mama had told me it needed repair, but this was ridiculous! The large brown-shingled house was overgrown with great prickly mounds of wild blackberry vines, climbing roses, ivy and weeds. Built about 1898 as a summer house for San Franciscans, its shingles were now bleached and curled by the sun. The boxed-in staircase in front was falling away, and the painted gray canvas-covered floor of the porch, stretching around two sides of the house, was broken, peeling and littered with discarded furniture. Redwood varnish stain on the plasterboard interior walls gave us the feeling we were entering a bat cave.

The large garden had been landscaped artistically, but had reverted to rain forest strangled in a gigantic blackberry patch. Two tall Washington palms and a Canary Island date palm were side by side with a Norway spruce, a large

Southern magnolia, two large acacias, a small olive, a couple of holly trees, a hawthorn, two apples, an orange and a quince. The property sat in a small valley surrounded by hills heavily wooded with California live oak, bay trees, madrone, redwood and eucalyptus.

Marin's lush natural beauty captivated Papa, as it had me the year before. He was in his element. The botanical names of the trees in the garden rolled off his tongue.

To Mama, a house reflected its owner's personality and she had an emotional investment in it. To Papa, it was a mere utilitarian shelter for the body that freed the mind for other pursuits. As Mama spent several thousand dollars refurbishing the wreck, Papa's loud lecture voice reverberated from the surrounding hills in mock desperation, "Onward! Onward! Into the abyss!" Bud dubbed our refurbished home "Barker Manor," and the title stuck.

Papa joined the San Anselmo Rotary Club, taught a class at the Marin Junior College and tried teaching at San Quentin Prison. At the prison he felt restricted by regulations forbidding him to make friends with his students and soon quit. He walked to the post office every day and enjoyed the seasonal changes and friendly people along the way.

Most of that first year in Kentfield, I spent in the Southeast Asia of my mind. I perspired profusely and my muscles ached as I wrote my way out of Burma, across Thailand and island-hopped about Indonesia. My typing was agonizingly slow. One record day, I produced two and a half pages of double-spaced rough draft manuscript.

The area from Afghanistan through India to Indonesia was in a state of violent flux. In U.S. schools, geography gave way to softer subjects related to everyday urban living. Editor James Michener seemed happy with our labors and we were paid under the terms of the contract, but the book was never published. Mama wrote to Michener that I had written a large part of the manuscript. He replied that he remembered me from his Greeley days as a capable youngster.

As Mama became more proficient at driving from her daily commute to San Francisco, she liked to take trips in the car. We started taking day trips to Sonoma, Monterey and Carmel. Her late life love of driving slowly expanded to driving to Oregon, Washington and Vancouver, Canada. We made several trips to Greeley. She covered most of the U.S. and a good part of western Canada. Later on, she and I traveled the highways of western Europe, England, Scotland and Wales, and when she was over seventy, New Zealand. On all these trips, everything was lovely, except sometimes my bladder would be under pressure because Mama had old-fashioned ideas about gentlemen's and ladies' rooms. And never the twain shall meet.

As a college student I had subscribed to the English language version of the *Shanghai Evening Post and Mercury*, which was published in exile in New York during the war when the Japanese were occupying China. I found the paper intriguing. I dreamed of getting a writing job in Shanghai. With inexpensive, dependable Chinese help, I envisioned myself living like royalty with a beautiful Chinese lover. I wrote a letter to Cornelius V. Starr, the publisher of the paper, telling him of my love of China and my feeling that I had great potential as a writer, as well as about my disability. He replied that I had an impressive style and he would keep me in mind. I thought that was probably the last I would hear from him.

One spring day, Mama, Papa, Bud and I were finishing lunch on our newly-screened porch when a Porsche pulled up our driveway. A plump man and two women got out. The man introduced himself as Randall Gould, editor of the *Shanghai Evening Post and Mercury*, in the U.S. for a brief visit. Cornelius Starr was interested enough in my writing to ask him to come see me. I thought he had come to look me over for possible future reference.

He said the Chinese had lost faith in Chiang Kai-Shek and it was probably only a matter of time until the Communists took over. Corruption was rife. Before inflation, a dollar would buy three yuan, but now on the black market it would buy 25,000. He brought newspapers showing a loaf of bread or a box of pencils costing thousands of yuan. This was no time to go to China, he said.

I could tell he was not very impressed with me, and later learned he doubted I could handle newspaper work. He had great difficulty understanding my speech. He had prepared for his journalistic career by learning shorthand in business school, then majoring in journalism at the University of Minnesota. He could type ninety words a minute. I couldn't talk right, couldn't write longhand, except to scrawl my name which took several minutes, or type more than six words a minute when I was in top form. I never expected to see him again.

In high school, I started writing verse for my own pleasure, but didn't show it to anyone. I thought of being a professional poet until I learned how little appreciated and poorly paid they were. But I continued writing verse because it gave my spirit a lift. In 1949 William Rose Benet published a piece of my blank verse in his column in *Saturday Review of Literature*.

Rain
Hungry Hopi child
Huddles in his pueblo
Sobbing silently
About his empty stomach.

His father dances
Clutching a rattlesnake
Between white teeth
Humbly imploring
Rain.

A Texas tenant farmer
Watches his wheat
Droop and die
For want of water.
He sifts a dusty handful
Of soil
Through work worn fingers,
Humbly imploring
Rain.

A doe mule deer
Fawn by her side,
Nuzzles a water hole
With crusted nose.
Lifting her head
Stares dull-eyed
At cloudless skies,
Humbly imploring
Rain.

The *Review* didn't pay me, but when my high school and college literature teachers, who had collaborated on a widely used junior high literature text, saw my poem, they included it in their book and paid me fifty dollars. I was especially glad to have done something of which Papa could be proud. He had great faith in my ability to write and now his health was failing fast.

His decline began with swollen ankles. He had known for several years that he had high blood pressure. Now he went to a doctor in Mill Valley where he learned he had a tired heart. The doctor put him on digitalis. Then came the crowning blow. The small blood vessels in his eyes began to rupture, and he was no longer able to read. He had been happy in Marin but now everything seemed to be against him. He died in December, 1948. Mama took his body back to Greeley where he was buried next to my natural mother.

I got my first job as a book reviewer for the *San Francisco Chronicle* by writing to Joseph Henry Jackson, the *Chronicle*'s literary critic. I was twenty-four and without experience beyond taking a journalism class and having a few short articles and an editorial published in the college newspaper in Greeley.

Mama's job as Supervisor of Student Teachers at San Francisco College for Women took her to schools all over the city, so it was not difficult for her to deliver reviews and pick up books for me once a week at the *Chronicle* offices at Fifth and Mission Streets.

My first review was an Andrew Jackson biography. It was only an inch and a half long with my initials in tiny print at the bottom. Within a year, I sometimes had the lead review on Sunday, over half a tabloid page, with an illustration and full by-line. I reviewed three or four books a week for about five years. This was heady stuff for a small-town boy from the plains of Northern Colorado.

Bud stayed with us while he attended College of Marin for one school year. He and I were drinking quite a bit. He declared, "I'll have to quit college or drinking." He graduated from rye whiskey to Christian Brothers brandy, but never from College of Marin. With my parents unwilling to pour money into my drinking glass, I drank fortified wine. We got stuporous on weekend nights.

Bud was fun. He used to bring weeds for my mother and me to cook. We cooked and ate pig weed, which was so-so. He gained a love of botany from his year in college. He read a lot and had a fondness for philosophy. He kidded me about my Oedipus complex.

During the summer he went back to San Diego to help his uncle on the turkey ranch. Back in Marin, he lived at Ross Hospital where he worked as a janitor. He embraced alcohol with uninhibited passion. He came to visit me often and we drank together.

After two years, Bud went north to Lake County to work on a pear ranch. After he became a pear orchardist, the only times I saw him were when he came down for a few days visit, about four times a year. Life became lonely for me. Bud married, returned to Marin, bought a house in San Rafael and worked for a manufacturer of fiberglass plastics. He quit drinking, except for a large glass of table wine before bed. He stopped by the house for a visit every Friday afternoon after work.

Mama made my lunch, cutting it into bite-size pieces that I could handle with a fork and putting straws in my glasses of coffee and sherry. I still had to chase food around my plate and aim painstakingly at my wide-open mouth. Because I couldn't trust my hand not to knock over a glass, I had to lean over and grab the straw with my lips.

Everything I did was time-consuming. On my old IBM electric typewriter I turned out three or four words a minute, XXX'ing out mistakes. I could get up and down from chairs and move about on my callused knees, but every time I had to pee, it took twenty minutes to go to the bathroom and back.

Being alone was not so bad. Barker Manor fairly overwhelmed the senses with quiet. I lived in the world of ideas through the books I read and reviewed. The large glass of sherry beside the typewriter gave wings to the imagination and enhanced my sense of power. My writing was more cocksure and strident than it is today.

Most of my favorite American writers—Hemingway, Faulkner, Steinbeck, Jack London, Tennessee Williams, Thomas Wolfe—were two-fisted drinkers. My admiration for them made it easy for me to follow a tradition on Papa's side of my family. I don't think Papa was an alcoholic, but he was a problem drinker on weekends. Back in Colorado, he would take the bus to Denver every Friday to teach an extension class and bring back exotic foods and two fifths of Scotch. By the time he returned home, he was half-loaded. Sometimes he became cruelly sarcastic. Mama hated the idea that I might follow in the footsteps of the well-lubricated side of the family.

Papa had asked Dr. Phelps about alcohol as a treatment for my tension, saying it worked for him. The doctor had said yes, alcohol was relaxing, but it lasted only for a while, then left one more tense and nervous and worse than before. As I became older and more independent, I found this to be an exchange I was willing to accept. I bartered relaxed days for more and more nights of tension and little sleep. Around three o'clock in the morning, I secretly endured many a dark night of the soul, rocking back and forth, sitting on the edge of my bed trying to keep my stomach down and fighting the burning sand in the desert of my spirit.

My spirit was being assaulted from another side also. Faith healers saw me as a challenge and I got more than my share of them. I told them I didn't have that much faith, but they insisted I didn't realize how much I believed. They tried to make me feel I was missing being cured out of pure stubbornness and worked on my feelings until I felt guilty. So I promised to read Mary Baker Eddy's *Key to the Scriptures*. I looked at it and tried to read it, but it was so boring. I was a young healthy guy in the prime of life and wasn't much interested in the esoteric teachings of an old lady in Massachusetts.

I still felt I could improve with professional help, and began looking for some kind of physical therapy. Vocational Rehabilitation sent me to a psychiatrist for an evaluation. He asked me what I wanted to do more than anything. I said, "I'd like to walk." He suggested I have a complete evaluation and had me admitted to the neuro-psychiatric ward at Stanford Lane Hospital, Stanford's teaching hospital in San Francisco at that time.

I didn't realize what I was getting into. It was the locked ward and most of the patients were mentally disturbed and some were in padded rooms. It was pretty quiet during the day but at night all hell broke loose with people screaming and yelling, and having hallucinations of rats and snakes and spiders. A lady across the hall kept complaining about the man in her bed and said that a doctor told her to close her eyes and hold out her hand, then placed his penis in it and asked her what it was.

The doctors wanted me to try an experimental drug, a plant-derived poison Amazonian Indians put on their arrows and blow darts to disable or kill prey. It worked by relaxing an animal's heart and lung muscles. I had read of *curare* and was eager to see if it would relieve my tension.

It worked too well. One injection and I was so relaxed I could scarcely move. It was like turning off a light switch. They had to watch me to be sure I didn't stop breathing. They tried tinkering with the dosage and giving it in peanut oil solution to slow down its effects and make it last longer but even then I went limp as a rag doll.

A small, sturdy-looking, brunette physical therapist with a Boston accent evaluated me, took me down to the Physical Therapy Department and gave me some exercise. Thus, I became acquainted with Beth Phillips, Stanford's Supervisor of Student Physical Therapists, and she introduced me to Dr. William Northway, Professor of Physical Medicine, a fast-moving, serious, gray-haired man. They let me come for physical therapy twice a week for five years and stay all day while Mama visited schools as part of her job supervising student teachers. Their generosity puzzled me a little. When I asked, they sloughed it off, saying they would charge if I insisted, and that I was the Department mascot. I took this to mean they felt their students could learn from observing me.

Beth asked if alcohol helped me relax. "It sure does," I grinned. She was interested to see how it affected me. The next time I went I drank about twelve ounces of sherry. As I exercised, I felt released from the chains of immobilizing tension. The therapists commented on how much more relaxed and able to move I was. Dr. Northway, a strong Methodist, said "It's against my religion but it works for you so I can't object."

After that, I always drank twelve ounces of sherry before therapy. Dr. Northway decided I should be evaluated with and without my wine. So I took it in a bottle in my brown lunch bag, and a group of doctors observed as I took range of motion exercises and tried to walk without wine and later with it. I did everything much better with wine. Now I felt wine had the seal of approval of the Stanford Medical Faculty!

Beth loaned me medical literature, including articles by my old doctor in Baltimore, Dr. Phelps. She shared details she thought would interest me on the background of some of the other patients. I learned a lot and was flattered that she took me into her confidence. Several years after I met her, she moved from Palo Alto to Mill Valley, only a few miles from Barker Manor. She took me out now and then for a movie or a couple of drinks. I found her bright and attractive, and pestered her to let me kiss her. She told me in every way she could that she wasn't interested. Finally, she introduced a large masculine woman in a lumberjack shirt as her roommate and later, when she moved to Marquette University in Milwaukee, her friend went with her.

Bud said my motto should be *Semper Gallo*. Gallo Cream Sherry gave me the most alcohol for the money, and I ordered a case of six half gallons every ten or twelve days from Grise's Liquor Store.

Beth tried to enable me to handle crutches by fabricating some that were weighted down with a great load of lead, to keep my arms straight as I lifted on them. One of my biggest obstacles to walking is a permanent contraction of my left Achilles tendon which points the foot down and puts me on my toe. Surgery could lengthen the tendon but not the nerves that serve it. So she then attempted to keep me on both toes using cowboy boots. Finally, she made my right foot level with the left using a six-inch-high elevated shoe.

The built-up shoe made it possible for me to walk, very precariously, on my own. I concentrated like an Olympic athlete, mentally rehearsing every move over and over and shutting out all distractions. It also required alcohol. Doctor Northway told me the fact I was able to walk at all was a feat. After I fell at home and bashed my head against the corner of the bathroom cabinet, gashing my forehead and spilling pools of blood on the floor, Beth made me get a football helmet.

Some mornings, walking in from the Emergency Entrance parking area with Mama beside me but not touching me, I would be surprised by the sight of Dr. Northway arriving at the same time. Glad to see him, I would lose my concentration. He would come running to catch me if needed. I think it made him nervous. Eventually he recommended that I give up trying to walk alone. Anyway, it was not of much use if I had to get semi-drunk to do it.

Doctor Northway was Acting Dean of Stanford Medical School at the time. He said I had good insight into my condition and encouraged me to apply to the school. I had taken all the biology, physiology and chemistry available at Greeley, which could be counted as Premed. I had always dreamed of being a doctor.

Bud drove me to San Francisco and helped me into the classroom for the entry test to the med school. I think that in those days to ask the school for special favors would have disqualified me. There was no one to assist me. I had imbibed a generous quantity of sherry beforehand to help me control the pencil. I worked with great difficulty to mark the test sheet with my spastic fingers. I knew I was too slow. It was not terribly difficult, but I wasn't half done when time was up. Most of the others, sharp-looking, competent youngsters, had already turned in their papers. The fellow who monitored the exam quickly looked mine over and told Bud I did very well as far as I went. I felt so frustrated, I was almost physically ill. I never tried to find out how I scored.

A tough-looking, tough-minded member of the Board of Admissions further discouraged me in my interview by pointing out that sick people wouldn't have the patience to deal with my difficult speech. He also questioned where I would get the $25,000 a medical education required in those days. With this meeting, my secret dream of being a doctor died.

At San Francisco College for Women where Mama taught, some scholarly Sacred Heart nuns read my verses in *Saturday Review* and book reviews from the *Chronicle* and *Examiner*, and told Mama I had a gift from God that I should treasure. I was developing confidence in my writing style and skill. At my electric typewriter I felt I could beat the world.

I made friends with some of the student therapists at Stanford Hospital. Dolly Valez had a degree as an R.N. from a university in Bogota, Colombia. She was Spanish and German with dark hair and remarkably large blue eyes. I was so enamored with her that I wrote her several letters in Spanish, a language with which I was only slightly familiar, and depended heavily upon an English-Spanish dictionary. She came from Palo Alto to visit me over several weekends. Mama gave Dolly her big bedroom and went downstairs to sleep.

Dolly was well read in English, Spanish, and French. I was one of the few people she knew in California who was acquainted with the famous South American writers of the day. Since I couldn't even speak my native tongue, the college authorities in Greeley had let me satisfy the language requirements with a course in Latin American Literature in translation. From time to time, Dolly sent me choice quotes. I particularly liked one from Baudelaire to the effect that those who condemn people for drinking are fools.

One night when Mama had gone to bed, Dolly and I were on our knees looking through the bookcase. We looked in each others eyes and kissed. I think we were both a little surprised but Dolly said, "We are human, too." Thus encouraged, I continued kissing.

When Mama took her sabbatical, my one thought was to go to Bogota and see Dolly. I worked up an itinerary that took Mama and me to visit our friends in Colorado, then her relatives in Virginia and North Carolina, and on to Key West, Florida to see a college schoolmate of hers who was a navy doctor. From

Miami we could island hop by plane, spending a week each on Puerto Rico, Antigua, St. Lucia, Granada, Trinidad, a month on Barbados and three days in Caracas, Venezuela. Now, since we were that close to Bogota, Colombia, we might as well spend a week visiting Dolly.

Dolly did everything a person could to make our week in Bogota enjoyable. She took Mama and me on the funicular rail up to the church on top of Monserrate, drove us out to the country town of Zipaquira where we visited the cathedral in the salt mine, and visited the villa where Simon Bolivar had lived with his mistress. I had a good time, but Mama was sick with diarrhea, and full of complaints.

Mama said Dolly was nice, but a bit neurotic. I knew Mama made herself neurotic thinking about me and Dolly. After I returned to Kentfield we still corresponded, but it was obvious that Dolly understood how Mama felt and our letters were a bit awkward.

Several weeks before Papa died, I had overheard my parents commiserating that I was the end of the Barker bloodline. After me there would be no one to appreciate the fine Candlelight sterling silverware engraved with a B which they had chosen together. Their words cut me like a knife. In their minds, I was unfit for marriage. In the society in which they grew up, anyone who would marry a disabled man was throwing her life away, was emotionally unstable or had ulterior motives.

Bertrand Russell, the British Nobel-winning mathematician and philosopher, wrote in his book *The Conquest of Happiness*, "To fear love is to fear life, and those who fear life are already three times dead." These words reminded me of Mama and most of her relatives. Russell felt that people who found themselves among those who couldn't accept them as they were would be wise to seek happiness elsewhere. I felt life was passing me by and that the Far East might be a more congenial atmosphere for me.

In November, 1955, Edith, my Chinese classmate from college, came from Hong Kong, where she lived with her husband Fook Kow Li and their four children, to visit her father in San Francisco, who was ill. She asked me, "When are you coming to Hong Kong? You must come. There's lots to write about over there. Everything is so different." Suddenly I knew I must go.

When I wasn't busy reviewing books, I read everything I could about Hong Kong. In December, I wrote saying we'd be over in the summer and that I planned to stay on a while after Mama left. In January, Edith replied: "Really glad you are coming over finally. I'm already inquiring around for a houseboy for you who'll speak English, wash, clean and cook."

Mama and I managed to go everywhere we wanted. The concept that there might be things I couldn't do never entered her mind. "I can't is a coward," she used to say. In her mind no stairs were too difficult for us to handle alone. On our travels we never asked for special favors, but people usually rushed to help us when they saw we were having difficulty. I tried to make myself as inconspicuous as a thirty-year-old man teetering on a fifty-year-old woman's arm could be. I felt people were thinking, "Look at that big lug leaning on that poor woman!" And I was still so self-conscious that every meal eaten out was an ordeal.

In late May 1956, Mama rented Barker Manor to a doctor's family for the summer, and we took off for Hong Kong. On the way we took a two-week tour of Japan and spent three days on Taiwan.

Above: Central District from MacDonnell Road, 1956.

Below left: Ah Lee; center, Ah Chong; right, Mei Ying.

Hong Kong, 1956

Chapter 3

Some things are better than sex, and some are worse,
but there's nothing exactly like it.

- W. C. Fields

Rain pelted the plane windows as we approached Kai Tak Airport. We felt a momentary thrill of danger as the wing tips narrowly missed the sides of the Nine Dragon hills, then emerged. Soon the wheels were splashing on the runway. Mama and a stewardess helped me down the steps of the plane to a waiting wheelchair. Rain poured down and mingled with the June heat.

We hurried through customs and Edith introduced us to her husband, Fook-Kow Li, a tall, plump, sleek man who did not engage much in small talk. A graduate of MIT and independently wealthy, he was prominent in Hong Kong's Government.

Edith indicated the frail little old fellow dressed in blue servant's pajamas struggling with our luggage. "This is your boy, Ah Tan," she said. I blinked hard. Then I remembered that any male servant, regardless of age, was a "boy" in the Orient.

I thought, this skinny little guy isn't strong enough to help me; he can scarcely lift our bags. Edith noted my consternation. "If he isn't satisfactory, we'll find someone who is. He understands he is on trial."

Her car threaded its way through the Kowloon traffic toward the auto ferry which would take us to Hong Kong Island. A black-clad coolie carrying two baskets of vegetables balanced on a pole across his shoulders trotted across in front of the auto, barely missing the fenders, and continued on his way unperturbed.

Ah Tan was willing to help me in every way, but I had to let him go. He lacked the strength and coordination to help me walk and to lift me in and out of the tub. Besides, I wanted someone young and lively for my companion.

The influx of refugees from Red China caused the Colony to burst at the seams. Old buildings were being torn down and replaced by expensive apartment houses. The pounding pulse of jackhammers and pile drivers was starting to change Hong Kong from a living relic of British colonialism to a cosmopolitan city.

Housing in Hong Kong was expensive. For three days, Edith drove Mama and me around as we looked and dickered. At Welsby House, on MacDonnell

Road, part way up the Peak, two signs caught my eye. One was the American eagle insignia and "U.S. Military Attaches Offices 4th floor;" the other, a crudely lettered chunk of cardboard saying "Caretaker Office."

Edith went into the office and emerged with a small, quick-moving Chinese, cigarette in hand, who grinned broadly and gestured eloquently. She brought him to the car. He helped Mama walk me to the nearby elevator up to the first floor where he showed us a large, three-bedroom apartment with a grand view of Hong Kong Harbor.

Edith did the bargaining—for forty-five minutes, broken by frequent interruptions while the cocky Cantonese phoned the company in Kowloon. "This is the reason some people say we Chinese have such even tempers," said Edith. "We take it out in bargaining. This fellow's name is Lee. He's a sharp trader and plenty fresh. He asked what my name is. When I said Li, he said, 'Good, we belong to the same family. We should do business together, Big Sister.'

"I told him if he is my Little Brother, he should give us a better deal. He's trying to make a big commission. That's why he phones so much. I wish he'd stop that Big Sister stuff. It rubs me the wrong way."

Lee flicked his cigarette and smiled with self-assurance.

"You should get this guy to show you the night life, George," said Edith. "He's been around."

We signed a three-month lease and rented furniture. My IBM electric typewriter arrived by ship, along with my gift for Edith, a footlocker full of books I had reviewed. I had the typewriter put on a large desk in my bedroom and was back in business, writing an article for the *Examiner*'s Sunday Book section about my visit to Tokyo's Kanda Street, where books from all over the world were sold in Japanese translation.

Edith had an *amah* ready for us. Ah Chong was about forty, neat, efficient, a pretty good cook. Her wealth resided in her teeth, liberally covered with gold. Her English was sketchy but adequate. She lived in the servant's quarters, a small room by the kitchen with a bunk bed, a toilet and a bucket for bathing. She was on twenty-four-hour call with only Thursday afternoons off. It seemed hard to us, but in Hong Kong in the Fifties this was standard practice.

At six-thirty each morning she was up and flapping about in her sandals and black lacquer cloth *amah's* pajamas, sweeping the floors at a measured rate. She also washed, ironed, bought her own food, and let our food stay in the refrigerator and spoil rather than eat it herself. When we were happy, she was happy: when we were glum, so was she. She brightened up at a word of praise or a joke. The biggest joke was when Master George or Missy tried to say something in Cantonese.

Ah Chong was in a state of constant vigilance against "the bad mans." She kept all entrances hermetically sealed. When we were gone she even tied the door to the verandah shut, though it was forty feet above the ground and I could scarcely bear to look down.

I asked Lee to show me Hong Kong by night. His English was sometimes difficult to understand, but he was surprisingly strong for such a slight man. We went to Laichikok, Hong Kong's amusement park. Chiang, the apartment house janitor, came with us to help me walk.

Chiang, tall and with extra-broad shoulders, handled me with the ease of my high school buddies. In one hand, Lee held my "relaxing medicine," a fifth of Johnny Walker scotch whiskey, dirt cheap in Hong Kong at that time. With me between them, Lee led the expedition, by taxi to the Star Ferry across the harbor to Kowloon, and then by bus through miles of shopping, industrial and residential areas teeming with humanity.

Lee and Chiang helped me walk to a small carnival-style tent. We sat on folding chairs in front of a wooden stage to watch four young women posing bare-breasted on a turntable. Their faces said, "You can make us do this, but you can't make us like it." We sat through fifteen minutes of this. "Not very good show," said Lee.

In the next tent a belly dancer executed uninhibited bumps and grinds to the beat of drums and Oriental music. She whipped her hips back and forth in a dizzying staccato, all the while laughing, smiling and making what I took to be raunchy remarks to her all-male audience. Lee said, "Chiang say girl very good." Anyway, her heart seemed to be in her work.

From another canvas-walled enclosure came sounds of a great commotion of gongs, drums, strange violin music and a big crowd. I suggested we look in on that but Lee dismissed the idea, saying, "Chinese opera. You no like."

I watched Lee and Chiang try their luck at carnival games similar to those I had known as a child at rodeo time in Greeley, in which they tried to win junky prizes by knocking down a moving target with a thrown ball or a cork shot from an air-rifle.

We ate chow mein in a little outdoor cafe and observed crowds of happy, loud-talking, escape-seeking Chinese strolling on the sidewalk. We caught a taxi to the ferry back to Hong Kong Island. The lights of the city glittered like sequins, dancing and reflecting in the moving waters of the harbor.

I glanced at my watch: just midnight. Still plenty warm and my clothes were soaked with perspiration. I took a couple of slugs of whiskey through a straw and relaxed back on the ferry's wooden bench, enjoying the breeze and the wonderful view.

Lee tried to tell me something for which his English was woefully inadequate. Something about a hotel room and a girl. "Japanese do. Chinese do. Maybe American no do." What did the Chinese and Japanese do that Americans didn't do? I tried to imagine.

"Make you feel good," grinned Lee. "You want try?" He pounded my tense-muscled leg with his clenched fist in what I took to be a display of exuberance.

A taxi driver on the Hong Kong side of the harbor received his orders in rapid-fire Cantonese and drove to a crummy district. He stopped at a run-down, disreputable-appearing hotel and we entered a dinky lobby where a bevy of pretty girls stood around in high-collared dresses slit to their hip joints. I entertained erotic thoughts.

Lee guided Chiang and me to an aged elevator and up two floors to a tiny room furnished with a single cot covered with a Formosa straw mat. A faded smear of scarlet lipstick stained the pale green wall. From the ceiling a feeble light bulb tried unsuccessfully to dispel the gloom. A brass spittoon and a tiny bedside stand littered with jars and bottles and a roll of tissue completed the decor.

Lee helped me partly undress and indicated I should lie down, patting the dazzling white, Lysol-odorous pillow whose sterile appearance was in marked contrast to the rest of the room.

An anxious half hour later, Lee arrived with a sturdy young woman in pink-flowered *amah's* pajamas. Her features were chunky and squarish, a peasant type. She sat on the cot while Lee haggled with her, paid her and left the room with Chiang in tow.

I smiled wanly and said, "Hi." She unsmilingly replied in kind, then carefully and deliberately opened her collar, removed her sandals, swung one foot up on the cot and started pounding my leg muscles—giving me a massage.

I felt sorely frustrated.

One night out with Ah Lee convinced me that he was not as worldly-wise as Edith thought. He had been fresh with her and was a big talker, but his choice of attractions left me feeling that he had not been around at all. Edith laughed when I told her. She knew by intuition that one reason I had come to Hong Kong was to meet women and get a little sexual experience. "You should take Mr. George to a ballroom and introduce him to some girls," she told Lee. But now I thought I would wait till Mama left.

On the Fourth of July, the temperature was ninety-nine. Sweat from my elbows made small, neat puddles on each side of my typing chair. That night, Edith and Fook Kow took Mama and me out to the Floating Restaurant on Aberdeen Bay for my birthday dinner. Fook Kow had to stick his well-bathed arm under my wet armpit in order to help me walk and board the little sampan that ferried us out to the large restaurant. I felt badly about that.

Aboard the Restaurant, I was seated ten feet from an attractive young lady in a *cheong saam* split well up her gorgeous thighs. It was hard to keep from staring. Edith laughingly said, "That girl is advertising too much. The style this year is for less exposure."

One of Mama's students in San Francisco was Bella Sun, a Chinese married woman from Hong Kong. Bella had visited us in Kentfield and we found her attractive and charming. She had returned to Hong Kong and started a school. When Mama called her, she and her husband invited us to dinner at their old, broad-verandahed home in Kowloon.

Dr. Sun made me feel at ease. Slender and quick, he knew how to joke about my disability without being offensive. He was a highly respected dentist who also did charity work for the poor and the Catholic religious orders in Hong Kong.

The next week, the Suns entertained twenty Jesuit priests. Dr. Sun thought to give me an opportunity to get an exclusive story. Two of the guests were American Jesuits only ten days out of Shanghai prison after seven years' incarceration. Their Order was sheltering them from the press. Father Clifford from San Francisco, a quietly intense man, generously gave me an informal interview for the *San Francisco Examiner*, with Mama helping interpret.

The Communists had deprived him of food and subjected him to great psychological pressure, but he refused to confess to spying. His hair had turned from dark brown to snow white. He required Dr. Sun's immediate attention for several infected teeth. The other priests expressed great admiration for him.

Typing till two in the morning, I hurried an article off, which the *Examiner* promptly published.

Edith recommended that I visit Tiger Balm Garden, a hill covered with grotesque plaster figures from Chinese mythology, a tourist attraction. Edith said the *amahs* loved the place because they knew all the myths by heart. Ah Lee helped Mama and me take a taxi. As they struggled to help me walk up and down the hill, a polite young man asked to take my picture. I said okay, but that I did not want to buy one. He said he did not want to sell it, but could he have my address? I thought he meant to send me a picture in the mail. That afternoon a reporter and photographer from the *Hong Kong Standard* came to the apartment to take more pictures and ask how I had overcome my disability.

Overcome my disability? I could not take a step without help, bathe, feed or dress myself, and writing my signature was a five-minute ordeal. I couldn't be understood by half the people I tried to talk to. All I felt I had accomplished was a scrapbook full of book reviews and a couple of published verses. The question seemed unreal. I said I didn't think I had overcome it, but I hadn't let it overcome me either, and I was still struggling to lead a normal life.

The next morning, Ah Chong shuffled in with our Sunday paper and held it up with a big grin. In the middle of the front page was a big photo of me and a flattering article. Edi phoned to tell me the same article was on the front page of the Chinese language version of the *Standard*. Both papers were owned by Aw Boon How, the millionaire manufacturer and promoter of Tiger Balm and owner of Tiger Balm Garden. Now, everywhere I went, people recognized me and smiled or waved. I knew for a while what it was to be a minor celebrity. I liked it.

Edith drove us across the harbor and beyond the Nine Dragon Hills of Kowloon to the New Territories to help me gather material. It was a picturesque area with Hakka villages and farms, rice paddies with water buffalo, duck ponds, banana trees and green hills.

Hakka women worked in the fields, dressed in black pajamas and their distinctive wide straw hats with three inches of black cloth hanging around the rim for protection from the subtropical sun. The younger ones carried babies in cloth slings on one hip or straddling their back. Some were quite attractive with olive skin, bold eyes and a proud, independent bearing. I would remember them four years later.

Along the main road, white-barked, twisted eucalyptus trees added a touch of weird wildness to the feeling of living in a fantasy travelogue. We drove to the road leading to the Peoples' Republic of China. Ahead of us appeared a no-man's-land of grassy hills between England's leased property and the Reds.

For about a month, in the apartment next door to us lived a friendly U.S. Army sergeant who treated me to a wild jeep ride up the peak for my birthday. He was with the U.S. Military Attaché's office on the top floor of the apartment building.

He told me, "The Major upstairs says he knows you. Says he drove your dog to a dog show in Denver. Name's Otho Payne." I remembered Otho well. He was the student Papa hired to take me, one of my buddies, and my cocker spaniel, Dudley, to the Colorado Kennel Club show.

Mama found a shopping companion. Thea, a sprightly young English woman, and her husband Stan had moved into a flat on our floor. Stan was a Royal Navy nurse stationed at the English hospital on the Peak. He worked long hours. Thea was glad to walk downtown with Mama in the morning and to visit us in the afternoons. She was just twenty-four and had been a librarian in Liverpool. We four became close friends.

I was determined to stay until November or December despite Mama's efforts to dissuade me. With $1,000 from Uncle Kim and several thousand left from Papa's insurance, I could have my fling in the life and excitement of Hong Kong, then retire to the solitude of a Kentfield winter when the beauty of the heather and acacias and flowering plants make approaching spring a paradise.

It was the end of July. My immediate problem was to find a dependable houseboy to look after me when Mama returned to the States. Stan said he would ask the labor foreman at the hospital to try to get me a helper. He thought it was ridiculous for me to pay more than HK$180 a month because that's what the Royal Navy paid its Chinese orderlies. However, I doubted Stan would find anyone willing to work for me for just six months for the kind of wages he thought proper.

Lee said, "I very like to service Mr. George."

He was fed up with his job as caretaker of Welsby House. "All day long something for trouble," he said.

Tenants complained Lee wasn't on the job. But it seemed to me he was always on the jump to the oft-repeated shouts of "Lee!"

An English couple on our floor woke to see a Chinese man going through their bureau drawers at an early hour of the morning. The woman screamed and the burglar vaulted out over the verandah rail, taking two watches and the money and stamps from her husband's wallet. She demanded the building be protected by a barbed wire fence.

As a compromise gesture, Welsby House's management decided that Lee should wake up and walk about the building three times a night to frighten away any prospective prowlers.

Little Brother was already unhappy with management because they had not paid him a promised commission. He offered his resignation. The owners didn't accept.

"Very bad the business! They talk, no quit! My Auntsie recommend me for the job. My Catholic Father sign a recommend for me. I don't know what to do. Too much the troubled matters."

I hesitated to hire Lee because he was employed. But I liked him and he had the gift of enthusiasm, a trait I found pleasing. If he was quitting his job and wanted to work for me, then I would like to have him.

We had Edith to breakfast along with Little Brother. I asked her to talk to Lee about working for me, as his English was difficult. She did, but said he seemed very reluctant and she did not want to press him. Later in the day, Lee came and wanted to sit down and talk. I said okay. He said, "I very much the heart to work for you, but you no understand my case."

Then he poured out his troubles. His wife was going to present him with his sixth child in about two weeks. "Too many baby. Very sorry matter." He told me the entire family lived in a room thirteen feet square in one of the government settlement blocks. I offered him HK $300 per month, about U.S. $45, to work for me.

The next day he went to see his priest and got approval to quit working for the apartment company. Then he gave the company ten days notice and came directly to tell me.

I thought it was settled.

The following morning Lee was back again. Now he wanted a guarantee of a big bonus when he was released in December. Edith came over and helped translate. She was angry. She told Lee he must make up his mind; that I would promise no more; that I had refused one boy the job and now he was keeping me from getting someone else. "Either you want to work for Mr. George or you don't. Now you go outside and think it over. Don't come back until you have made up your mind." Edith treated Lee as though he were a naughty child. Little Brother went sheepishly out of the room.

Lee was back in two minutes with the information that he did indeed want to service Mr. George and that all my terms were acceptable.

The day Lee started working for me, he arrived at eight a.m. He tried to suppress it, but he was radiant. I asked him whether it was a boy or a girl.

"A boy! Very strong boy! Him weigh half past seven pounds!" he exclaimed proudly.

In hopes of relaxing and cooling off a little, I drank more and more whiskey—ten fifths of Johnny Walker in fifteen days. Mama was upset. She asked me if I didn't think I should slow down. I said I thought so.

The next case of whiskey I bought, I had Lee line the bottles up on the floor against the wall of my bedroom. My idea was to keep better track of the amount consumed and ration myself.

The theory was commendable. The practice left much to be desired.

In order to remind Lee that I wanted things kept shipshape, I had Mama buy some poster paper and crayons and then asked Thea to letter me these signs: WASH HANDS WITH SOAP BEFORE COOK OR FIX FOOD; POUR BOILING WATER OVER DISHES AFTER WASHING; COVER FOOD AND KEEP FLOOR CLEAN TO DOWN THE COCKROACHES; DEFROST TUESDAYS; REMEMBER MR. GEORGE IS BOSS! I resisted the strong temptation to add an Orwellian touch with: BIG BROTHER IS WATCHING.

Armed with Scotch tape, Little Brother put the defrost sign on the refrigerator door. He taped the REMEMBER MR. GEORGE IS BOSS! sign on the open bedroom door, where only I could see it. Lee did not want to put up the kitchen signs, saying they were not necessary. "I live with European people long time now. I very clean man." I suspected he felt he would lose face, so I said okay.

Lee seemed to me to be hardworking, alert and thoughtful. He was a devout Catholic. I had seen enough to know that professing religion does not automatically change human nature and make a man honest. But Lee had a seemingly lofty conception of what was expected of the faithful. When he said, as he did frequently, that he did not do this or that because "I am Catholic Church member," I was reassured.

While Mama was preparing to go home, I discovered good gin was much less expensive than scotch. From then on I would smell like juniper berries rather than a charred oak cask.

Then came the morning Mama was to go. She worried about leaving me, but at the same time determined to let me lead my own life. We kissed and said good-bye. But there was more of a tear than either of us would readily admit. She was my nurse, my best friend and my confidant. I stood clutching the cyclone fence with one hand while trying to wave at the taxiing plane with the other, with Ah Lee and Edith holding me up on each side.

Back at Welsby House, Lee set to work with a vengeance. He commandeered his brother and Chiang to install a bell system. Lee had procured his old job for his brother, a dour, shifty-eyed fellow. Within an hour after our return to the apartment, I could ring the bell in the servant's quarters from my bedroom or the living room.

Lee's little boy, Georgie, would come to my room and do a little jump-up-and-down dance to announce when meals were about to be served. The plump little fellow ate with Lee and me. He could empty a rice bowl in the twinkling of an eye. The approved Chinese technique was to place the bowl to the lips and use the two chopsticks as a paddle to shovel the food into the yawning abyss.

Georgie often had little appetite because he was such a pet of the Welsby House *amahs*. "*Amahs* all the time giving Georgie too much eat," said Lee. "They very much love the baby."

I had told Lee that Georgie could eat with us sometimes; Lee stretched it to mean all the time. But I delighted in Little Georgie's presence at the family board. I enjoyed Lee, too. We still had trouble understanding what the other said, but there was precious little we could not get across when we took the time.

We laughed and teased. Lee was having trouble with the iron and he got one of the upstairs *amahs* to help him with the ironing. I teased him about the *amah* and his red-hot iron. We went to see Marilyn Monroe in "The Seven Year Itch"; he teased me about my thirty-one-year itch.

He called Little Georgie by the Hong Kong slang term "cowboy." The Cantonese kau means "play," so "cowboy" means "playboy." Often Lee talked about "Little Cowboy Georgie" and "Big Cowboy Georgie."

Lee had Chiang help him with the cooking. Between emptying garbage cans and sweeping the courtyard, Chiang would double as my chef. I could only hope he washed his hands. He looked impeccable. Lee said Chiang was teaching him. Chiang was a good cook, within his limited repertoire. He did well with eggs, egg rolls, fish cooked crisp in thick, black soy sauce, and he made excellent chow mein with pan fried noodles. But he was often heavy-handed in his use of lard and onions.

I enjoyed the rice-based Cantonese diet. The long-grain rice from Thailand that Lee bought had a delicate, almost perfumed aroma. Lee said every Chinese man must eat five bowls of rice each day to keep his power. Lee certainly kept his power while eating at my table. He downed the required rice like a butcher stuffing a sausage.

Lee was a good washer and ironed well, but spots of starch on my dark blue rayon-linen trousers made me look like an unaproned milkshake maker at the Dairy Lane. The floors were swept daily and things were fairly tidy.

I used to go to the kitchen to watch the cooking and try to learn. I would occasionally attempt to direct operations for a simple American meal. But no matter how easy a dish was, they managed to spoil it. They made soup of the canned corned beef hash and cooked the wieners in lime Jello. I concluded that Lee wanted the cooking left to him and Chiang.

Bud had told me several times that, if I ever cut my umbilical cord, I would spew all over. While not exactly spewing, thinking of Mama alone, rattling around Barker Manor, tended to make me blue. The saving grace of my situation was that I had plenty to occupy my thoughts. And I did feel unfettered from the bonds of Mama's unrealistic expectation that I would spend my life in a state of celibate bliss.

A week after she left, I developed a badly infected foot. It made wearing shoes painful. When I crawled on my knees it rubbed on the hard parquet floor and hurt like hell. Stan took one look, frowned and insisted in his pleasantly firm manner that I consult a doctor. "We're in the tropics and something like this can turn quite nasty," he said.

Thea called Edith. She evidently gave an alarming account, because within two hours Dr. Henry Li, Fook Kow's brother, was at the flat. Dr. Li was a large, robust man who gave the immediate impression of good health and intellectual vigor. His charm appeared to conceal tremendous drive.

He took my pulse and blood pressure. "Very good," he said. He examined my foot. "Nothing serious. I'll give you something that'll fix it."

Edith came shortly after he left. She assured me that brother-in-law Henry would want to operate, probably amputate.

"He loves to operate. He isn't happy unless he's slicing up someone's insides. But he is a wonderful doctor. Did you like him?"

"Very much," I said.

The medicine Dr. Li gave me brought the infection to a head. Lee went downtown to see the doctor and tell him it was ready to lance. He reported, "Sick business very good. Many people waiting in doctor's office."

Lee and Chiang tried to make some cookies for me while I was incapacitated from the infection. They emerged from the kitchen into the bedroom carrying a biscuit tin covered with beautiful cookies. Lee had watched Ah Chong and now he was doing it, but the best intentions are not always enough. He had missed something. Baking powder and vanilla, I think. The flavor was good, but they were like bricks. They had the texture and taste of some tough Seaman's Biscuit that Papa bought in Nova Scotia on the trip through Eastern Canada. Lee said very bad. I said, never mind, they taste good.

With my foot cleared up, I felt the need of some good red meat untouched by sauces and not chopped into little pieces. We took a taxi to the Parisian Grill and Lee and I had Chateaubriand. All the way home Lee was muttering—"Very dear. Very dear." He described the meat to Chiang in minute detail, spouting machine-gun Cantonese to him for half an hour.

Lee went to the Central Market and bought a cut of meat that he told me would make about five servings of Chateaubriand. Lee had never tasted top quality beef cooked medium-rare before. He imagined that the retired water buffalo meat that passes for beef in the Central Market could be transformed into Chateaubriand by use of meat tenderizer and seasoning.

Little Brother's Chateaubriand, translated into Cantonese, came to the table as thin slices of tenderized, but still leather-tough meat cooked almost white inside, colored pink with cinnamon and flavored with onions.

Since Stan worked many evenings, Thea acquired the habit of popping in at odd times of the day to give me the latest apartment house news. There was something kind and commonsense and very English about her. Mama had suggested to Bella that she would be a good teacher. That was how she got the job at Bella's school. I lost a lot of good conversation, but she did drop in after school and tell me about her school work.

Thea's opinions were strong, especially about the Chinese. She seemed to think one could never trust the blighters. A British friend who lived in Hong Kong for twenty years told her the Chinese invariably disappoint one. I didn't think so.

Thea directed her *amah* much better than I did Ah Lee. She was kind but firm. Ah Lan knew exactly what to do and how to act. It was hard for me to imagine any servant telling her, as Lee so often told me, "But Mr. George, you no understand this matter."

Some evenings Lee and Chiang would come into my living quarters. Lee was not as worldly as Edith thought, but it took no detective ability for him to know I wanted a woman.

Both Lee and Chiang talked about girls to me. Lee said he had a friend. A beauty girl. A nice clean sixteen year old. She would charge me $70 HK for the night. One hundred dollars including hotel and room. Then he added as a sort of clincher that she would go to America as my wife if I liked her.

This seemed utterly ridiculous. I did not believe for a second that a hooker and I could have much in common, much less a sixteen year old. I could see myself telling Mama who taught in a convent college and was somewhat strait-laced in her respectability: "Mama, this is Mui Mui. She cost me seventy dollars the first night. I liked her so much I decided to bring her home. I know you two will be happy together."

Lee asked me how I would like to marry a Virginia girl and take her home with me.

"A Virginia girl?" I queried.

"I explain. A Virginia girl, no have husband, no have lover. Her is Virginia. Understand my meaning?"

He added, "Chiang say he think her not very pretty. But maybe you like. Him say girl same as flower. One man like rose. Other man like some different. Him say this girl face him no like. Maybe you say very good. Him say her have good chest—very much!"

Their ideal seemed to be a dumb virgin with big tits, the younger the better. Lee seemed to regard my declining their efforts as most unnatural. What I wanted was short term liaison with a pretty woman with enough sexual know-how to compensate for my utter lack of experience.

Lee and his brother were gifted amateurs on the Chinese two-string violin. This beautifully carved, lion-head instrument produced an anguished, wailing quality that seemed to typify much Chinese music.

Disturbed by some raucous, off-key screeching noises, I asked Lee, "What is that?"

"Chiang is learn to play violin," he grinned and added, "Chinese say, 'make kill chicken noise.' "

When Lee bought a guitar and played it while his brother played the violin and Chiang accompanied on the mouth organ, most of their selections were from Cantonese opera. It was some of the most disturbing and haunting music

I had heard. It grew on me until it got to be an actual hunger. I missed it when I was two days without it. My evenings of Chinese music helped convince Thea I had gone dotty.

One night, Little Brother played the two string Chinese violin into my tape recorder. He turned the violin over to his brother while he sang some Cantonese opera—including, at my request, a selection from *The Red Chamber Dream.* Edith had taken Mama and me to see the opera and I had reviewed two translations of the epic novel of several generations of a Chinese family on which it was based, so I was much interested.

I hadn't finished Han Suyin's new novel that I was reviewing for the *Examiner.* Dr. Sun tried to arrange for me to meet Han Suyin and interview her, since Mr. Nichols, my boss at the *Examiner,* suggested it might be worth a try. But her friends told him she was living on a plantation in Malaysia with her new English husband.

At Dr. Sun's house for dinner, he irritated me. He told me I should watch my drinking, that my liver could not take so much abuse. I felt embarrassed when I had to ask for an extra drink after dinner, but I did not want to become tense and shaky in his presence. He said I must learn to take it easy and put my faith in something. I knew he was right, but the question for me was: faith in what?

Perhaps Dr. Sun sensed there were many things about the Catholic church which strongly appealed to me—the grandeur of its history, the mysticism of its ritual and the high quality of the priests and nuns I had known.

I thought of myself as an agnostic. If there was a God, why was He so wretched to some people? Evidence of the absence of a caring God was abundant everywhere in the world.

Yet, out of desperation at some unknown, foreboding, I had been silently saying the Lord's Prayer each night since Mama left Hong Kong. Not reeling it off by rote, as many people say their prayers, but thinking it silently and slowly, a phrase at a time, trying to analyze it and wring some meaning from it for my life.

One might have thought that being in the Far East, I would have remembered Buddha. But his ideas were not in the entrepreneurial spirit of Hong Kong. The Colony's mottoes seemed to be, "He who hesitates is lost" and, "Life belongs to him who dares." Those had become my feelings, too. Further reading convinced me desire is the essence of man. A man without passions has no motive to act. All constructive human activity was prompted by desire. I began to have a more all-embracing vision.

Lee had belatedly grasped the fact that I did not wish to become involved with his "beauty girl friend" or Chiang's "real Virginia girl *amah.*" "You is some unstandard thinking," he would say sadly, shaking his head and glancing at me with signs of uneasiness.

At dinner he talked about the Chinese way of thinking. "Chinese say, 'Food for the stomach, then food for the penis.' You know?"

I nodded, yes. I knew Taoist philosophy was based upon the integration of Nature into one's life and one's life into Nature. Lee did not need to convince me of the importance of sex in life. I was already converted.

Uncle Kim, who helped finance my stay in Hong Kong, wrote to me, urging me to mingle with all kinds of people. Not just my well-to-do friends. And such was my inclination. I wanted to have a relationship to those about me, not be emotionally separate and self segregated. I tried to become friends with Lee and Chiang, and I finally mingled myself very freely with a woman acquaintance of Lee's.

I asked Lee to get a woman and bring her to the apartment for a night. I would rid myself of my thirty-one year itch. I must have overdone my admonitions about no teenagers. She was a plain-looking, middle-aged, muddy-complexioned, unwashed Tanka boat woman in wrinkled, black lacquer-cloth pajamas. Being introduced, she immediately straddled my lap and pinched my cheek.

Lee's idea of a proper bedfellow for me was rather discouraging. By now, I had seen lots of pretty cheong-saamed cuties trying to be anyone's "girl friend" for a night. Instead, Lee must have gone to the far end of a dark and dirty alley to find this woman. She stank of stale sweat and tobacco. Even her underwear was dirty. After she felt she'd earned her money, I woke her several times, and she took to "playing possum." Had not my stomach been blessedly anesthetized with gin, I was certain I would have been ill. I thought, if this be sex, I will relinquish my share gladly. I'd had it and I wished I could give it back.

Attempting to extract more money, she exaggerated and told Lee I hadn't let her sleep half an hour all night. Lee insisted on handling the money on this transaction. I did not care. I was just glad when the woman left.

I asked Lee why he chose such a dirty woman for me to sleep with. He looked at me directly and spoke earnestly. "Her is very sorry case. I know her many years. Five children. Sick husband. Very poor. Need money. I thinking, you like to help her and she help you." Lee almost made me feel virtuous, like I had given to the United Crusade.

The next morning, Little Brother was waiting at the drug store. He bought enough oral penicillin to outfit a medical battalion. While I did not want to take any venereal souvenirs back home with me, I doubted that oral penicillin would do the job.

For a week afterward, Lee kept working on me to have the woman back, but I said, "No more." Although he kept talking about how unstandard I was, he knew I meant it.

I wrote Dolly, my Colombian friend, who was back in New York working for the Rusk Rehabilitation Institute. I told her I was in Hong Kong and asked her if she would consider marrying me, and, if so, now was the time and this was the place. I suggested that she read *A Many Splendored Thing* which gave a good account of life in Hong Kong at that time. She replied that she was flattered but she didn't think she could leave her job. She read *A Many Splendored Thing* and thought it was a good love story but she didn't understand the politics. Anyway, I was glad she didn't say she didn't love me. Though, she did not say she loved me either.

Maybe she didn't really care for me that much and this was just something that I had built up out of a number of kisses. I often wondered what would have happened if I had pursued her more assiduously. She was certainly the most physically attractive, brightest, most literate woman I had known as a young man.

Lee and I had a fight over money. The item in contention was a chicken. I pounced upon the bill with much rancor. Lee said it was a large chicken and reminded me that he had told me a week before that some foods become 50% higher before the Moon Festival. I said among other things that it made me unhappy to be unhappy with him. That I liked him very much. He said, "No need be unhappy. Because you is gentleman. Better for well you say this things than no say and then some day 'boom.'"

Lee showed me the chicken. In a separate package were the entrails. "Man at market ask, is for European or Chinese peoples? When I say European people, him throwing away insides. I say no, no! Very funny. I take home anyway." When I told Lee that I didn't relish the idea of eating chicken insides, he smiled with ill-concealed pity and said, "I understand. I give to Chiang."

I received a note from Dr. Sun. "You are invited to our house for dinner tonight. Please do not say no. It is the feast of Mid-Autumn and mooncakes will be served. Dinner will be served at eight, please come before that—Francis Sun." Of course, I accepted.

At Dr. Sun's house, as usual, we had more superb food. The dinner was a large, delicate fish with shredded ginger, sweet and sour pork, a big wintermelon full of soup, chunks of stewed chicken, and mooncakes followed by fruit. They had Cantonese and Shanghai mooncakes. The Shanghai kind were full of slivered almonds and truly delicious.

Doctor Sun told me that during the Mongol Dynasty, all highly placed Chinese families were required to employ one Mongol servant. He was an informer. By sending messages to each other inside of large cakes, they decided that all Chinese families should kill their Mongol servants on a certain date. The date being that of the full moon in the seventh month on the Chinese calendar. The Chinese killed their Mongol servants, overthrew the Mongol Dynasty and founded the Ming Dynasty and henceforth celebrated Moon Festival with moon cakes.

Edith had spoken of the public baths in Hong Kong. Fook Kow went to one about once a month, mostly for the pedicure. He was going to take me, but never got around to it. I decided to get Lee to take me.

I was allotted a towel covered cot in a curtained cubicle. Men dashing about in various stages of disarray reminded me of a men's locker room in the U.S. The bath itself was a waste of time and money. A big pot-bellied brute of a Chinese gave me a brisk scrubbing with a sponge in a tub. And that was it. But afterwards, resting, relaxed on the cot, getting an expert and much needed pedicure, I thought it highly worthwhile and enjoyable. Both Lee and Chiang had come along to help me.

Lee and Chiang talked. Lee turned to me and said, "Chiang say him want to get girl for you." By then I was ready for more sexual adventure. I said okay, and Chiang was gone.

They took me by taxi to the Tennoche Hotel in the Wanchai. It was a sparkling place with a ballroom connected to it. The parquet floors of the room were polished to a dazzling shine. Much Cantonese passed between the room boy, Lee and Chiang.

Time passed. Two girls walked in the room dressed in traditional Chinese cheong saams, half covering their faces with handkerchiefs, turned around and walked out. "You take girl you like," Lee said. I chose the one with the direct gaze and the shy smile. I found her appearance attractive and her manner pleasing. Lee and Chiang stripped me to my jockey shorts and left me on the bed.

The girl reentered the room and smiled reassuringly at me. With ease and deliberation, she pulled her cheong saam over her head, unhooked her bra and slid off her panties. It was the first time in my life that I had seen a real-life totally nude woman. (I didn't count Lee's disgusting boat woman.) This girl was built like a gymnast—trim, strong and graceful, but definitely female in the breast and hip department. She squatted on the bed to pull off my shorts and, still squatting, eased my penis into her pink vagina. Spiritual release engulfed me. It was the pounding surf on a soft tropical beach; the warm musky clean woman fragrance.

I simply had to take her back to Welsby House. In the taxi, Lee learned her name was Mei Ying which means Beautiful Swallow. It fitted her perfectly for she was small, bright-eyed and very pretty. She was only four feet ten inches tall and weighed scarcely ninety pounds. Well bathed and scrubbed without a hint of heavy perfume. She said she was twenty-three years old.

"Her a very wise girl. Her very good thinking," Lee said.

Lee discovered Mei Ying loved Cantonese opera and had even sung in some minor roles with a small company. Nothing would do except an impromptu performance. Lee much admired her knowledge of Cantonese opera and her singing voice. No catlike shrieks, but a different minor key sound. She said she wanted to become a professional opera singer, but her voice was too deep and masculine for the high-pitched female roles, and she was too small for the male parts, which are often played by tall women. I drank gin and tea and watched her lose herself completely in her role.

After the others had gone to bed, she wanted to sit at the window and look at the lights of the cities of Hong Kong and Kowloon and the ships and ferries on the harbor. She tried to help me to the window. I slipped and fell. Tears leapt from her eyes and were instantly turned off by biting her lip. I regained my feet and she, with surprising strength for one so small, continued to assist me. Seconds later she was sitting completely and serenely lost in the beauty of the harbor. Such was her mercurial temperament that she could turn from weeping to reach exalted heights of the spirit within a minute.

I began thinking. Perhaps I could keep this delightful kitten for a month. It would be expensive, I knew. But it would be a once in a lifetime affair. It would be a chance for me to experience some of the joys of life which I felt had been denied me. I thought about it most of the night and by morning my doubts were resolved.

I would hire this lovely creature. She would have no claim on me. I would have the experience I had been clamoring for since my early teens. I had to handle the transaction through Lee because he was the only one who could speak both languages in whom I was willing to confide. It would have been too embarrassing to ask Edith to interpret.

Lee saw I wanted her badly. He held a long conversation with her in Cantonese. He told me the price she wanted. I thought it was too much and told him so. But it was evident he had made a deal with her.

"Ah, but you is high class gentleman," deplored Lee. "High class gentleman needs high class girl." I was suspicious of Lee, but I thought, what the hell! It's only for one month. I said "Okay." It was decided the month would begin in two days on the first of October.

Mei Ying arrived at Welsby House shortly before noon on October first, bringing her belongings in a calfskin suitcase. For a month, she would be a member of my little household. Dressed in flowered pink pajamas with her hair curled almost kinky, I had to look twice to be sure it was the same girl.

She put her suitcase in the extra bedroom and hung her brightly flowered towel in the bathroom. When the noon meal was over, we went to the desk and studied my First Year Cantonese textbook.

As a part of my get-the-most-out-of-Hong-Kong plan I had subscribed to all three daily English-language newspapers to obtain a well-rounded picture of life in the Colony and China. I also engaged a woman to tutor me in Cantonese. She advertised in the *South China Morning Post* as a "young University lady." As she went out the door Lee snickered, "She is young and I am ten years old."

I was writing Mama four or five letters a week. I had always been open and above board with her and made no effort to hide Mei Ying's existence. I believed she would take the news of my acquisition of "a good little bad girl" calmly, even if she would be disappointed.

Thea questioned the wisdom of telling my mother about the situation. She could not realize how close we were and that when I went home I would want to be able to talk to Mama without having to wonder if I'd told her this or that. I thought that being perfectly frank and straightforward was the best policy. But maybe it was more like a naughty boy showing off what he could get away with. I didn't expect her to be thrilled with the idea, that's for sure!

Thea said Paul Gauguin had nothing on me, that the flat had become quite exotic. She professed surprise that the mild-mannered Mr. Barker should become so involved in Oriental mysteries and blossom forth with a Little Lotus. I said that no one wanted to be that mild-mannered.

She told me I was too analytical and urged me to quit dissecting situations and people and enjoy myself. I told her it was part of the disease of being a writer. It was true. Some nights I would lie awake thinking about writing, down to the last punctuation mark.

But I was not at all objective about Mei Ying. While I feigned a detached attitude, I was mad about her. I adored the smooth rounded curves and creases of her athletic young body; admired her quick, easy movements and ready laughter; and thought her totally charming and highly intelligent.

I told Thea I wasn't going to try to conceal the fact we were living together. "How do you want me to break the news to Bella?" she asked. "Wouldn't it be best just to say that she's Lee's cousin here for a visit?"

"My God, no! The Suns are already afraid that Lee's going to take advantage of me."

"I see your point. But they do bear a striking resemblance. Are you sure they are not related?"

The truth was I wasn't sure. Both had the surname Lee, and they looked enough alike to be brother and sister. "All I know is what Lee tells me. He says there is no relationship."

"Well," said Thea, "there are probably a million Lees in China!"

"Lee says he knew her father in Kwangtung. He owned a factory that manufactured pots and pans for cooking. Lee said he took some guns and bayonets there to be repaired when he was in the Nationalist army. Then he says he remembers Mei Ying as a little girl of thirteen or fourteen when she took tickets at the ferry in Sek Kee."

"But what should I tell Bella?"

"Let's see," I pondered. "I am a little bit afraid of Dr. Sun. He is supposed to have a terrible temper. You know Bella's always talking about it. It might be well if we broke the news to them gently. If he should stumble in here someday and find I have a girlfriend, he might blow a gasket."

"All right," she said. "I'll just say that George has a girlfriend at the apartment and leave it there."

"Good," I said.

"No! She'll want to know where you met. What do you want me to say?" Thea's eyes twinkled with mischief because I had confided in her the story of the evening I met Mei Ying.

"Just a minute, let me think. Tell her we met at the Dairy Lane Restaurant. That's a nice clean place. And Mei Ying is going to meet me and Lee there tomorrow noon because I want to buy some things from the Dairy Lane Store."

"How very American of you, Barker. Meeting your girl friend at a milk bar. Really, I would have expected something more exotic from you."

Thea came back from school the next evening to say that her revelation had been met by a moment of stunned silence and then, "Tell me about her. Where did he meet her?"

Thea perjured herself on my behalf. I thanked her for it because I was particularly anxious that Bella should not know the whole story. She was so genteel, I was sure she would have been shocked.

Early in October, a cool dry breeze began to blow out of China. We closed some of the windows and I no longer typed and sat around shirtless. With the cooler weather the mosquitoes, flies and cockroaches largely disappeared. It was a relief to be able to sleep without the buzzing sound of two or three hungry little bloodsuckers.

Lee commenced having chest pains. I felt sure they were due to the strain on his pectoral muscles caused by lifting me. He went to a Chinese herb doctor and got a herb paste which he applied energetically to his chest.

Mei Ying and I had joked about being husband and wife, and Lee had called our month together a "trial marry." I told him not to be silly. He countered by asking, "Why not? Mei Ying make a very standard wife. Her have good thinking. Her is good cook, wash, ironing. And her very love for the baby." It was true Mei Ying loved and looked after Little Georgie. She relieved Lee of all duties connected with the Cowboy. She scrubbed him, dressed him and was knitting him a blue turtleneck sweater.

Through the prisms of Lee's poor English and Mei Ying's and my private bedroom sessions with the First Year Cantonese Text, I tried to imagine Mei Ying's life in China. She was born when her mother was forty-four, the tenth and last child. Her father was a man of ability and power who owned three factories employing sixty-five men.

Just after his death in 1949 when Mei Ying was fourteen, the Communists took over China and took everything from the family simply by labeling them Nationalist reactionaries and capitalist exploiters. Mei Ying came to Hong Kong penniless and friendless.

She worked first as an underpaid amah in a Chinese family, but soon moved on to a factory in Kowloon making batteries. Eventually she emerged from the cocoon of dreary factory existence into the exciting, if tawdry, world of Hong Kong taxi dancer. America used to have taxi dancers who charged for dances as a cabby charges for rides. In the Far East the term was usually a euphemism. Dancer, hotel girl, bar girl or just plain prostitute, I will probably never know Mei Ying's whole story. It is clear she needed money, and not surprising to me that she was induced to exploit her petite charms.

Her mother was old now. Her brothers and sisters were quite selfish and left Mei Ying to shoulder the responsibility of their mother, who was sick with failing eyesight and required expensive medical care.

I began to envision myself as a quirky Don Quixote in tarnished armor, rescuing the beautiful Dulcinea-Mei Ying from the conniving rogues of Hong Kong.

Mei Ying bought herself a pair of spectacles, not for vision but to put on a respectable appearance. She also had a tailor make a severely cut suit and had Lee and Chiang tell everyone she was my Chinese teacher. Whenever she went out shopping or to visit friends, she took Little Georgie.

Now when Lee went to visit his wife twice a week, I wasn't alone. Generally, Mei Ying sat in the chair beside me, feet in my lap, knitting away on Little Georgie's sweater, humming or singing Cantonese opera as I typed. She helped me walk, saving my always-sore knees from crawling on the parquet floors. When Lee and I got into an infrequent shouting ruckus, she walked around waving her arms and begging, "No talk, no talk!"

I was glad I'd decided to stay in Hong Kong, even though I usually felt tired between my love life, gin, studying, trying to keep my thumb on the household expenses and writing, writing, writing. I told myself that when I got home to Kentfield I would have plenty of solitude, rest and quiet. Better live my months in Hong Kong to the hilt.

One Sunday morning, Cathay Pacific airlines was selling plane trips around Hong Kong for a pittance, with the proceeds going to the Royal Air Force. I thought I'd give Mei Ying and Little Georgie a thrill. I tried to get us up and out and over to Kowloon early because I was afraid there would be a crowd. They dawdled around and took it easy. I had yet to learn the Cantonese attitude was that one was on time if he was no more than half an hour late. When we arrived at Kai Tak Airport at almost noon, all the tickets were sold and several hundred people were left waiting. I felt frustrated.

I had bought tickets to the Anglican Church's Michaelmas Fair the next afternoon which would afford us a good chance of meeting Edith in happy, sanctified surroundings where questions about Mei Ying's background would not occur. Then we planned to go to a Peking restaurant for dinner and after that to a movie.

Mei Ying informed me through Lee that she didn't want to go to the Fair. That she wouldn't know when to kneel or when to pray, and would feel completely out of place. Lee suggested that I go more slowly and teach her the Bible first.

I tried futilely to explain that, although the Fair was sponsored by the Anglican Church, it was not church. But I had made the mistake of agreeing with Lee that it was a Christian's duty to support his church. He spoke very understandingly. However, it was obvious he doubted me when I said we would take Little Georgie and have a good time. He again advised me, "Not so fast."

I became irritated and said, "We go at two o'clock. If Mei Ying doesn't go with us, we don't go tonight."

She said, "Okay, we go."

It was then one-thirty. She went to the bedroom, got her pillow and said, "Mr. Georgie, I go sleep. Okay?" Since it took her about half an hour to get ready to go anywhere, I took this to mean she was telling me by her actions she would not go.

I said, "Okay!" and tore up the Michaelmas tickets. I told Lee to tell her we were staying at home that night.

She came running out of her room and gaped for a moment at the tickets. She got some scotch tape and tried putting the tickets back together.

I said, "No good."

She started to sob and said, according to Lee, "Maybe I give your money back and I go back to hotel!"

I said, "Okay! Go back!" I told Lee to help her pack her bags.

She dissolved in tears. "Her say her is only talking. But you get mad," said Lee. "Her say you no have love for her. Her say you is no good *lo gung*." *Lo gung* is Cantonese slang for husband.

So saying, Mei Ying fled into her bedroom and slammed the door.

Ah Lee spoke to Dr. Li about my constant drinking. The doctor told him to have me cut back on the gin and instead drink several bottles of beer each day. "Him say, too much gin hots up your inside." I brought a case of beer, but couldn't bring myself to down a bottle of such insipid brew every day.

In early October I began noting signs of instability. My notebook entries were very emotional. I would sit at the typewriter and get carried away on a wave of tears or a gust of laughter. In sleepless hours at night, stray noises would be transformed into a cappella choirs or violin solos.

I'd had a similar experience on Barbados when Mama and I rented a pink coralstone bungalow by the beach. That month I drank many bottles of the island's fabled Mount Gay Eclipse rum. On sleepless nights after days when Dolly dominated my waking thoughts, the roar of the waves became an eerie Gregorian Chant, the Latin litanies rising and falling with the sound of the surf, muffled in the distance, but now and again clear and distinct above the noise.

Mei Ying asked if she might go to Kowloon to give a friend money to take to her brother in Canton who was ill with tuberculosis. She said she would be back before ten. I said all right, but come back *fai-dee, fai-dee*, quickly, quickly.

It was Lee's night off to visit his wife and children in one of the government's huge resettlement blocks in Kowloon. He was feeling muscle pain in his chest from helping me walk through the Central Market. I thought a bottle of Sloan's Liniment might help him, since he had been going to a herb doctor without noticeable improvement. I gave him the name on a slip of paper.

I was tired from typing all day. When Lee and Mei Ying left at the same time it annoyed me, but reason told me it was only natural that they should take the same taxi to the Star Ferry.

I gulped the gin and tea Lee had left me and typed on. When ten o'clock rolled around, I commenced to get angry. Visions of passion between Lee and Mei Ying clattered noisily across my inflamed brain. All one hour I sat and brooded. No Lee. No Mei Ying. My anger mounted and I decided to barricade the door. To hell with them, I'd show them! They wouldn't lie to me and get away with it.

I got on my knees and, mustering all my strength, shoved the heavy bureau and a foot locker against the door jamb. This will keep them out and cause them a bit of mental anguish comparable to what they are causing me. They could wait till morning to see me. Hadn't I waited long enough for them? Who was boss anyway? I flopped in a heap on the floor, curled up and dozed off.

At about 11:15 there was a great banging on the bedroom door.

"Mr. George! Mr. George! Open door!"

"Go away."

Then from the verandah near my window, "Please Mr. George. Open door."

Nuts to you, I thought, and remained curled up. Chiang applied his broad shoulders to the door and it came bursting open.

Lee and Chiang picked me up off the floor. "Let go! Leave me alone!" I yelled. As they sat me on the edge of the bed, I lifted my foot and gave Lee a shove that sent him reeling back against the wall. When I was loaded, I thought I was Zeus.

His face became a menacing mask. His small eyes crinkled fiercely. "You is for fight me!" he shouted, bubbling over with Cantonese anger.

"Hai!" I shouted. "I fight you." My face was flushed and contorted.

"Okay, I quit tomorrow. You is no gentleman!"

"Okay, quit!"

"If you no pay my doctor bill, I go police and I go Labor Board."

"You can go to hell. Don't try to scare me with the police!"

"No talk! No talk!" said the tearful Mei Ying.

Chiang dragged the voluble Lee out of the room. Lee was back in a minute, his arms full of parcels of clothes that Mei Ying had purchased, which he dumped on the floor with an angrily dramatic flourish.

"Mei Ying is for shopping," Lee shouted indignantly. "Chiang and me is follow her go many stores. She buy this and this and this." He helped Chiang bring in at least twenty boxes and bags of shoes, clothes and scarves and dumped it all on the middle of the floor.

"This is what I am doing! All night long!" Lee spread his arms in disgust. He said that they had gone three places before they found her friend. And in tones of high-pitched indignation he said he had spent an hour and gone to nine shops before he found the American medicine—Sloan's Liniment!

"I go pack now. Tomorrow morning I go," he blazed.

"Okay. Go on, pack," I fired back.

"I give you honest service. But you is very small heart man," he shouted as Chiang dragged him away again. "You make Mei Ying cry. You small heart!"

I lay sprawled on the bed. I was a stranger in a strange land. All this incomprehensible gabble—like the shouting now echoing from the kitchen. I felt boozily self-pitying. Tears began to flow.

Mei Ying put her hand on the back of my neck and sobbed, "I sorry, I sorry."

That opened wide the floodgates of my tear ducts and we were both sobbing mightily when Chiang arrived back dragging Lee in tow.

Chiang tried to get us to shake hands. Neither of us was agreeable. I said I did not like to be threatened and that I did not like his "small heart" talk. Lee said that many things are said in anger that are not true. We both sulked around for a while longer and at length grudgingly shook hands.

This should have been a warning to me that I was dangerously close to a mental precipice. Instead, I fairly reveled in the emotional vortex in which I found myself.

When October tenth, Double Ten, the Nationalist holiday, came, Mei Ying wanted to go out and celebrate. I was behind in my typing and did not want to go. She said then maybe I would give her the evening off. I refused at first. But she had the sulks and I relented. Just two nights before, I had made an ass of myself by barricading the door.

From now on I told myself, I'll trust her completely unless she gives me ample reason not to. Yes, she can go out and celebrate Double Ten. Anyway, I needed a little solitude now and then. What the hell. Let her go. Just be certain they leave me three water glasses full of gin and tea.

They left at eight p.m. and, knowing how they liked to make a night of it, I didn't expect anyone to return before one. But at ten-thirty, Lee came bursting into the apartment. Close behind him were Mei Ying, Chiang, Lee's wife and little Georgie.

Lee was very excited. "Big fight! Big fight! Kowloon! Many people is for fight!"

After he calmed down, the story emerged. They had been eating in a small restaurant near the resettlement block where his family lived. All at once, a great commotion. People running through the street at great speed. Shouts of, "Fight! Fight!" Bricks thrown. Glass shattering. The police in hot pursuit, firing tear gas.

Fumes drifted into the restaurant. Lee told the group to dip their handkerchiefs in water. Using these as masks, they cleared out and headed for the ferry as fast as they could. Soldiers with rifles and bayonets directed traffic at the Star Ferry pier.

This was an incident in the Kowloon Riots of '56. The fighting began when a Hong Kong Government official removed a Nationalist flag from the walls of a resettlement block. Their policy was to maintain strict neutrality between the Nationalists on Taiwan and the Communists on the mainland. The Nationalists protested, and for two days sporadic rioting kept the situation tense. Soon the Chinese criminal Triad Societies, a very powerful group going back to the old Dynasty period, accelerated the chaos by stirring up anti-Communist, anti-foreign feeling. The wife of the Swiss Consul ventured into the riot area and burned to death in a taxi. We, on the Hong Kong side of the harbor, were afraid the violence might spread and involve us.

Thea's servant, Ah Lan, was in the Shushimpo area of Kowloon visiting a friend when the rioting broke out. The Government suspended Ferry service between Hong Kong and Kowloon. Thea showed me a genuine blister she had acquired washing Stan's white shirt. In Hong Kong, *amah* power replaced kilowatt hours.

I glued myself to the Radio Hong Kong news, devoured press accounts, and wrote like mad. I sent Lee to the cable office to send my account of the affair to the *Examiner*. Lee came back and told me he had sent it without punctuation because it was cheaper. I've often wondered what the editor thought when he received it. Oh well, it was secondhand anyway because I lacked the credentials to enter Kowloon.

As soon as the Government lifted martial law, I visited the riot area by taxi. With Lee and Chiang's help, I walked around the administrative office of the Resettlement Block where the crowd gathered to protest the ripping down of the Nationalist flag. I saw broken windows, smoked walls and piles of papers evidently from the files. But the *Examiner* was not much interested in stale news.

Mei Ying brought home a paper bag full of giant diving beetles. I'd heard of these from people who had seen them in Chinese medicine shops, but I hadn't known they were a fall season snack food.

I pointed out to Lee their striking resemblance to our few remaining cockroaches. "No! No!" he said positively. "No cockroach! I don't know English name. Grow in farmer's water."

Among the books I had brought to Hong Kong was Zim's *Insects*. Near the back of the book I found a picture of Mei Ying's delicacies and read they were Giant Diving Beetles that live on underwater refuse. But Mei Ying said they were good eating and an aphrodisiac, too, which she explained by pointing to my penis and straightening her drooping finger.

She sat at my desk, broke off the head, wings and legs, popped the body in her mouth and crunched contentedly. Little Georgie, who at age four surely had no use for an aphrodisiac, gleefully grabbed some and chomped happily away, gaily scattering wings about the bedroom floor. My gang ate them like peanuts, with great gusto.

Lee said, "Very good eating. You want to try?"

"Sure."

Mei Ying prepared one for me, as Lee munched on a handful. It tasted good, like fried chicken with a slight varnish flavor, but they needed salt.

Stan thought I should be more careful about what I ingested. I think the idea of my "going native" bothered him. He said I should get more rest. I was usually hot and perspiring when he dropped by. He thought my ever-present glass of gin and tea a terrible combination.

I could see myself daily growing more fond of Mei Ying. The nights were getting cold and I felt I'd freeze to death without her to help keep the covers on the bed. She wrapped herself around me to go to sleep.

At one a.m. one morning, I dropped out of bed and crawled to my typewriter. I took a big gulp of gin and tea. The words just wouldn't come. All I got was, "The lights of Kowloon are sparkling like a treasure chest of diamonds, rubies, and emeralds. From Hong Kong Island it looks like any other night." It was trite and I knew it.

Mei Ying came to me in a t-shirt of mine that reached half way down her thighs. She placed my jacket around my shoulders.

"You sleep," I told her.

She answered quietly, "You no sleep, I no sleep."

She knew my writing was very important to me, and sat down in a chair beside me as I tried once more to get on with it. A mental cog was stuck.

Mei Ying checked the bedroom door. Soon after her arrival she had stuffed the keyhole with cotton, saying that Lee and Chiang were peeping. When she was sure it was securely closed, she returned and opened the Cantonese text on my desk to a page with many words and phrases written in both Chinese and English.

She pointed to "white ants" as she said, "Ah Lee no good. You money go, go, go." She made motions like tossing money to the winds. She put her finger on the words "dishonesty" and "liar" and said, "Ah Lee" with curled-lip scorn. She pointed to "commission" and "big" and said, "You give money me, Ah Lee take! Ah Lee no good!"

I had suspected as much. This made me angry. "How much did Lee take?"

She was reluctant to tell me, and begged me not to talk to Lee. She said she was afraid of him.

She made a nibbling motion with her fingers, and went on to say that Chiang and Lee's brother were termites too, eating from my kitchen.

After we went back to bed I lay awake for some time, listening to Mei Ying's regular breathing and wondering how I would take Lee in hand. Something in me rebelled at letting him get away with graft.

I was relieved to know that my suspicions about Lee were not just the ugly product of my imagination. I had began to wonder if I was developing a kind of evil eye which imputed dark motives to everyone around me. At the same time I felt very warm towards Mei Ying. She trusted me enough to confide in me. She obviously was not a cohort of Lee's, which was good to know.

Thea had seen Chiang carrying dishes full of food from my kitchen to the Caretaker's apartment. When she told me, I had expressed indignation. She reminded me that Lee, like most Chinese, was very poor and had to be watched. "Don't expect to make saints of Lee and his gang. My guess is you'll be doing good if you keep the graft within limits."

I told Mei Ying about halfway through the month that if she wanted she could leave and not return any of the money I'd paid her. She said she didn't want to leave. That she felt very much love for me. Maybe she was pretending. But I didn't think so.

When we were alone at night Mei Ying would get out the book and we would talk as best we could. The word "matrimony" started to take on a smudged appearance in the book.

I was beginning to take marriage seriously. Mei Ying was attractive. Lee was right; she would make a "very standard wife." I tried to analyze my feelings and list the reasons I loved her. I could fill a page with her good points, but it went beyond mere reasons. She satisfied in me the crying need of every creature to love and be loved.

My image of a prostitute had resembled the coarse, cow-like figures in drawings by Lautrec of the loose ladies of Paris. This was not Mei Ying. She had a school-girlish air of wide-eyed innocence, which seemed without artifice. Her love for movies and avidity for mah-jongg amused me from my lofty eminence of thirty-one years. I thought marrying her would be like taking a delightful child to raise. At the same time, I realized that it was presumptuous of me to consider a twenty-three-year-old as a child.

What would life be like until she learned English? I envisioned it as similar to the slow opening of a lovely flower as we were able to share more and more of each other's lives. She could open to me unfound doors into the world of Chinese culture. In America, I would perform a similar miracle for her.

Would she be happy in the woods of Kentfield? I rationalized she would—with me, my few friends, television and puppies. She loved me; I loved her. Kentfield would be awfully quiet after the hustle and bustle of Hong Kong, but the Mei Ying I had seen possessed strong inner resources.

The bittersweet melancholy of Lee's Chinese guitar drifted from the servant's quarters.

Above left: Edith, 1956; above right, Thea, 1956.

Shadows on the Dream

Chapter 4

Joy and grief are never far apart. In the same street the shutters of one house are closed while the curtains of the next are brushed by the shadows of the dance. A wedding party returns from the church; and a funeral winds to its door.

- Robert Eldridge Willmott

The night of October fifteenth Mei Ying asked me by way of the Cantonese text for a holiday to visit her mother in Canton to discuss marriage. I was willing to let her go. I needed a chance to look things over in the cool light of reason. I knew my first acquaintance with semi-domestic life had been so pleasing it might have overwhelmed my doubtful good sense.

Then, too, Mei Ying's absence would give me an opportunity to work on Lee to make him admit he had taken a commission. I rankled at the idea that my often sanctimonious "We-is-Christian-people" servant was operating as sort of a pimp. But to be fair, he was doing exactly what I wanted in finding Mei Ying for me.

Thea tried to calm me down. "Don't take it so hard, Barker. It's nothing new. It's part of their culture to get squeeze where they can." Perhaps I had expected too much of Lee with six children and a wife to feed. In his eyes, any American who could fly halfway around the world and take a luxury flat for five months was rich and could take a little fleecing without pain.

The stabbing in Lee's chest would not go away. The night he applied the Sloane's liniment, he scarcely slept. It practically burned him up. Worried I had injured him with my homespun prescription, I sent him to the doctor of his choice, who told him that he might have TB. Now, I felt sorry for Lee.

We made an appointment for him to see Dr. Henry Li, Edith's brother-in-law. I was left alone for an afternoon with nothing to drink. Mei Ying was on her way to Canton. The apartment was a mess and I needed a bath. I felt depressed and moody. November is the month I go home, I told myself. I'll tell Mama I'll be home by Thanksgiving.

But then, with Lee back, a bath, a drink, a cleaner house and the prospect of about ten hours' sleep following a satisfactory chicken dinner, I wrote Mama I might marry Mei Ying and stay till mid-December.

The evening after Mei Ying left on her holiday, Lee came to where I was typing and sighed, "The great God is punish me for many sorry matters." I looked up to see his eyes red and moist from weeping. His eighty-four year old blind grandmother was seriously ill. "Her say this world is only trouble. Her no want for live in this world anymore."

"Well, eighty-four is a good age," I said, trying to console him.

"But I very love my grandmother," he gasped, trying to control himself.

"I'm sorry she's so sick," I said.

"I want you should give me holiday tonight. My brother and I want for go hospital see my grandmother. I very afraid her is for die."

"Okay" I said. "Just leave me plenty of gin and tea. I'm going to go to sleep pretty soon, but I want to get up early in the morning and type."

"Thank you, Mr. George."

Next morning about eight-thirty, I had just finished a letter when Lee came in weeping. His grandmother had called his given name, Kuo Wah, several times in the night. He said if she lived, it would cost him a small fortune to keep her in the hospital. And if she died, the cheapest Cantonese funeral that would give her "face" would cost about $1600HK. This included casket, lot, "bury clothes," undertakers, hearse and band.

The thought of his calamity brought forth a fresh outburst. He sat by my desk and sobbed openly. "This is my unlucky time. Last year my mother is for die, now my grandmother."

"Well," I said, "Maybe I can help you a little with the money."

He wept even more uncontrollably.

Lee and his brother had scraped together enough money to place their grandmother in a hospital. Now, Lee said, the hospital wanted her to move, because if she died there it would hurt their good record. I could scarcely believe anyone could be so unfeeling and I expressed my doubts to Lee. He swore it was so.

I gave Lee the afternoon off for him to arrange the change of hospitals. Lee told Chiang to look after me. Chiang cooked me a good lunch and also a raisin cake, a sensitive gesture to help me keep down the serpent of latent homesickness.

A cool, clear moonlit evening October eighteenth kept me plugging away at the typewriter past ten o'clock. Even then, I hadn't done my self-imposed quota of writing, partly because I'd been upset by Lee's troubles. He returned still in emotional turmoil.

He had been to half a dozen hospitals before he turned to his priest in desperation and got his grandmother accepted by a Catholic hospital in Kowloon. Then Lee had to take his laughing, crying, hallucinating grandmother by taxi across the harbor to change hospitals. He looked dog-tired and about ten years older. I told him to try to get some sleep.

The next morning Chiang got me up, washed me, dressed me and made my simple breakfast. I worked a while, and then Miss Tse gave me my Cantonese lesson. After she left, Lee came into the room with his wife, his eldest daughter and Little Cowboy Georgie. All were dressed in their most formal clothes. Lee's wife had been keeping a bedside vigil and had come to tell Lee his grandmother had died. Lee wept quietly.

The next day Lee returned from the requiem Mass bearing his grandmother's death certificate. He said he, his brother and his aunt spent a years' wages for a funeral that sent her to glory in the proper style. I was thankful to see him dry-eyed.

When I told Thea that I'd given Mei Ying the opportunity not to return if she didn't want to, she was shocked. She had shown me some articles in the newspaper about unscrupulous Chinese girls who had led English boys to believe they would marry them and got them to give them large sums of money and then disappeared into China. She thought Mei Ying would just keep the money and go back to work in the Wanchai. But when she looked in Mei Ying's room and saw her prettiest clothes still there, she said, "Well! She must be coming back!"

Dr. Henry Li came by to tell me that Lee didn't have TB, just muscle strain, as I thought. I asked him to take some of my blood to test. I might have been exposed to God-knows-what venereal disease in my encounter with the boat woman, and Mei Ying could easily have picked up something plying her trade. He came by again to say, nothing serious, but he wanted to give us both a shot after Mei Ying returned. Dr. Li was so jolly and not at all pretentious. I really liked him.

I was still driven by a compulsion to have Ah Lee admit that he had taken a commission from Mei Ying. I called him into my room, had him sit down and asked him about it. He readily admitted that Mei Ying had given him a big bite of the money I had paid her, and said it was "a very common case." That night Lee was so frank and open and seemingly relieved, I had to laugh. I almost felt as though he really were my little brother.

Several days later, I asked Lee to take me by taxi to Edith's stately, old house on Conduit Road. She had been ill and I had not seen her for a month. I was bursting to tell her the news. As we seated ourselves in her living room, I said, "You should drop around to the flat and meet my girl friend."

"Your girl friend?"

"Yes," I laughed.

"When did this happen?" she asked delightedly.

"Just in the last month."

"Tell me all about it. How did you meet her?"

"At the Dairy Lane."

"What's she like?"

"Of course, I think she's really beautiful."

"All your girl friends are," said Edith. I detected gentle sarcasm.

"Well, I think I'm going to marry this one."

"You're joking!"

"No," I laughed. "I'm serious."

She appealed to Lee. "Is he joking?"

"No. Mr. George no joking."

Edith was so surprised that we three were all laughing.

"I can't tell when you are serious and when you're kidding," she said.

"Mei Ying, that's her name, is in Canton right now visiting her mother. She'll be back on the ten o'clock ferry day after tomorrow. If you'd like to take me to pick her up, you can meet her then."

"That'll be good. I'd like to do it. This is such a surprise. I do hope it all works out as you want. But—gee, George—I wish you knew a little more about this girl. Don't be in too big a hurry to rush into this thing. Some of these Hong Kong girls—well!"

I asked Edith if she would check with the American consulate and ask if I could get her into the U.S. if I married her. She was a citizen of Red China, and our relations with that government were virtually in the freezer at that time.

Edith picked up the telephone and learned from the U.S. Consulate that I could take Mei Ying home if she had never been a member of the Communist Party. If she passed the screening, it would take three months, more or less, to process her papers. The Consulate could not do a thing about it until we got married. In other words, marry her first and gamble on being able to take her home.

I thanked Edith and bade her good-bye, but she insisted upon driving us back to Welsby House. On the way, she reiterated several times her wish that everything would work out as I hoped.

At the apartment, I found a letter from Mama raising several objections to the marriage, but saying the right sort of Chinese girl might make the best kind of wife for me. She added it was my own life to lead, but admonished me to think carefully.

The day Mei Ying returned, Edith drove us to the ferry to meet her. As Lee helped me out of the car at Welsby House, I asked Edith what she thought of Mei Ying.

"She seems very nice, but I'll have to talk to her for a while before I can express an opinion."

"I need to talk to her too. Lee doesn't understand half of what I say. I want to discuss things with her. Could you come and interpret for us tomorrow?"

"Sure, George, I'd be glad to."

It was wonderful to have Mei Ying back. We laughed, teased, made love and talked. She said she had told her mother my legs were no good, but that my heart and mind were very good. She told me this by pantomime, patting my legs, pointing to my heart and head. She got Lee to tell me that her mother said it was her own life to live, that she should use careful thinking, similar to what Mama had written me.

Edith came the next morning to translate. There was much Cantonese between the two women. Mei Ying sat cross-legged on the bed and Edith sat primly in a chair.

I asked Edith what kind of Cantonese Mei Ying spoke. "Is it grammatical? Does she use slang?"

"She speaks perfect 'Classical' Cantonese—much better than I do—very formal, no slang."

After they had talked for a while, Edith turned to me and said, "She wonders whether they will let her into the U.S. She says she was a call girl."

My surprise at Mei Ying's frankness must have shown, because Edith said, "Don't look so shocked, George. Many nice girls from good families have come to Hong Kong where they didn't know anyone and have become call girls out of desperation."

She told Edith that since her father died in 1949 she had accepted the responsibility for her mother. That was why she had become a call girl. But if she could give her mother enough money to buy a house, she would feel her obligation had been fulfilled. I had Edith tell her that I had little income of my own and simply could not afford that much money.

After much Cantonese passed between them, Edith's manner became gently scolding. Mei Ying's posture sagged, and she looked sulky and petulant. Mei Ying told Edith she was afraid she wouldn't be able to adjust to life in America with no one to talk to and no friends.

"She has raised so many difficulties," said Edith. "Should I just tell her that you are sorry, but if she isn't sure in her own mind that she wants to marry you, you say, all right, never mind?"

I was dumbfounded and hurt, but what else could I do? "That's good," I said. I could feel antagonism growing between Edith and Mei Ying.

Edith said, "I'm sorry George. I know what a disappointment this must be. Perhaps it needs more time. But I don't exactly trust her. I'd like to see her on the plane to the U.S. before you give her any more money."

Edith left. Mei Ying and I sat looking at one another. Tears rolled down her silent, impassive face. Our eyes embraced and would not let go. I went to her on my knees, hoisted myself up on the bed, and took her in my arms. Clinging to her, I felt calm and peaceful. Come what might, I knew she had to go to America with me.

That night we locked the bedroom door. Sitting on the edge of the bed with my Cantonese text, we talked. I offered her an amount of money that she felt would take care of her mother, about two-thirds the cost of one round-trip air fare across the Pacific. She smiled and said, "Good!" This would not be enough to buy her mother a house, but it would pay her rent for a long time.

I went to the desk on my knees and took out my checkbook. Standing on my knees at the desk, taking fifteen minutes, I laboriously scrawled out a check for a large amount, the remainder to be paid in the States. I felt like a bulldozer on a downhill run—nothing could stop me now!

Moisture glistened in Mei Ying's eyes. She said, "I talk thank you, Georgie. Me the mudder talk thank you, Georgie!"

Looking back, I realize that despite my worldliness in some ways, in others I was like a peasant from the provinces. Mei Ying had a pair of silk stockings with the black lace halfway up the calf in back that seemed to me risqué. I persuaded her to purchase a plain pair, but whenever something important came up and I was anxious for her to look respectable, the plain pair was always conveniently dirty or wet.

I thought she should have some medium-high heels in addition to her usual spike heels. I gave her the money for them and indicated the height of the heel with my fingers. She came back with a pair of dancing shoes with spike heels of plastic glass.

I said, "Cowgirl shoes!"

Mei Ying said, "No cowgirl! Very good!"

Lee was filled with admiration for the "beauty shoes." I asked Thea if she'd be caught dead in a pair of shoes like that.

"Why these are lovely dancing shoes," Thea said. "Wish I had a pair like them." She held them up to the light to admire them. "Of course, I'd only wear them dancing." Turning to Mei Ying she said, "Very pretty, Mei Ying. I like."

I retired as Mei Ying's clothes consultant. When she went out in the daytime she wore plain black slacks, white blouse, black sweater and flat shoes. She put her hair in a small ponytail and declined makeup. She was as cute as a little, brown mouse. Sometimes she wore her "teacher" glasses.

I asked Thea if she would help us fill out the American Consulate's biographical data sheet in triplicate. This much we could have ready when we were married. Knowing it would be impossible for me to fill it in longhand, she said she'd be glad to.

That afternoon Thea came to the apartment. She was tired and hungry from teaching in Kowloon. Lee interpreted Mei Ying's answers to the Consulate's questions and I interpreted Lee's English for Thea.

Thea noticed a conflict of dates about when she entered the Colony. Mei Ying hedged about her work both in Hong Kong and Canton.

"Be honest. Tell the truth," I pleaded.

Thea became provoked. I was a bit embarrassed and mumbled something about it being a Chinese characteristic to be vague on dates.

"But this is ridiculous," said Thea. "Why, I can jolly well remember the dates of every place I've ever worked!"

After several more uncertain replies from Lee and Mei Ying, Thea put the pen down and said, "All right! I'm dying of hunger I'm going home and eat. I'll come back tomorrow and finish the bloody thing when she and Lee decide to tell the truth."

I was angry, too. All through supper I alternately pleaded and scolded. "Tell the truth. It will all be investigated. If the Consulate finds you have been lying, there will be trouble."

I was upset as much by Mei Ying's lack of faith in my judgment as her lack of honesty filling out a red-tape government form. That night as I sat typing, my anger grew.

On my desk were two five-dollar bills Thea had brought as change from money I gave her to develop a photograph she took of Mei Ying. I tore them into nickel-size bits, then rang for Lee. Both he and Mei Ying came. I asked for more gin and tea. They spied the money torn in a neat pile. They laughed and were a bit incredulous.

"What for?" asked Lee.

"Money is nothing compared to having a wife who doesn't trust you."

"You no understand this matter," said Lee. I had been hearing this refrain increasingly from him.

"Maybe I don't understand Chinese ways, but I know American ways!" I shouted angrily, in a foot-stomping manner. "And if we don't tell the truth, there will be big trouble!"

Mei Ying went to her bedroom, put on her jacket, clutched her purse and made ready to leave.

"Her say you no love or trust her," said Lee.

Tears were streaming down Mei Ying's cheeks as she said defiantly in Cantonese-English patois, "I come tomorrow for my clothes. I give money back. You me no more. You no good husband!" She turned abruptly and headed for the door.

I said, "Okay, go!" I'd be damned if I'd plead with her.

She was weeping copiously. Lee told Chiang to grab her. Chiang forced her back into the room, rather savagely. As he seized her he accidentally inflicted a cigarette burn on her wrist. Lee seemed to be enjoying the spectacle of Mei Ying weeping and struggling to escape Chiang's vise-like grasp.

I told Lee to tell Chiang to let her go, that I did not capture women. We had all been to see the movie "Bus Stop," in which Marilyn Monroe was manhandled by a cowboy. When Lee realized I was adamant, he relented. Chiang let go. Mei Ying, sobbing, fled down the corridor, the echo of her high heels fading into the night.

Chiang told Lee, "Now that she has his money, he will not see her again. You no sleep tonight. You watch Mr. George. He may try to kill himself." Fresh in his memory was the night I tried to barricade the door. He knew I was an unreasonable person and insisted Lee remove any poison medicines from my bureau drawer.

To reassure Chiang, I had Lee tell him that writers live only to write a story. But I had no doubt Mei Ying would return. I told Lee she would be back that night. He said skeptically, with half-averted eyes, "I think so," and "I hope so!"

I drank another gin and tea and passed out when my head hit the pillow. About 1:30 a.m. I woke to see Lee putting Mei Ying to bed. He said the watchman in the courtyard had called him about twenty minutes earlier to come pick her up. She had collapsed, dead drunk in front of the apartment house elevator.

This was very unusual. Ordinarily she wouldn't touch a drop of alcohol.

Lee dragged her up to the apartment toilet where she was sick. He put her in the bathtub and bathed her. He sprayed her with deodorant and put her to bed.

"Boy! Cigarette! Whiskey!" she mumbled.

She clutched the pillow and passed out.

In two or three days Mei Ying would be leaving for her final trip to Canton. In the meantime things continued to happen at a rapid rate.

We went to make our appointment to be married. The Registry Office required us to have our picture posted for two weeks, because many people with spouses on the Mainland try to marry again in Hong Kong. The Registry was booked with weddings until March. Lee said, "This is marry weather. Marry business very good." The Registrar, an elderly Englishman whom Lee called the "judgeman," listened sympathetically to my plea for speed. Edith helped explain my need to get the Consulate working on Mei Ying's papers. As a special favor, he gave us an appointment in only fifteen days. I could foresee a race between my dwindling bank account and Mei Ying's visa.

The weather was cool and dry. Flanked by Lee and Mei Ying, I climbed thirty steep steps to the photographer's studio in my heavy tweed jacket, Dacron shirt and bow tie without perspiring a drop. For the suddenly cool nights, Edith brought me a wonderful goose down comforter, three or four inches thick.

Stan, Thea, Edith, and Fook Kow all raised arguments against the marriage. They were mild enough that I could tell myself that every prospective groom must expect some doubtful voices. The gin and tea I drank gave me the exalted feeling that life belongs to him who dares. I regarded all cautioning voices as those of cowardice.

Bella wrote Mama not to worry because she was sure it was just a "passing fancy." The same day I wrote Mama I was definitely going to marry the girl.

That evening Mei Ying put on her slacks and sweater and took Little Georgie shopping. Lee came to my room to talk to me. In his hand was a letter in Chinese.

"Many troubled matters," he said.

"What's the trouble?"

"Mei Ying's auntsie is write me. Want me to tell you no marry Mei Ying."

Mei Ying's aunt! What business was it of hers? Mei Ying had brought her to the apartment for two days just before she went to Canton and had taken her home with her. During those two days, she had not lifted a finger. Her laziness irked me, and Mei Ying agreed with me that she was no good.

"And why not?" I asked.

"Her say Mei Ying have a husband and a baby girl in Kwangtung."

This knocked the wind out of me. "I don't believe it," I said.

"Her say you marry Mei Ying, you have much trouble."

"Well, I just don't believe she's married or has a baby!"

"You are my master," said Lee. "I am for service you. I don't know this matter. But I think is funny. Mei Ying's aunt give Mei Ying letter. I gave you honest service. I see Lee on letter and thinking it for me. I read. It say Mei Ying no marry you. It say her marry you her have many troubles. I think some strange."

I knew Lee read my mail while I was in the bathroom, but there was nothing I could do about it. For once, however, his inquisitiveness pleased me.

"Well, what do you think?" I asked.

"Mei Ying's auntsie very unstandard. Why her write two letters say same thing?"

"I think she's afraid Mei Ying will leave Hong Kong and she won't be able to get more money from her." On one of our trips to Kowloon, Lee and I had waited for Mei Ying while she went to a squatter shack behind a resettlement block to take her aunt some cash.

Lee smiled. I deduced we had reached the same conclusion.

The next morning I rang for Lee and asked him to show Mei Ying the letter. He was reluctant. I insisted. Mei Ying was sitting up in bed when Lee confronted her with it. She was incredulous. She doubled up her small fists and said her aunt lied. The words poured forth in a torrent, tumbling out so rapidly they tripped over one another. She wept angry tears. She was all for going to Kowloon and fighting her aunt. Two long strings of mucous dangling from her nostrils, the avalanche of words continued to pour forth. Lee, who was weeping a little himself, wiped her nose and eyes.

I didn't need to know Cantonese to tell that her story was heartbreaking. She said when her father was dying, he had called her to his bedside and told her the other relatives were no good and that he was counting on her to take care of her mother. With the family business ruined and her mother sick, she had gone into this "hard work" to see she got proper care. She told how when she was last back in Canton, she had bought a chicken dinner for her relatives and this aunt had slyly taken chicken out of her mother's rice bowl.

Lee finally calmed down enough to help me quiet Mei Ying. We had to talk her out of her narrow-eyed vows of vengeance. I feared she would get herself arrested and jeopardize her chances of getting a visa. She calmed down.

This was the day she was packing to leave for her last visit to China and her mother. Once she married me, there was no turning back. She would be crossing the Bamboo Curtain not to return to the land of her birth in the foreseeable future.

The writer collecting his material.

Gin and Fantasy

Chapter 5

Never lose a holy curiosity.

- Albert Einstein

Mei Ying left for her last visit to Canton on Saturday morning. We said our good-byes at the apartment and she promised to return in ten days. Ah Lee went with her to help her with her luggage as far as the Kowloon-Canton Railway Station across the Harbor.

I settled down to catch up on my correspondence. Lee returned about noon and told me all had gone well seeing Mei Ying off to Canton. He prepared a simple lunch of hot dogs, rice and bok choy. He said he would like to go home to Kowloon Sunday morning to spend the day with his family. I said sure, just leave me some toast and three glasses of gin and tea, that I planned to type all day. He left at nine and returned about six.

The evening wore on and I was still trying to write, though fatigued and starting to make mistakes. About nine, I felt nauseous and crawled to the bathroom and vomited blood. Stomach acid and alcohol burned my throat, causing it to swell. My throat felt as though it had been seared. I could not swallow. I couldn't stop vomiting. Even more frightening, I could scarcely breathe.

I told Ah Lee to phone Dr. Li who lived nearby. He came right over, gave me a sedative and told me to go to sleep and that I was not to drink any more alcohol. I said okay. He said he'd come to see me the next day.

Monday morning I breakfasted on milk and toast and went back to bed. There was still a full glass of gin and tea on my desk. I was tense, jerky and restless and thought that maybe just a sip of the gin would soothe me, but I resisted. I had asked Lee to order eight half-pint bottles of milk because I knew what my stomach needed, but Lee let the store boy come and go without leaving an order.

As I lay on my bed I heard voices on the balcony above our apartment. The lady who lived up there was asking, "Do you know what '*lo poh*' means?"

'*Lo poh*' is a term of rough affection in Cantonese. Literally, it means "old grandmother" and is used in much the same manner as an American might speak of his wife as "my old lady." Not exactly proper, but not lacking in a slangy sort of tenderness. I called Mei Ying my '*lo poh.*' Now I imagined the lady upstairs had been listening to our pillow talk. I felt embarrassed.

When I told Lee about the lady upstairs, he pretended to think it was a good joke and told me I had better get some sleep.

Then I heard Lee and Chiang and all the amahs in the courtyard laughing and shouting. "Do you know what *lo poh* means?" Their voices assumed a hollow, gong-like sound, echoing and reechoing around the courtyard.

I rang for Lee. I was furious.

"For Christ's sake, you didn't have to tell everyone!" I scolded.

He looked puzzled. "What I talk? I no talk anything."

I said very nastily, "You know what I mean!"

"You careful. No thinking more this matter," he cautioned.

I had crawled to the other room to escape the voices. But the lady upstairs moved too, so I had Lee take me back to my bed.

Then I heard Lee upstairs. He was weeping. "Mr. George is for die."

"Who told you that?" the lady asked.

"Li Fook-Kuen say last night," sobbed Lee, using Dr. Henry Li's Chinese name.

A discussion followed about what ailment was to be my demise. I lay shaking like a leaf, sweating and straining my ears to catch all the conversation. With the aid of a Cantonese-English dictionary, they narrowed it down to bronchial and finally to bronchiectasis, a rather rare disease about which I knew absolutely nothing except that Papa's first wife died of it. The husband of the lady upstairs expressed shock. "Of all the diseases in the world, it is absolutely the most fatal," he said with finality. My poor burned throat throbbed with soreness.

All this news worked me into a frightful state. As I was sitting on the edge of the bed, Stan came in the room. Thea had told him I was sick at my stomach the night before, because she had come over to talk about three minutes after I started vomiting. I had asked her if she and Stan had any medicine to soothe the stomach. She said they had nothing at their flat, but that they should, and that she'd ask Stan to get something the next day.

Now Stan appeared like a searchlight in my darkness.

"I'm just off work and thought I'd pop in and see how the old stomach is," he said brightly.

I immediately assailed him with a lurid account of the developments. Being a surgical nurse, he instantly recognized that I was sick in a region considerably higher than my stomach.

"Take it easy, fellow," he said. "You're just on edge. Even if you did have bronchiectasis, which I'll wager you don't, it isn't necessarily fatal. Probably not half as dangerous as that gin and tea you drink."

"I want you to promise me one thing." I begged. "If Dr. Li thinks it's serious, I want you to see that I'm sent home right away. I want to die at home, not here in Hong Kong."

"Certainly, George. I give you my word. But it's ridiculous. I've been telling you that the things you eat and drink would make you sick."

Just the week before he said that I must have the constitution of an ox to eat and drink the things I did. I took it with a grain of salt. I knew that some of the things I ate outraged his British sense of proper dietary habits.

Dr. Li came. His rotund, cheerful face helped to reassure me. I told him that I hadn't had a drink all day and was very nervous. He, of course, could see that I was shaking, glitter-eyed and that my voice had an unnaturally shrill pitch. He said he would give me a shot that would settle my nerves.

Dr. Li and Stan went into the other room for a moment and then came back. Dr. Li said, "I think it would be a good idea if you go to the hospital for a few days. You need a rest and we need to make some tests. Don't worry. You'll be all right.

Stan and Thea offered to accompany me and Lee in the ambulance. I was grateful to have them with me. They saw me settled and said they'd come to see me often. Lee was to provide my nursing care. I felt a little better.

But on the hospital elevator one of the Chinese orderlies glanced at me casually and said what sounded to me like, "Dying?"

The other replied, "Yes" in Cantonese.

Today, I'm sure what he said was, "Dai-ng?" or "number five?" in Cantonese, which is pronounced quite similarly to "Dying?" It shoved me deeper into the cobra pit of my poisoned imagination.

After Thea and Stan left, I was certain that Mei Ying was trying to come to see me but was being kept away. I believed she had been brutally beaten or killed in her desperate attempts to search for me. I heard her weeping and calling my name in the hall outside my door.

I would call and on several occasions I crawled out into the hall on my knees. The nurses frowned upon my crawling half clad through the halls, shouting "Mei Ying! Mei Ying! Come here, Mei Ying!"

As Lee tried to take care of me, I kicked out at him. I fell out of bed several times. He was replaced by two nurses, one night, one day. There was talk of moving me to another hospital where everything in my room would be padded, but I quieted down somewhat when Lee was removed.

The hemorrhage from my stomach stopped. I was placed on a milk diet. A consulting physician was called in. He was a craggy Scot from the University of Hong Kong. He wanted to know how much gin I had been drinking a day. I told him from two-thirds to three-fourths of a fifth. And before I came to Hong Kong? A quart of cream sherry wine a day, more or less.

He wanted to know if I had ever seen him before. I said his face was vaguely familiar.

"Where do you think you might have seen me?" he asked.

"I think maybe I saw you once at Stanford Hospital in San Francisco," I replied.

"Yes," he said. "It's possible. I've been there."

I gloated, supposing I had scored a big triumph.

A voice said, "He's never been there. He just said that to make you feel good."

Someone told me my mother had been sent for. That only confirmed my belief that I was dying. My voices had changed the diagnosis from bronchiectasis to cancer of the throat.

Dr. Li's B-complex injections looked and smelled like mustard gas. I told him so. My voices were proud.

"He told Li Fook Kuen that it may be B-complex but it looks like mustard gas to him," my voices told each other.

"Gee, he's brave," said a voice larded with sarcasm.

The nurse would try to give me a pill.

"Don't take that medicine, Georgie! Li Fook Kuen hates your guts for dragging the Li family name in the gutter. Don't let them give you that medicine. It's potassium cyanide!"

A man who is dying of cancer isn't very afraid of being poisoned. I was frightened of Dr. Li, but I didn't trust my voices either.

One of my voices said, "You stick with Dr. Li, Georgie. He's the best friend you've got right now." This must have been my voice of reason. I decided to be poisoned or cured like a man. I took the pill.

The blank white walls began to take on kaleidoscopic patterns like ever-changing wall paper. "That's the cyanide pill! Quick, while the nurse is out of the room. Go to the bathroom and burp it up. It's your only chance. Do you know what the death agonies of cyanide poisonings are like?"

I dropped to the floor and crawled to the bathroom. The nurse was right behind me. "What do you want?" she asked.

I felt a little chagrined, "I er . . . uh . . . want to urinate." She turned her back and waited, then she took me to bed.

Some of my voices were nurses too, but Americans, and they spoke my language. The Chinese woman who was my day nurse spoke a little English and was pretty good. My night nurse knew almost no English and the less said about her the better.

I overheard several nurses talking about a big air crash in the Aleutians.

"This poor guy's dying of cancer and now his mother's killed on her way to say farewell!"

Who else could they have meant but me? One was reading the details aloud. "A Northwest Airlines plane bound from Seattle to Tokyo and Hong Kong crashed at an early hour this morning in the icy waters off the Aleutians. Aboard the ill-fated plane was a San Francisco college professor on a mercy mission to comfort her son who is dying of cancer in a Hong Kong hospital. Professor Barker was not among the survivors."

This news broke me down. I tried to get the details but none of the morning papers seemed to have an account of the crash. I grabbed a copy of the *China Mail* from Dr. Sun that afternoon when he came to visit. Not a word.

My voices told me that Edith had spent a thousand dollars to have a dummy copy of the paper printed in order that my last hours would be happy. That sounded rather like my generous friend.

Edith wrote my mother:

November 6, 1956

Dear Mrs. Barker:

Soon after you left, I was under treatment at Queen Mary Hospital for my long and painful headaches, which lasted for weeks at times. I was constantly under some kind of drugs which made me dopey—and hence didn't see George for a month and a half—but would send my servant over to see how he was.

During that one and a half months, George became acquainted with Mei Ying and fell deeply in love. He came to tell me at the middle of October that he wanted to get married. I've been the translator for George on two serious occasions and met her two other times casually—George has probably written to you about her—so you probably know more than I. As for my views (perhaps you want to hear from someone who's seen and talked with her), she seems to be thoughtful of George's every concern, quiet and mature for her twenty-two years of age.

I've told George about women in H.K., to be careful—trying to discourage him from going deeper—but he's made up his mind, and once he's done that, you know how hard it is to say anything else. I've told him repeatedly and warned him that this might not come out as he wishes and he said he'll chalk it up to experience. Mei Ying has gone to Canton again to have a last visit with her family before her marriage. Their engagement is registered and the date is set for November nineteenth at ten a.m. George has asked Lee and me to be his witnesses.

On the day of Mei Ying's departure, George had gastritis with a small hemorrhage. Dr. Li, my brother-in-law, thought it best to have George in the hospital for a few days' rest—away from his gin, as that was probably the cause of it. He gave him a few injections to relax him. George has been on a milk diet for two days now, and Dr. Li said he can have a very diluted drink tomorrow, one part whiskey to twenty parts water. George said he doesn't want it. Your son is certainly stubborn at times.

We all thought a few days' rest would do him well, but George's mind seems to be a bit disturbed. He speaks of things which are not true—but are connected to his daily life, such as "someone was at his apartment reading his notebook" (and had Lee rush home to lock it up); "that you were flying out," and "I had cried all night." Outside of these statements, he seems perfectly logical and well. Dr. Li came tonight to say that he wants to call in a nerve specialist, the best in H.K. (the one who treated me for my headaches), and I said—I'm sure you would agree.

Dr. Li is confident that he can cure the gastritis and the hemorrhage has already stopped. It's George's mental disturbance that worries all of us. I go to the hospital at least two times a day, and Lee is staying with him. Please don't worry, and I shall write again soon. George has asked me to write a letter for him tomorrow, probably to you. Before he became ill, George asked me to book two seats with JAL for December eighteenth.

Love, Edith

P.S. Lee just called from the hospital to say that George keeps on calling for Mei Ying and there's no way we can get in touch with her.

On November 7, 1956, at 11:30 A.M., in my room at the Central Hospital, I sat up in bed and dictated a letter to Edith. It was a last farewell to my friend, Bud, in the States. I spoke unusually clearly and distinctly, emphasizing each syllable in cold anger.

Dear Bud:

Things around here have been moving at a rapid pace. Edith and others tell me it is only fantasy, but even if it is only fantasy, I believe it.

First, I will tell you about Mei Ying, the girl I am very much in love with. To some people I suppose she would be just another snub-nosed Cantonese, but she means the world to me. We had planned to be married on November nineteenth, but tragedy has marred our plans.

I came to the hospital on Monday, November fifth, with an illness of uncertain nature. Some people thought it very grave. Others thought not. And, of course, I do not know.

The day I entered the hospital, I heard some people sending a wire to Canton, asking Mei Ying to come back. This she did. But she was not permitted to see me.

Mei Ying is a girl of very determined mind. In order to keep her from me, someone thought up the bright idea of telling her I was dead. She did not know what to do.

I told my servant, Ah Lee, to send Mei Ying a note. Of course, he pretended that she was still in Canton. He addressed the envelope to Canton. Then he went around the corner out in the hall. The whispers about whether to give her the note reached my ears and there was much drama about how she had wept all night last night because she thought me dead.

Several hours passed and Mei Ying read my note. She was here at the hospital begging to get in. Some of the nurses said yes. Others said no—to come back during visiting hours. She tried, but still no admission.

About ten or eleven p.m., there was a great commotion in the hall and I heard Mei Ying's voice crying, "Georgie! Georgie!" It appears she had climbed up the outside of the building—brick by brick and stone by stone—to the fifth floor in order to try and see me. She got to this ward and pleaded and pleaded, "I have love for my Georgie and Georgie have love for me!"

The nurses were almost ready to give us an hour together. But the night supervisor came along. She was willing to give us five or ten clandestine minutes after the nurses pleaded with her. But my servant, Lee, for some unknown reason, did not want us together at all. He cornered Mei Ying and kept her from coming to the part of the ward where I could call to her.

Once, she got away from Lee and into the elevator. He pushed a button and off she went. He followed her down and beat her rather severely, but she came right back. She was in pretty bad shape, I guess. She had been drinking, anyway.

Again Ah Lee corralled her and I could hear her crying and pleading. I called Ah Lee a number of times but he wouldn't come, so I got out of bed and crawled out to the main hall where a nurse came and told me to go back to bed and go to sleep.

I said I didn't want to sleep but wanted to see Mei Ying. The nurse said, "All right, go to bed and I'll bring her to you."

She took me to bed and gave me a strong sedative instead. I told her I would not sleep until she brought me Mei Ying. She said O.K., she'd go get her, thinking that no doubt the sedative would put me right under. I was only able to stay awake half an hour or an hour, although I tried, maybe not even that long.

When Dr. Li came this morning I asked him if it would be all right for my girlfriend to visit. He said he thought she was in Canton. I said no, she flew back as soon as she heard I was ill.

Shortly after the doctor left I heard her in the hall again, evidently quite drunk, asking to see me. The nurse said I was on the bedpan and told her to come back later.

The next thing I heard were screams: "Don't let her fall! Don't let her fall! Mei Ying! Mei Ying! Don't!" And then a gasp.

Five minutes later someone said she was bleeding to death on the concrete paving of the courtyard. I finally heard many times that she had a fractured vertebra and can never walk again.

I've asked many people if I could go to see her, but they deny that any such person as Mei Ying ever existed around here. So, you see, I feel rather trapped. If she is conscious, I would like to see her. But I doubt that I will ever he able to see her in this hospital environment.

The happiest month of my life was spent with her.

They tell me I have nothing serious wrong with me. But I can feel the sloughing off of the cells in my throat. And this, of course, means something very serious indeed. I cannot trust anyone to tell me the truth about my health any more than I can trust them to tell me about Mei Ying. I am probably dying of cancer.

Please drink plenty of wine for me and remember the good times we had together.

George

The same day I dictated the letter to Bud, Edith wrote my mother:

November 7

Dear Mrs. Barker,

The doctors advise your presence and to take George out of this environment as soon as possible before he becomes more serious. They are trying to put him into Queen Mary Hospital tomorrow and into a safe room with padding and bars as he tried to open his room window last night, imagining Mei Ying to be climbing up to the sixth floor brick by brick. It's a protection for him.

I don't know how to express my regrets and how sorry I am over this whole matter, Mrs. Barker. We all like George very much and in some ways feel some responsibility—if he would only listen to someone—but he is completely hypnotized by Mei Ying and I can't help feeling that Lee is mixed up in this somewhere.

We all think that George's experiences these past two months have been too much for him—the physical relationship with Mei Ying, the mental anxiety of whether she would come home and stay with him, the mental strain of juggling his finances to meet her demands have strained him both mentally and physically. The yearning for her and the anguish of doubt seems to disturb him no end—and there is no one who could

*make him listen and realize the situation he's in and the damage it is
causing.*

*We all know how difficult it will be for you to come over—but it seems
there is no other way—especially when George is in this mental state.*

*I am at the hospital constantly, chatting with him and trying to get his
mind off Mei Ying. This morning George asked me to write a letter to
Bud telling him what he thought happened. Please tell Bud, George is
not well. This hospital is quite nice—it's where I had two of my babies.
My brother-in-law does all his surgery there. But where George is to
be moved tomorrow—the Queen Mary—they're very strict on visiting
hours.*

*Outside his mental state—physically—George is all right. The gastritis
and hemorrhage stopped the second day and he's still on milk and
congee was added to his diet today.*

*Everyone George knows in Hong Kong seems to have gone to see him.
All are most thoughtful and George seems quite relaxed when we chat
on other matters. The doctors don't think that bringing Mei Ying back
would help matters at all. The only thing is for George to leave here
and all the problems that he's surrounded himself with.*

Let us hear from you,

Edith

I wondered how I could hear the voices when no one else could. The
answer was simple: I had super-sensitive eardrums combined with an innate
ability to converse silently by brain waves. How stupid were all those who
thought I didn't know exactly what was going on! I picked up the news that
Mama had survived the crash, but had a broken spine and would never walk
again. Then the dismal news that several uncles had committed suicide at
hearing of Mama's death. She insisted upon continuing the journey to Hong
Kong on a stretcher. Then I got word she was having a hemorrhage and had
died at the Tokyo airport.

I simply did not know what to believe. Edith showed me a telegram from
my mother. It said: ARRIVING SUNDAY JAL FLIGHT 608. A put-up job,
said my voices. Edith tried to reason with me. It wouldn't work. I was wise,
Mama was dead and evidently they thought I'd be dead by Sunday or they

would not have put Sunday on the cable. If I continued in fair health, they'd just have one made: FLIGHT POSTPONED.

The most horrible night in the series of horrible nights, was when the doctors were trying to patch up Mei Ying. She seriously injured herself when the elevator in which she was riding to escape Lee had gone out of control and plummeted to earth. I could hear the doctors working on her in the next room. They made a terrible racket and were quite frenzied in their desperate efforts to save her life.

They kept knocking her head against the floor with a terrible, sickening 'cluck' every time she regained consciousness because they couldn't administer an anesthetic. The cry kept going up every five minutes or so: "More blood! More blood! More morphine." And there would be a great scuffling and tramping of feet as more blood was rushed to the scene.

This was a class A emergency, but only a few residents and interns were at the hospital at that hour. These amateurs were trying to patch up my beloved. Evidently they were bungling the job.

The voices of my friends upstairs kept me morbidly informed of the whole bloody proceeding. "She surely is messed up!" said one. The floor was so slick with blood and the air was so fetid with the odor of blood and viscera that several inexperienced nurses vomited.

These amateurs were not sewing her up properly, my friends said. They were going at it patchwork fashion. What was needed was a master surgeon like Li Fook-Kuen!

"More blood! More morphine!"

"Oh God, no! Mei Ying's vomiting again. Every time she has a paroxysm it tears out some stitches and they've got to open her up again."

"More blood! More morphine!"

"Georgie! Georgie! Wonderful news. Dr. Li and his brothers are coming to operate. The world's greatest surgical team. If anyone can save Mei Ying's life, the Li brothers can do it. Bless Li Fook-Kuen!"

I will spare my reader all the grim and gory details of how the Drs. Li laid open the body cavity and with swift and sure strokes of the surgeon's knife eliminated all that was damaged and useless. How they sewed the torn and broken organs together with neat stitches. And how they saved the life in her womb of our child-to-be.

My voices were unanimous in congratulations on impending parenthood. I was jubilant to think that I had kept faith with my germ plasma and had planted the seed of a new generation just before I died. I thought too, or rather my voices told me, that my remaining relatives would see that Mei Ying got out of Hong Kong if she had a child by me.

I was tearfully grateful to Dr. Li for saving Mei Ying's life and when he came to see me the next morning there was a catch in my voice as I said, "I want to thank you, Doctor, for cutting up Mei Ying and putting her back together." Doctor Li seemed somewhat taken back. I guessed he didn't think I knew.

With the logical part of my mind I did not think it was morally wrong for Mei Ying and me to live together unmarried. Morals are largely a matter of time and place, anyway, and it seemed to me that it was natural for a man to have a woman. I tried not to be hypocritical. Besides, I was certain that having Mei Ying was good for me physically and mentally.

But despite this, there were faint stirrings of guilty feelings hidden deep in recesses of my mental library that made me vaguely uneasy. We do not unceremoniously discard the ideas and examples of our parents. I knew many people, including good friends, who would have been shocked and disappointed had they known that I was "living in sin." Remember, this was 1956.

Mama was unhappy about it, I knew. So, evidently, was the Episcopal Bishop of Hong Kong, for he sent a priest named Father Heather to scold me for living in sin with Mei Ying. Typical of my confused state of mind, this Anglican minister was supposed to take my confession, give absolution and then administer the last sacrament.

One reason I think I pulled Father Heather and the Bishop out of my subconscious was that Edith, uncertain about Mei Ying, had suggested that I confer with the Bishop about marrying. He understood the Chinese, she said. But I did not think he would be very likely to approve, so I said no.

I could hear someone just outside my door engaged in conversation with Father Heather. It was one of my voices and he was telling the Father: "He won't do it. He doesn't think it was sinful at all."

"His mother dead! His relatives dead! His girlfriend suffering the agonies of the damned! He—dying of cancer in a few days! And the Bishop sends me up here to tell him his last moments of happiness were sinful," said Father Heather.

"I don't envy you the job," said a voice. "Especially when having Mei Ying was so good for Georgie. Relieved his tension. Doctor said it was fine."

"This is the damnedest thing I ever heard of. Having a woman as medical treatment. I wonder what the Bishop would say about that!" He pondered a moment. "I'm going to go back to see the Bishop and ask him to let me out of this. If having Mei Ying was a medical treatment, how can it be sinful?" He flushed with embarrassment and laughed. "I'll probably be defrocked for this, but I can't go through with it."

"Could you baptize Mei Ying?" my voice asked. "She isn't conscious now."

"Yes," he said piously, "I can baptize her. At least she'll die a Christian."

There was described the painful scene of the minister weeping at Mei Ying's broken condition and the courage with which she bore her suffering and the tragic situation in general.

Instead of going to see the Bishop directly, Father Heather volunteered to go to a hospital in Kowloon to get more blood. It was a desperate race. Mei Ying was spurting like a broken hose. By the time he got all the blood rounded up, it was two or three in the morning. One could hardly blame the Bishop for being sore and adamant at being awakened at that hour.

"A sin's a sin," he told Father Heather. "Stealing relieves kleptomania, but that doesn't make it right. George Barker is a good-for-nothing sinner and you should know it."

That's the report my voices gave me—but I never saw Father Heather, so I really don't know.

A blood-and-thunder melodrama about the tender and gentle Mei Ying bringing death to the evil, arch-villain Ah Lee, consumed most of one night.

The girl who had leaped from the sixth story window was really the notorious Lee Anna, perpetrator of every crime imaginable, who had been confused with the sweet and true Mei Ying.

The real Mei Ying was being kept from me by the evil genius, Ah Lee, and had been so brutally beaten the nurses were afraid the shock of seeing her might kill me.

The nurses kept her away from me for hours and got her to join them in bedpan drill. Some people have never heard of "bedpan drill." I confess it was new to me. It was kind of a game with the laudable purpose of eliminating sloppy bedpan handling. The object of the game was to fill a bedpan with water, speed up to the roof in a freight elevator, run to other freight elevator, whiz down, slam open the door and pour the water into a bucket without spilling a drop. This was timed with a stop watch. As the door slammed open and the water was poured into the bucket, I could hear a voice calling out the number of seconds that each participant took to complete the job.

Mei Ying started out slowly. She hadn't had the experience with the elevators, for one thing. She was inclined to come down too fast and apply the brakes so quickly that there were at least half a dozen times she had to be removed from the elevator on a stretcher and her face repatched. But soon she had set a new record for the hospital and I was proud when I heard everyone congratulating her.

Then, like a devil out of Hell, Lee appeared. He was going to capture her again and beat her for coming to see me. Twice before he had trapped her with his superior knowledge of elevator operation. But now she was ready for him. She saw him coming, shot up to the roof, waited till she saw him start up in the other elevator, shot down to my floor, filled a bedpan with water while everybody was urging her not to fool around—he's coming! She shot up to the roof and as he stepped from the elevator two floors below she dropped the bedpan of water on his head, squashing it like a watermelon. "He never knew what hit him," said one of my voices. "It's the first time I've ever heard of a bedpan used as a deadly weapon," said another. The rejoicing was great that the world had been rid of that bastard Lee!

My voices lashed me about my notebook. They told me I had written unspeakable things about my friends, especially Edith and Thea. They kept screaming at me about my "dirty, filthy notebook." Since I was dying, they said, all my friends were reading it, some were nauseated, and all were angry. I was angry too at what I considered an invasion of my privacy.

I begged Edith to forgive me for writing that her husband was a boor. My voices told me that my friends were revolted at the lurid, vulgar manner in which I described my meeting with Mei Ying. They quoted some disgustingly filthy passages and said I had written them. They sounded off on them until I half believed I had.

Later, when I got out of the hospital and mustered up the guts to look, one of the first things I did was to leaf through my notebook with trembling fingers. I need not have worried for there was nothing offensive in it.

When I first heard that everyone was going through my notebook I instructed Lee to go home and lock it up along with my Cantonese books. My voices told me my friends were going to destroy them to keep Mei Ying and me from communicating.

Miss Tse was a regular visitor at the hospital. She told me I should be glad my girlfriend hadn't come back from Canton. "There are too many of that kind of girl in Hong Kong," she said. "Now you are going home, I understand. Too bad we did not have time to finish the First Book. I am sorry, for you were a good student." This was the first inkling I had of the suggestion that I should leave the Hong Kong environment as quickly as possible.

I received another shock when Edith told me she had written my mother "the facts about Mei Ying." She said she had written two letters, one fairly mild and then, when I got worse, one in which she really told how she felt. She intimated that she had attributed my illness in part to Mei Ying. From the manner in which she told me, I thought the letter must have been a bit of a scorcher.

At about the same time, Uncle Kim, who I had hoped might send me more money, wrote me he was temporarily broke.

One glorious morning after I had been in the hospital six days, Lee came in dressed up in his gray suit and blue tie.

"Mr. George" he said, "I go ferry now for get Mei Ying. Her coming on ten o'clock ferry from Macao."

I waited, half fearful, lest it be another trick. My voices told me it was a deception.

At ten thirty, Mei Ying came. She was dressed in her black silk traveling pajamas which were dusty from the journey.

"Georgie, Georgie! What for, Georgie?" she exclaimed. Tears glistened in her eyes.

"I don't know, baby. I don't know. But I'm okay now."

I was never so glad to see anyone in my life. I grabbed her and hung on. I was laughing and crying a little and kissing her hands and her face. As I held her, I became more and more certain that she was the real thing.

And she wasn't battered, bruised or beaten at all. Maybe since Mei Ying was all right, my mother was all right too. Maybe I wasn't dying of cancer after all. Funny thing! My throat was no longer sore, come to think of it.

With Mei Ying's arrival, I began to get things in perspective. I commenced to realize that the whole experience had been a hideous nightmare.

When Mei Ying returned from Canton, she came straight to the hospital and that night took over my care from the poorest nurse in existence. She was tiny, but she slipped off her slippers, jumped up on the bed, planted her feet squarely on each side of me and heaved me up. She kept me in good shape.

She was completely worn out and needed sleep after traveling all night. There was a small nurse's cot across the narrow room Mei Ying tied one end of her bathrobe belt around her wrist and tied the other to the head of my bed. All I had to do was pull the sash and she woke up, saying, "Whatuwan, Georgie?" While no remarkable feat, it showed a little ingenuity.

Mei Ying bathed me, trimmed my nails and shaved me with loving tenderness. The day nurse, while pleasant and willing, had somewhere acquired the weird notion that the way to shave a man was to rub dry talcum on his face and then attack him with a safety razor. After one painful experience, I refused to let her approach me when she had the razor in her hand. Mei Ying knew that powder was for the electric razor, soap and water for the safety.

I tried to talk to Mei Ying and tell her some of the horrible things I had imagined. But she said, "No talk!" Her idea seemed to be that my troubles were over now, so I should forget about them.

Mei Ying cranked the bed up to the sitting position and crawled in with me. Sitting there with her head on my shoulder, she said "Ah Lee telephone you sick. I talk me mudder. Me mudder talk, you darling sick, you go quickly!"

"I am sorry you had only four days in Canton," I said.

"Never mind," she said. "Suppose I no come quickly, I no good *lo poh!*"

The next morning I had Edith cable my mother after receiving a FLIGHT POSTPONED cable from Kentfield. I felt better now and had Edith cable back: OVER DTS. FEELING FINE. DON'T COME UNLESS YOU WANT TO ATTEND WEDDING. OFF BOOZE FOREVER, LOVE GEORGE.

Then, on the thirteenth of November, Edith wrote:

Dear Mrs. Barker,

George is all well now and laughs over the delusions and crazy ideas he had. We're all relieved to have him back to normal and I know it must have given you a big scare as it did us.

Mei Ying came back on Saturday morning the tenth and George is completely happy and contented. His life seems to be complete with her—and I feel so frustrated not knowing what to say about all this. My last letter was frank and so are my opinions. I've told George I wrote you about the situation. I sometimes wonder whether—if they live happily ever after—I shall feel badly about writing as I did. And yet, if I keep silent my heart will not feel at ease.

Mei Ying stays all through the night—being his night nurse—and partly during the day. She goes back to the apartment to wash up and cook his meals, which he eats with gusto. And a few days ago he didn't feel like eating anything! She takes care of him with understanding and consideration.

I've received your letters of the ninth and tenth about keeping him in the hospital. I showed Dr. Li the telegram and he said he'd call me tomorrow morning. So I'll continue after he calls and after I have seen George.

On November 16th, she wrote agaain.

I've just received your long typewritten letter and feel so badly that I've upset you so. There's nothing to be ashamed or humiliated about.

George is only human. I've talked with him about the possibility of his not being able to bring her to the States. Then he said he'd have to go home alone without getting married as he can't possibly make a living in Hong Kong. The wedding date has been postponed till the twenty-ninth of November after George finds out definitely whether he can take her back or not before proceeding with legal action. He leaves the hospital tomorrow. The first thing he will do is type a letter to you; secondly, a letter explaining the situation to the American Consulate.

Out of all this there is just a possibility that she will take good care of George after they marry—what then? And if George is so determined, I would feel terribly badly that your ill feeling toward her was the result of my opinionated letter. At present, she's devoting herself to helping George recover.

As friends we all want George to be happy. There's not much more I could say to persuade him—though I go to the hospital every day and talk to him. He's quite made up his mind to try and get her over. If he fails, then he'll return alone—which is all for the best and nothing more need be said. If he succeeds, Mei Ying will be his wife and your daughter-in-law by then. I think that you must make the best of things. Sometimes kindness and understanding can do miracles. I know I am very bold to offer you this advice and hope you'll understand George's situation has been on my mind constantly ever since he came and told me he would get married. I feel so unwise and helpless and frustrated.

I'm so sorry all this happened—the added expense, the worry and anxiety it has caused you, Mrs. Barker, especially when you've always had such a favorable outlook on the Chinese.

Love, Edith

After I asked Dr. Li, "Doctor, have I been having the DTs?" and he replied "You sure have," one might have thought I had the problem licked. Not at all. My voices were still with me.

In hospital, they were constantly with me, tormenting and vilifying me, leaving no stone of my private life unturned, no pretense unshattered, no hole in which to hide.

My room was on the sixth floor and I thought there was a long verandah outside my window. One of my unseen companions, the weird woman on the verandah, haunted hospitals in hopes of procuring a handful of morphine tablets to assuage her addiction. She had a remarkable gift for mimicry. She would go from window to window and pick up snatches of conversation and then peddle them around the hospital.

Somebody told me not to listen to her. That she was an idiot savant who was attracted by my ravings. But she said no, she had been a nurse in a great hospital. One night while on duty she developed a toothache and took a little morphine to ease the pain. It made her feel so good that she quickly acquired the habit. Her conscious mind was so drugged that she acquired the capabilities of an idiot savant. She certainly put me through hell before I found out.

I still heard voices. But they were no longer weird, at least not like the woman underneath my window.

I suspected they were in my head—"We're TB patients in the ward above you. We're sorry we had to do this to you. But, gosh, Georgie, we're so darn bored. And you were the first real fun we've had in months."

I thought that over—accepted it momentarily—then rejected it. "You can't fool me," I said. "TB patients don't stay awake all night."

"Don't pay any attention to them, Georgie," said a voice from the window next door. "They're just a bunch of screwed up psychiatric nurses, interns and orderlies. They're driving us crazy too."

Then another voice from the same window, "You kids ought to be ashamed of yourselves. You put George Barker through hell."

But then I began wondering why all my voices had American accents. I said, "You guys can't fool me anymore. You're all in my head."

"He knows. He knows," said a voice in mock horror. "Little Georgie knows everything that goes on in this hospital. He knows everything about every-thing."

Another voice, "Little Georgie don't know nothing about nothing. Why not tell him the truth. We're Fulbright scholars at the University of Hong Kong. Georgie, I knew you at Stanford Hospital. We wanted to study a CP with the DTs. I will tell you frankly we were amazed."

"Yeah," came a cynical voice, "We were amazed all right—amazed that anyone has such a damn filthy mind! You have the filthiest mind I've ever listened to in years of studying filthy minds and that's the God's honest truth."

"Don't listen to him, Georgie. Your mind is no cleaner or dirtier than anyone else's. But when you were babbling away, you really let the barriers down."

Then a woman's voice sobbing, "It's that goddamn whore. She's dragging our Georgie into the gutter."

"She is not a whore. She's a respectable call-girl. That's what Georgie wrote his mother. Isn't that right, Georgie?"

"A whore is a whore is a whore."

"Mei Ying is not a whore and Bok Pin is a respectable dancing instructor. She runs a respectable dance hall. I've been there myself many times and have enjoyed myself each time."

"Bok Pin is not a dancing instructor. And she runs the dirtiest, filthiest, whoriest whore house in Hong Kong."

"Mei Ying is not a whore. She's a call-girl. Men take her out for dinner and they dance afterwards and sometimes that's all. Just like America, only here they get paid for it. I wouldn't mind that kind of a life myself."

"Oh, how can you say such a thing?" sobbed the weeping one.

"It beats juggling bedpans," said the bolder nurse.

"For Christ's sake, do you have to broadcast my affairs from the rooftops?" I said. "Haven't you any respect for privacy? How would you feel in my place?"

"We wouldn't be in your place for a million dollars, Little Georgie, and that's the God's honest truth."

My fears, doubts, love and hatreds had gushed forth in a mighty torrent. I had a complete mental catharsis administered by a multitude of voices, each of which was a part of my own being, fractured like a pane of glass catapulted onto a concrete floor.

I remember vividly the day Stan and Thea came to see me at the hospital in an effort to dissuade me from marrying Mei Ying. Thea started out by trying to arouse suspicions of Mei Ying, saying that there might be something to all my imaginings of an affair between Mei Ying and Lee. But that was long past. I asked her if she knew something that I didn't and she replied, "No, but I wouldn't trust her as far as I could throw her!"

"Well," I said, "I trust her. And as soon as we are married we're going to dispense with Lee's help and move to a smaller place."

Thea said she doubted that I could get Mei Ying into the U.S., the Consulate had sounded so doubtful. I said I thought they were encouraging.

Stan said, "I know what Her Majesty's government would do to me if I tried to take a girl of that caliber to England!" This only made me silently resentful. I did not regard Mei Ying as low caliber.

"Mei Ying has never been arrested," I said. "Anything else is hearsay." I was quoting what I had learned at the Consulate.

Then they told me my mother would never accept her. I was sure Stan and Thea were wrong. I told them so.

Stan said the only smaller, cheaper places to live were in Kowloon or Wanchai, and I'd be back on that Chinese food—Stan thought the rice and vegetable Chinese diet was unhealthy, compared to the meat and potato English fare of that time—and the weather would get cold and I'd wind up in the hospital again. But I didn't think so.

Finally, Stan said in very biting tones, "I know it's not my place to say so, but I think Mei Ying is taking you for the damnedest, biggest ride any man has ever been taken for."

"I'm sorry you feel that way," I said.

They said good-bye and as they were going out the door, Stan said, "I think we'll have to give you up as a bad job."

I couldn't forget their aggressive attitude or the unusual vehemence with which they had expressed themselves. I thought about it and considered the idea that their visit might have been just a last gasp of my DTs. Several times later I was on the point of asking them, "Did you and Stan come to the hospital and try to talk me out of marrying Mei Ying?" But I did not care to open the painful subject again.

As I became increasingly aware of the extent of my derangement, I asked for Lee, who had been staying away from me—probably at Dr. Li's suggestion. "I have done you a grave injustice," I said. "I am very sorry and apologize for my crazy ideas."

Lee radiated understanding and forgiveness, as he tapped his forehead and grinned, "Never mind! You no worry. I understand this matter." He added, "You was for fight me. Remember?" And he grinned some more.

"Yes, I remember." I had to grin too. I had repeatedly tried to kick him away as he struggled to keep me in bed. I'd kicked so vigorously that I landed on my back on the floor and he had to fetch a nurse to help me back in bed. "I was crazy," I said.

We shook hands and another weight was lifted.

Just before I left the hospital I received a cable from my mother: DOCTOR NORTHWAY SAYS YOU ARE IN NO CONDITION TO MARRY. NOW I OBJECT.

The Wedding Dinner:
Stan Major, Dr. Sun, Fook-kow Li, Edith, Ah Lee, me, Mei Ying,
Bella and Thea.

No More Hamlet

Chapter 6

He who hesitates is lost.

- American proverb

All the way from the hospital to Welsby House, my voices rode up the hill in the taxi with Lee, Mei Ying and me. When Dr. Li asked me if I still heard them, I lied. I was sure he wouldn't let me out of the hospital until he thought I was all right. I knew I was a little insane, but felt my dementia was temporary and I was on the mend. The quiet, privacy and familiar surroundings of the apartment beckoned me to a speedy recovery. My voices, while still frightening, were no longer babbling about bloody violence and I was now aware they were living only in my mind.

Apart from the worry I caused my friends and Mama, I felt no shame. I had made a silly ass of myself with my hallucinations but that was to be expected of one gripped by insanity.

Going up in the Welsby House elevator, I had a chance to glimpse myself in the mirror. My face was gaunt and haggard, and a wild, penetrating glitter lit my eyes. My God! Vincent van Gogh's self-portrait! It shocked me. I'd not seen my face of madness till then.

Among the letters and bills which awaited me on my desk was a scathing note from Mama. The story of Mei Ying's wanting "gold and diamonds and jade" hit her like a blow to the solar plexus. Despite my gin-induced mental haze at the time, I felt certain I would have remembered anything that important. I felt I had to win Mama's acceptance of Mei Ying because we would be living with her, in her house and on her budget.

My stomach felt and acted better than it had in ages. I no longer had my little cough and the world seemed a bit brighter. I was able to sign several checks and was functioning normally, and didn't feel pooped with gin and work. I developed a real affection for Dairy Farm Fresh Milk.

Dr. Li asked me when we were getting married. I said the nineteenth. He beamed and exclaimed, "Good!" Dr. Northway told Mama I was in no condition to marry. I figured he thought I was still mentally disturbed. He also told her, "We cannot judge people. Trust George to find a way." I wrote Mama again.

The following Sunday I received a cable: USE YOUR JUDGMENT BEST WISHES—MAMA. I laughed with joy and relief, and Mei Ying and Lee joined me.

However, all my problems were not solved. I had $1,000 HK in the bank when I got sick. Against that was balanced the unpaid Chung Kee Store bill and pay for the two nurses Edith had hired to care for me after I became violent with Lee. These wiped out my bank account.

Hospital, medicine, X-ray and ambulance bills had to be paid before I left the hospital. That was roughly another $1,000. The rent was due in two days—$840.

When I got home to Welsby House, I found a red-lettered "Final Warning" from the Hong Kong Electric Company and a notice of disconnection from the South China Gas Co. The doctors' bills loomed like a specter on the horizon of month's end. Mei Ying needed an overcoat because the weather was plenty chilly. We needed money to get married—for the registry fee, for a taxi and for a wedding dinner.

Just before I got out of the hospital, I asked Edith if she would loan me some money. "Why sure, George," she said. "How much would you like?" I thought that about $2,000 HK should take care of us until I got some money from the U.S. Edith promptly wrote out a check for that amount. Two days after I got out of the hospital, I had gone through all the money, and with some embarrassment asked her for $500 more. We had to eat off the credit of the Chung Kee Store, ordering every day in our "store book" and having the groceries delivered by the "store boy." Thus the day of reckoning was postponed until month's end.

My stomach flared up again, this time in response to Chinese sausage which Mei Ying cooked. Dr. Li gave me some weak hydrochloric acid solution and advised me to eat more pork for vitamin B complex. He said that vitamin B was helpful in alcohol-related disorders. I now ate about half the meat, which was not very much. Lee and Mei Ying seldom ate meat, preferring tofu, fish and occasionally chicken, which they ate with lots of vegetables and white rice.

I had always imagined I would suffer from an intense craving for liquor if I quit. But such is not the case. I don't crave it, I don't even miss it—except as a stomach sourer. The pills Dr. Li prescribed for me were "tranquilizers," one of the first. Like alcohol, they were a depressant and fuzzed up one's acuity as they relaxed, but not to the extent of alcohol. A muscle relaxant, they also disconnected my mental processes in a not unpleasant manner. I thought of them as my "don't give a damn" pills.

Mama wrote me that some Senators were saying that Ingrid Bergman should be kept out of the U.S. on the ground of moral turpitude because of her affair with Roberto Rosellini. She suggested I should make certain Mei Ying could not be kept out. These and the doubts raised by my DT's convinced me to check again and see whether I could get more satisfaction from the Consulate. I asked Edith to make an appointment at the Consulate and go with us as my interpreter.

Mr. Dunnigan, consul in charge of the Visa section, had a private office in a corner of the huge desk-cluttered room. When Edith entered the room with me, we attracted considerable attention. I, being helped to walk on each arm, was a curiosity in Hong Kong and Edith was instantly recognized as the beautiful wife of one of the most influential and wealthy men in Hong Kong government. People at the Consulate always awakened from their pall of bureaucratic boredom whenever she entered.

As we were being ushered into Dunnigan's office, Edith asked me, "What do you want me to say?"

"Find out what the moral turpitude provisions of the Immigration laws are and if her being from Red China will keep her out."

"How much should I tell him about her, uh, work?"

"Well, don't be too frank. Tell him she was a taxi dancer at a ballroom. That's at least partly true."

Mr. Dunnigan, a clean-cut looking executive type about thirty-five or forty, with a crisp manner of speaking, introduced himself. Edith explained the situation to him and asked about the moral turpitude laws.

"Do you have any reason to suspect that this little lady is guilty of moral turpitude?" Dunnigan asked me.

"Well," I said, "she was a taxi-dancer and we've been living together for two months."

"The moral turpitude provisions of the Immigration Code are very flexible," he said. "We consider moral turpitude to be conviction for theft, conviction for prostitution, conviction for forgery, conviction for murder, things of that nature."

I heaved an audible sigh of relief at the stress he placed on the word "conviction." Mei Ying had been in no trouble with the law. "She'll have to explain all those trips to Canton," he said.

"About the affidavit of support: just how much money do I have to have?"

"There's no definite amount. We just have to be satisfied that she will be supported and not be cast adrift to become a public charge."

"Well, I'm partially dependent on my mother."

"Then we would need a statement from her. What does she think of the marriage?"

"I can answer that," said Edith. "She had given her consent. Then George got sick and while he was in the hospital, his friends wrote his mother about it. I think we made rather a mess of things."

Lee and Mei Ying were sitting quietly in a corner of the small office, Mei Ying with her "teacher glasses" and without makeup, striving with considerable success to appear demure and mousy. She wore a loose black sweater, black slacks and her black hair in a small pony tail.

"How do you two manage to converse?" Mr. Dunnigan asked me.

Edith helped me out. "They have a Cantonese textbook and they talk by pointing to words. Anyway, when you're in love, who needs to talk?"

Dunnigan became very serious and looked directly at me. He said about 95% of those applicants who were denied admittance to the U.S. from Hong Kong were refused because they had tuberculosis. He suggested I see that Mei Ying had a physical examination, and particularly a chest X-ray, before I married her.

I knew Mei Ying's brother in Canton had a serious case of TB and Mei Ying, while not thin, weighed only about ninety pounds. She lived in the teeming, TB-riddled Wanchai and had what I hopefully thought was a cigarette cough. Yes, I'd have Dr. Li give her a physical.

As Mr. Dunnigan escorted us out of the office, he said, "We never advise anyone. Until you are married, our hands are tied. Then we'll do everything we can to help you. I've never stood in the way of romance."

I felt quite encouraged and determined to see the wedding through to the end.

I received more letters from Mama in which she was upset and worried about my contemplated marriage. I thought Thea and Bella were telling me how upset Mama was and at the same time contributing to the upset with inflammatory letters. Bella felt a righteous sense of moral outrage that anyone would consider marrying a hooker, being a proper person herself. Mama had been adding fuel to this drive to see me off at Kai Tak Airport unwed. When she got steamed up, she tended to let herself go at the typewriter. Many a San Francisco store manager's complexion must have turned ashen upon receipt of mother's torrid prose concerning an inefficient or nasty clerk or some fault of the management.

I placed Mama in the awkward position of seeming to condone prostitution if she gave her approval to the marriage. Mama was staunchly Victorian in her sexual ideas but did not detest prostitution as much as might be expected, defending a person's right to live one's life in any manner, so long as it did not interfere with the rights of others. She sometimes quoted the famous San

Francisco doggerel, "The miners came in 'forty-nine, the whores in 'fifty-one, and when they got together, they produced the native son."

The money I borrowed from Edith was from her personal account, money with which she planned to buy Christmas gifts for her friends and family. It would soon be the first of December. Edith was polite and generous, but I could detect a hint of uneasiness about when the money would come. I finally wrote Mama that the situation was becoming daily more desperate.

I find there are parts of my hospital stay that I don't remember. Thea had been careful not to let Bella know of Mei Ying's career, at my request. But when I was in the throes of the DTs, I told all. This caused Thea some embarrassment and she told me she was angry at me.

Mei Ying and Lee were very insistent that I must have a new suit for the wedding. It is Chinese custom that the couple wear everything new on their wedding day. I protested that I didn't have any use for a suit. Mei Ying was so stunned at the thought of my getting married in old clothes that she was almost speechless and uttered the Cantonese exclamation of despair—*aiyah!*—and smote her brow.

"Never mind," said Little Brother, "I will borrow $100 from a friend. We can get gabardine suit for $80."

When Lee and I got back to the apartment the next day from our suit shopping expedition, we found Bella Sun and Mei Ying in earnest Cantonese conversation.

I've just been talking to your girlfriend," said Bella. "She says you are going ahead with your plans to be married tomorrow."

"Yes," I said, "I was downtown buying a suit for the occasion."

Lee brought tea and retired to the servant's quarters, while we three sat around the table and talked. Most of the conversation was in Cantonese, of which I got only a small portion. But now and then Bella would pause and give me a synopsis in English.

As they talked, Mei Ying's face darkened and her Cantonese poured forth in a torrent.

"I've made your girlfriend angry," said Bella. "I just told her that your mother is from the Southern U.S. and believes strongly in tradition and is old-fashioned in her social outlook and would never approve of your marrying a girl of her class. It made her angry. She has been telling me about her family. She says she did what she did to support her mother and brother who has tuberculosis. Of course, she has a point and I can't exactly blame her for being angry."

Bella went on to say that Mama had indicated in her letters to her that she would never accept Mei Ying as a daughter-in-law.

"Don't you think you should give your mother more time to get used to the idea?" she asked. "I know she is terribly upset by this. Just give her a week or two longer."

Mei Ying suggested we wait and make certain it was all right with Mama.

"But," I said, "the wedding has already been delayed once. The Consulate won't do anything about her papers until we are married. As it is now, I don't have a chance of getting home before Chinese New Year. I don't want to go home without Mei Ying and I just can't afford a long stay in Hong Kong with rents what they are."

With Bella and Mei Ying prodding me, I decided to wait fifteen more days and get things squared with Mama. Mei Ying said the mother-son relationship is one of life's most precious things and she did not want to come between us.

I asked Bella to stop at the Marriage Registry on her way back to Kowloon and please ask the Registrar to change the date to December fourteenth. She said all right.

After Bella left, Mei Ying burst into tears.

"Her say," said Lee, "Suppose you know Chinese talk you cry too. Dr. Sun wife say many unkind words. Her is lose very much face. Dr. Sun wife say her is very low class girl. Say your mother no give you marry low class girl. I think this is Nineteenth Century thinking."

Mei Ying went shopping for her coat and wore her glasses and took Georgie with her. Having him with her made her feel respectable. Ah Lee went home to Kowloon and Mei Ying came home with Georgie at ten o'clock. Georgie was afraid to be alone at night, so there was only one solution—Mei Ying slept surrounded by Georgies.

When Edith came that morning to take us to the wedding and we told her it had been postponed, she went home and wrote Mama:

Dear Mrs. Barker,

Since I've poked my finger into the pie, it's too late for me to say, "Who am I to cast the first stone?" I've asked George quite frankly if he would be terribly unhappy if he does not marry Mei Ying and bring her back. He said, "Yes, I would be." I know from every indication that George loves her. George thinks that Mei Ying is sensible in her outlook. She has taken care of him well, doing all the cooking, trying to get him on his feet to good health. She seldom leaves him except for marketing. From what I see she's considerate in taking care of him and from these last few times translating for them she sounds thrifty, sincere and sensible. To tell the truth, Mrs. Barker—I still don't know what's what. Fine time to say it.

I'm sorry that our opinions and impressions of this situation have made you so unhappy. What can I say that will be comforting and yet the truth?

It's difficult to say what one should do with his life. I suppose it's unfair to judge on the surface. A person might change and might not. And a person is different through different eyes.

George is in desperate financial difficulties. Mei Ying sold her ring and they both pawned their watches. I've loaned George $2500 to settle the hospital, rent and running expenses. He's now completely broke. Mei Ying has tried to borrow from her friends and they've been eating off the credit from Chung Kee.

George looks with anxiety to you for help and has asked Lee to inquire at the bank whether a check has come from you or not. They've postponed the wedding for another fifteen days. Chung Kee Store will be asking for payment soon. George has so much on his mind.

I'll try to help in every way. Please write.

Edith

I began to weary of playing the indecisive Hamlet. I had diddled away a month wasting time I could ill afford. I no longer had the sense of power that alcohol gave me. The pills that replaced it were calming and tended to make me passive. I must be more decisive and not let myself be swayed by every doubting breeze from my friends and my mother. From now on, I would be as stony and unmovable as Egypt's Sphinx.

Lee found more and more excuses to be away from the apartment. It was not unusual to see Mei Ying with her pajamas rolled up above her knees, mopping the bathroom or kitchen.

"Ah Lee no good," Mei Ying angrily exclaimed. "He you the amah. I do amah work."

The wind blew colder and colder out of China and the sun was a rare, tired visitor. Most nights we went to bed early and snuggled under the comforter, listening to the wind whining around the corners of Welsby House, rustling the bamboo shades and rattling the windows. Mei Ying became more uneasy about ghosts and insisted upon sleeping with lights on and door locked. She clung to me more tightly and pulled the comforter over her head.

Despite Lee's disclaimer that he wasn't afraid of ghosts, he believed in them and lived in dread of meeting one. One night I had needed a drink of gin and crawled to the servant's quarters and wakened him, saying, "Lee" and shaking him lightly by the shoulder.

He sat bolt upright, flung his arms wide and, with his face a mask of terror, gave throat to a spine-tingling scream of horror. I recoiled in contagious fright.

"Oh, it's you, Mr. George," he said quickly. "I thought you was ghostie!"

He and Mei Ying fed each other's fears. Lee told me he thought it was very standard to believe in ghosts. "We is Christian people. We believe man have soul. Ghostie is soul of people who die before he is ready to go. He come back to see what is happen to his darling. But they can't hurt you," he assured me.

We had to move by the nineteenth of December. Edith, Mei Ying and I went apartment hunting. At the Cathay Hotel in the Causeway Bay District, we took a ground floor apartment in the Annex. Our new flat was old and had been well used. Trading the apartment in Welsby House for one in the Cathay Hotel Annex was akin to moving from a mansion to a cottage, but we were satisfied.

Mei Ying was delighted at finding a place in such close proximity to the movie theaters and near the St. Francis Hotel where her friend, Ah Fat, worked. I loved Mei Ying and wanted her to be happy. Mei Ying knew it too. "I very much like the moon," she teased. "You buy for me?"

"Maybe tomorrow," I said.

"I very love your head. Will you cut it off for me?"

"Maybe next week."

The day before our wedding, we moved. In my six months at Welsby House, I had drunk myself into the pit of my own private hell and crawled back out again. I had sought and found my sexual initiation in the person of the odious, unwashed boat woman. Having done my bit for charity, I had latched onto Mei Ying of the happy laugh. I was no longer as emotionally dependent on Mama. I had made friends in a different culture.

We piled all our things in Edith's car and made two trips. I welcomed the fact that we were on the ground floor only fifteen feet from the curb, since exhaustion started dragging me down when I had to walk more than half a block on a helper's arm.

Our wedding day arrived. Shaved and trimmed by the hotel barber and dressed in my absolutely cheap suit and seventeen-cent tie, I felt very strange. I made a last-ditch plea for my familiar tweed jacket and ascot tie, but it brought forth such anguished gasps of dismay and Cantonese curses that I subsided.

We arrived at the Hong Kong Supreme Court Building at exactly ten a.m. in a chill drizzle. Edith Li and Dr. Sun were waiting for us. They had consented to be our witnesses. The kindly, elderly English Registrar performed the ceremony. His message was that our marriage was binding until death and that our union could be dissolved only by a legal divorce. Should either of us marry again without a divorce, that party would be guilty of a heinous crime of bigamy. Thus inspired, we were ushered into the state of matrimony.

In keeping with the ceremony, the room was chilly and we all kept our coats on. We were seated around a long table with the Registrar and his interpreter standing at its head. Mei Ying was calm and poised. She repeated the words after the Registrar so perfectly that he probably halfway believed she understood what they meant.

It was necessary for me to scrawl my name four times on various papers. I was tense and nervous and my hand was shaking badly. The Registrar told me to take my time. Lee said, "Not so urgent." Dr. Sun instructed me to relax and take a deep breath. Edith laughed and said, "Gosh George, I didn't think you would be a nervous groom."

On the envelope which contained our marriage certificate was written in large letters—"ON HER MAJESTY'S SERVICE." Adorning the certificate was a crown and the letters E.R., Elizabeth Regina, I suppose. Our wedding had a touch of class after all.

At the conclusion, hands were shaken all around. Dr. Sun gave us his hasty and heartfelt good wishes and hurried off to his dental appointments. Edith handed us a wedding gift as we stepped into the taxi to return to our apartment. Six delicately worked silver coffee spoons with the Chinese character meaning double happiness or marital bliss.

I sent Ah Lee to MacDonnell Road to pick up my typing chair and bring it back in a taxi. The bride napped for an hour, then rose to answer the door. She scrubbed the kitchen and bathroom and washed all the dishes and scoured the pots and pans. Ah Lee arrived four hours later with three chairs.

We were ready to go to the Sky Restaurant. Mei Ying took the two bottles of gin left from my downfall and some oranges and apples. The gin was to keep down the liquor bill in case anyone felt alcoholically inclined. I was calmed by four cents worth of my "don't give a damn" tablets. My new medicine lulled me into a state where I was quite content with everything, though not as relaxed and euphoric as when under alcohol's diabolically sweet influence.

A big bouquet of red gladioli graced the center of our large round table. On each napkin rested a red carnation of the same shade, and matching the red plastic top on Gilbey's gin bottles. Red is as traditional to a Chinese wedding party as white is to an American.

The guests were all on time which in Hong Kong meant not more than fifteen minutes late. Mei Ying saw that the machinery was well oiled and everyone had enough of everything, getting up now and then to pour more gin in Stan's glass or pick out a choice morsel of unfamiliar food for Thea. With characteristic aplomb, Lee told everyone where to sit, urged the laggards to dig in and generally took over the duties of his inefficient host and boss.

All the courses were served on big dishes in the center of the table. Each person had two pairs of chopsticks, one with which to serve himself and one to eat with. Lee and Mei Ying helped me.

The dinner still staggers my mind. It began with a lobster salad heaped between the head and tail of a huge lobster. The eyes had been replaced by two flashlight bulbs which could be turned on and off by moving the lobster's whiskers.

Several plates loaded with huge fried crab legs came next. A large dish of scallops and bok choy was followed by a huge bowl of brown, gelatinous, shark's fin soup. Then a kind of shellfish similar to cockles, cooked with small pieces of liver. Next came a large platter of sweet and sour pork, with which the boys brought a big bowl of Chinese mushroom soup.

Now we were getting down to serious eating. A big garoupa was served, moist and tender and steaming with shredded ginger and other herbs. After the garoupa, chicken, cooked crisp in thick black soy sauce. Then tapioca in a casserole with sweet red bean paste.

"Good Lord, George," said Stan, "How much more is there going to be? You should have warned us."

"I don't know. I only saw the menu in Chinese."

"I don't think there is any more," said Dr. Sun.

A waiter walked in bearing a large plate of chow mein with soft pan-fried noodles. He was followed shortly by another with a plate of fried rice. The apples and oranges were untouched.

I thought it was part of the host's obligation to show enthusiasm for the food. Hence, I ate at least one serving of each dish, two of most, and three of some. It was the most Chinese dinner I ever had and I was proud to be its co-sponsor. Nobody told this Western barbarian that the bride and groom were supposed to partake very sparingly. Mei Ying modestly picked at her dainty servings.

Everyone wished us well and shook hands, and Fook-Kow and Edith drove us back to the apartment, where we spent our wedding night in slumber.

I gave Lee one month's notice, according to our original agreement that he would work for me until December. I would miss him. He was a loyal, likable, lazy rascal, but his habit of going on an errand downtown and coming back three or four hours later was just too expensive. He was not cut out to be a servant. He had an executive's genius for organizing things and delegating work to others.

He thought he had a job lined up as purser on a small Dutch ship that plied the seas between Hong Kong, Singapore, Jakarta and Bali. He was the picture of enthusiasm, grinning, gesticulating and saying at least ten times, "Now I see the world. Very good. Pay me for doing what other mans do for a holiday."

I wrote him a good recommendation and praised his accounting skills, hoping he would get the job. Mei Ying and I discussed how much we should give him and decided to be generous. He clasped my hand warmly and kissed my cheek in the kind of spontaneous gesture that made him so likable. He swore that he would be back very soon and that he would always be at my service, both of which I was sure he meant.

Before he left, Lee secretly told Mei Ying my trouble was leprosy, and if she let me make love to her often, she'd catch the disease and be just like me. For a moment I felt a sense of outrage. I thought Lee had devised this as a scheme to drive a wedge between Mei Ying and me. But I remembered the Chinese words for paralysis and leprosy were the same. Maybe, it was a misunderstanding born of ignorance. I could see Mei Ying halfway believed him. I had her call Dr. Li and ask him. She did and came back from the telephone and teasingly told me, "Dr. Li talk, 'Georgie no good.'"

She had been keeping her friend Ah Fat away from the apartment because she was afraid Lee would say she and Ah Fat had broken his rice bowl. According to Chinese ethics, one hesitates to cause anyone to lose his job.

Large, happy and immaculate, usually wearing a thin gray sweater, Ah Fat was a hotel "boy" at the nearby St. Francis. Light pock-marks scarred an otherwise handsome face. He grew up across the street from Mei Ying's family in a town halfway between Hong Kong and Canton. His family name was similar to Lee, so Mei Ying and her cousins often called him Uncle Lui.

Mei Ying liked an able-bodied man about the apartment at night because we were in a tougher neighborhood. When he wasn't on duty as a janitor at the nearby St. Francis Hotel, Ah Fat brought his blankets and a camp cot and curled up in front of the dining room buffet.

Mei Ying's cousin was detained in Macao on her way from China. Since she would be our amah when she got to Hong Kong, I had advanced her the money to come. Because of our language gap, we simply spoke of her as Macao Girl.

The telephone rang. It was Macao Girl's husband in Kowloon. He had talked to his distraught wife on the telephone and she said if Mei Ying didn't come and get her, she was going back to Kwangtung. Mei Ying said she would take the afternoon boat the next day and fetch her, returning in the morning.

Mei Ying arranged for Ah Fat to help me with my bath and dinner before he went to work at six. I typed until eleven p.m. and crawled to bed. The next morning at seven o'clock the doorbell rang exuberantly and Mei Ying burst in carrying six neatly stacked Macao crabs in a wicker cage.

With her was rotund little Macao Girl. She was Mei Ying's height, but fifty pounds heavier. Mei Ying told me she was her cousin, but I learned later that they were sisters. Macao Girl was a smiling, countrified version of my wife. She did not know a word of English. It was easy to see why Mei Ying had to fetch her; she would have been lost in the big city.

Macao Girl helped Mei Ying lift me in and out of the bathtub, which was built on a platform a foot above the floor. She was a better housekeeper than Lee, and a great Cantonese homestyle cook, which meant more boiled food and less stir-fried. She was almost always home, and when she did go out she got more food for the money. We were literally "eating mighty low on the hog." For four days we dined on soup made with watercress, ginger and pig's small intestine. A bit unusual, but cheap, nutritious and tasty.

On December 22nd I received a sizable check from my bank. Mei Ying ran to the curb where Edith was double parked, waving the check to show her we could pay our debts.

Christmas was overshadowed by impending Chinese New Year, but Hong Kong did have its decorated store windows and helicopter-borne department store Santa Claus. Mei Ying brought home some Christmas cards, and selected one of the Babe in the manger to send to her Mother. "Baby—very good," she said. We enjoyed a small Christmas, thankful for good health, friends, food, love and enough money to pay our bills.

Cable radio gave forth with familiar carols sung by a children's chorus in Cantonese, including "Hark, The Herald Angels Sing" and "Jingle Bells." Later that evening, the two women listened to amateur singers rendering carols and other songs, among them Auld Lang Syne, a favorite among my Chinese friends. Chiang played it on his mouth organ, Lee on the violin, and it was often on radio. Mei Ying said "Aul' Lan' Syne—very good."

Christmas morning, while I washed down my half-pound of dainty jam sandwiches with a large glass of hot tea, Mei Ying told me she was going out. She scraped her finger across her face, indicating, I thought, that she was going for the barber. She didn't think much of my electric shaver. The two times a barber shaved me, she stroked my chin with admiration.

Ten minutes later, she flew into the room and unwrapped a straight-edge razor. "Six dollar Hong Kong. Good or bad?" Taking a great gulp of boiling tea, I managed to say "Good" and look nervously pleased. She must have watched the barber carefully, because she took his bow-legged semi-squatting stance and lathered my face with the brush and proceeded to give me a really expert shave. She was pleased and told me how beautiful I was.

Stan and Thea had spoken well of the Chanticleer Restaurant in Kowloon. After reading its generous Christmas menu in an ad in the *South China Morning Post*, I decided I would give my Chinese buddies a festive Western holiday dinner with a Russian flavor.

Macao Girl, usually a hearty eater, picked at her plate with the unaccustomed fork and, though she was too polite to tell me, told Mei Ying Chinese food was better. Ah Fat made a brave show of stuffing his portion away, but I thought I caught a hint of grim determination behind his bland manner and his oft-repeated, "Very good." I had to eat half of Mei Ying's turkey and ham and all her plum pudding. Since I quit drinking, I had developed a tremendous appetite and was happy to help out.

I grew increasingly frustrated at my inability to make progress on Mei Ying's visa. After the night I tore up the money in an alcoholic rage, Lee had spent the morning helping Mei Ying write down the necessary information to fill out the Consulate's biographical data form. Whatever they had decided to say was now on a single sheet of paper in Chinese. Edith was going to translate it into English; but her children had chicken pox followed by sore throats, and what with Christmas and the holiday season, she had been too busy.

I filled out the application for an alien resident's visa. I wrote my mother requesting three birth certificates and the affidavit of support. Then I wrote the Consulate and asked if they would help by translating the biographical data for me. The Consulate phoned for us to come the afternoon of the 30th. A Mr. Salazar would help us as interpreter-translator.

Edith drove Mei Ying, Ah Fat and me to the American Consulate. After all the trouble I caused her, she remained the best of all my friends. She asked me several times. "Do you think I did the wrong thing writing to your mother?"

Mr. Salazar, a thin-faced Portuguese, and a plump, elderly Eurasian took Mei Ying to a desk behind a counter and filled in the blanks while I sweated it out in the main office. Thus I did not know how she glossed over recent employment or who she gave as personal references. I told myself, it was probably better that way. Mr. Salazar and the chunky Eurasian were smirking as they glanced at Mei Ying and me. I wondered how much they knew. When I got sick Edith told me half of Hong Kong was talking about the affair.

I had to have my signature on the application for Mei Ying's Alien Resident's Visa notarized. This would go to Washington, be approved by the Justice Department, be sent to Honolulu and there be approved by the District Director of Immigration, then sent back to Hong Kong before the Consulate could proceed with its investigation.

I saw Mr. Dunnigan looking through a three inch thick file on Mei Ying and spotted a clipping in it. I had sent the *Tiger Standard* a photograph of Mei

Ying and myself taken for the Registry. I wrote a well-scrubbed little account of our marriage for the paper. The photo was blown way up under the big headline, "The Year's News in Review," and captioned "Romance Blooms Over First Lessons in Cantonese." I thought publicity always helps a good cause.

After returning from our fifth trip to the U.S. Consulate in a month, I began to see why they said "maybe three months." It could easily take that long or longer. I had optimistically thought that Mei Ying and I would make it quicker.

I felt like a pet bird in a cage. People were pampering me, cooking good food to please me, letting me out now and then, saying sweet things to me, but I wanted to go home. No one spoke my language in the apartment or seemed in a hurry to leave Hong Kong. Mei Ying appeared content to listen to the cable radio, play mah-jongg with her friends and take me out to an occasional movie. We were behind bars. Big, sturdy, jail-like bars crossed our long front window. Our only entry had a triple lock on it.

The Consulate officials were polite, but emotionally distant. "These things take time"—so they continued to do the paper work in triplicate and wait for it to make the round trip to Washington and back.

There's nothing quite like the helplessness one feels as he waits for the cold, impersonal wheels of government to grind out the required poundage of red tape. Just sit and wait, hope and pray. I felt a prisoner of other people's patience.

My health was a matter of some concern to Mei Ying and her cousin. They cooked my food with medicinal herbs and brewed special teas to aid my digestion. They repeatedly made one tea with a distinctive bitter flavor. Struck by the lightning of remembrance, I identified it as cascara, a laxative inflicted on me and most patients at Children's Hospital in Denver right after I had encephalitis.

I found it in my dictionary and pointed to the Chinese characters for cascara. "Gwai Pei, Very good," they said. "No cough tomorrow!" They were referring to the croupy cough we all had at the tail end of our colds. They took it too.

Macao Girl said I was very shy. It was true that when I was enthroned in the bathroom and she popped her head in just to see how things were coming along, I would motion her away. I guess I was about the shyest fellow she'd ever met. She discussed my constipation with Edith, as she did with the grocery boy and probably anyone else who was handy.

Mei Ying wanted me to eat more and gave me plenty of pork, following Dr. Li's suggestion. Usually it was boiled with watercress. Sometimes it was cooked crisp. I liked it, but they always picked out the fattest pieces for me.

They were being kind and wanted me to get fat and reflect their good care. Fragrant long grain rice from Thailand was an integral part of every meal.

I watched Macao Girl squatting in front of her chopping board in the middle of the kitchen floor, chopping a chunk of fish to a pulp with her cleaver. As a good amah should, she cheerfully ate the leftovers from the previous meal before assisting in the consumption of the new vittles.

When Mei Ying bathed me, I came out of the tub steaming like the laundry on a cold day in Colorado. Everyone added another layer of clothing when the temperature dropped. Macao Girl laughingly showed me that she was wearing five shirts, thus adding to her natural rotundity. Judging from the number of colds around, this was a poor substitute for central heating.

Macao Girl's husband was with us on his off days. He was a clerk in a cloth shop in Kowloon and worked ridiculously long hours. Of average height and on the thin side, he seemed to be a serious person in his suit and tie. He instantly antagonized me by the way he scrutinized everything in the apartment—even the contents of my desk and dresser drawers. Mei Ying explained, "First time Hong Kong." Just a country boy goggle-eyed his first time in the big city—so she indicated with a gape-mouthed expression as she turned around flat-footed in the middle of the floor and rubber-necked at the walls!

Macao Girl's husband was entirely unselfconscious, whether dipping his comb into my jar of Brylcreme or taking a sheet of paper or examining my checkbook. If I should be so impolite as to give him a dirty stare, he would respond with a smile at being noticed. I grew to like him a lot. He was not the least bit sneaky, just very inquisitive.

I couldn't bend over the straw in my tea glass or fumble around picking up a piece of chocolate that he didn't try to help me. One night he came in at ten-thirty and I was in bed reading and Mei Ying was out playing mah-jongg. He thoughtfully poured me a glass of tea and brought in the big candy-store jar of candied fruit and stuffed us both. He was certain that he was welcome to share in my good fortune of being a "rich American."

Another night he surprised me by buying a barbecued duck and a bottle of brandy and insisting we share. It was the first drink I had had since my sickness. It was Chinese grape brandy and as far as I could tell was as good as American. I enjoyed it, but I no longer hankered for the stuff.

I took Mei Ying to a live performance of the San Francisco Ballet's *Nutcracker*, helped by Ah Fat. At the ballet, we were seated when I heard Bella's voice two seats behind us calling, "Hello George. How are you? I never expected to see you here." Mei Ying kept me company and remained seated during the playing of "God Save the King" and "The Star Spangled Banner." She punctuated the music of Tchaikovsky with the crackle of watermelon seeds between her teeth. After the performance, Bella and Dr. Sun came around and asked us to come visit them. But it was one of those vague, "Do come see us sometime" kind of invitations.

I wanted to observe a real Chinese New Year. Mei Ying got $100 in small bills which she placed in red envelopes embossed with the gold Chinese ideographic character for double happiness to become Lucky Money. She bought fireworks and sparklers to scare away any demons that might be lurking on the premises. We would have the special foods. Macao Girl's husband would be with us for three days. Everyone took it easy and enjoyed himself.

Mei Ying and Ah Fat brought home two big potted purple and white peony chrysanthemums. Plum and peach blossoms mean prosperity; peonies mean happiness. Fresh fruits overflowed our large dining table; four huge pomelos, apples, oranges, Japanese pears, mangoes and a lot of little tangerines. All houses entered the New Year spotless.

As darkness fell on New Years Eve, Macao Girl placed the red and gold incense pot in the window beside the improvised oil lamp, an inch of oil floating on a glass of tea with a cotton wick and a wire holder. Mei Ying enacted a little ceremony before dinner. Four long joss sticks were lit in the incense pot. She poured rice wine in three tiny wine cups and placed them carefully in front of the fragrant burning incense. Our whole soy chicken was positioned on the table decorated with red paper. Mei Ying and Macao Girl formally bowed three times and burned some of the gold papers. The fire dispatched these good things to heaven for the enjoyment of our ancestors. Papa would have enjoyed the scene for he often spoke of such ceremonies.

Macao Girl's hubby came about eleven to take me out in a rickshaw to the Fair. I took two "don't give a damn" pills and we took off. The Fair consisted of a collection of stalls: curios and household goods on one street and flowers on another. The flower street did a brisk business.

I'd read of throngs of people but it never meant much to me, but that night I saw the thronging masses. The Cathay Hotel was about six blocks from the park where the fair was located. Droves of happy, fire-cracker shooting humanity surged in a constant sea towards the Flower Market. Others came away with a peach or plum tree in bud and blossom, sawed off at the trunk, just like a Christmas tree. Some people carried hyacinth plants in pots. Glads, cockscomb and mums were prominent. It was by all odds the biggest flower market I'd ever seen, including Mexico. People were packed four or five deep in front of most of the flower stalls. Black lacquer suited coolie women with baby on back, happily held a single stem of gladiolus; while prosperous looking business men clutched a peach or plum tree.

Firecrackers rattled in strings or popped singly all night long. Not a second passed silently. Some of them went off with tremendous bangs that made me jump. At the flower bazaar, someone dropped a string of big blasters in the midst of the crowd directly in front of my rickshaw. People scrambled every way.

Mei Ying helped me bathe early that morning. To bathe early in the day on New Years meant one would have plenty to eat during the year. On New Years day no sweeping, dusting, cutting, or cooking for fear of sweeping out or frightening the God of Prosperity and the God of Happiness. Mei Ying put away her knitting needles.

To beat the cold, Mei Ying and I went to bed right after supper and she knitted while I read. We went to sleep about nine o'clock and at midnight we woke up and she said she was hungry. Well, so was I. She phoned the Waldorf Hotel on the corner and they sent us our midnight snack. I had boiled noodles with dim sum and Mei Ying had a bowl of rice and duck. No delivery charge except a small tip for the boy. This part of living in Hong Kong I liked.

We no longer slept between sheets. We discovered on MacDonnell Road that we were warmest with one of Edith's towel spreads under us and the comforter on top. That provided a sort of non-slip cocoon-like arrangement that was snug and warm.

The month proved dismal and cheerless: gray, dripping and very chilly. Each day I thought we'd had the worst and was certain that today was colder than yesterday. Then came the coldest February day on record in Hong Kong. Snow fell on the two peaks of Lan Tao Island.

One night we went to a movie and I came home riding in a rickshaw. The rickshaw boy was outdistancing Mei Ying and Fat. I jokingly shouted at them—*"fai-dee, fai-dee!"* which means faster, faster! The rickshaw boy thought I meant him and lit out as though I were after him with a whip. Fat and Mei Ying were left a block behind. When we reached the apartment it began raining and the rickshaw boy helped me in to the capable hands of Macao Girl. He grinned at the joke we had played on my friends.

Edith drove me to her home for lunch. She asked her amah to prepare an American-style lunch for us. Then we listened to some of Edith's records, including "South Pacific." I felt homesick for California.

A hawker of watermelon seeds called her wares outside the window. She was dressed in coolie black and her two large baskets of seeds were hanging from each end of a coolie pole. The seeds were big, ocher red things and were heaped in each basket. For a moment, I felt torn between the richly exotic environment and my desire to be back in familiar Marin County.

At the Consulate, they weighed and measured Mei Ying. She was four feet nine and a half inches tall and weighed only eighty-four pounds: tiny, but a perfectly proportioned young woman. Sometimes, when I looked at her tiny undies and slacks hanging on a hook in the bedroom, I marveled at their smallness. Did I marry a person or a doll?

I really couldn't blame Mei Ying for going out to play mah-jongg with her friends. Watching me type every evening got pretty dull. If only she did not make every game a marathon! She might be gone for hours. She lacked any sense of urgency about time. But I trusted Mei Ying. She was not sex-crazed and her passions were not volcanic. As Macao Girl told Edith, Mei Ying had two hobbies—mah-jongg and Cantonese movies.

When I woke, the wind out of China was whistling down the drain pipes in the courtyard of the hotel. The sound varied from a siren to a flute and the melody was punctuated by the occasional rattle-bang of a loose window. The sun came out and cast a different aspect on the land. My gloomy thoughts vanished like cobwebs before a feather duster.

It was eleven o'clock and Mei Ying telephoned from the Consulate that she wouldn't be home for lunch. I hoped it meant that they really were working on her case. My spirits were soaring at the prospect of springtime in Marin. Let more patriotic souls brag about freedom and bravery. Like *E.T.*, I loved my new friends but wanted to go home.

Mei Ying was at the Consulate till five o'clock. From her description of the proceedings I gathered she spent most of her time waiting while people told her, "Jussamoment." She said, "Consul talk me go *Mei Gwoh* very good." She had to get six more pictures made. They put her picture on everything. The next morning she was off to collect the pictures, go to the Consul doctor in Edinburgh House, and back to the Consulate. When she returned, she said she talk, talk, talk. "Consul say he want me one more talk."

Mei Ying was out playing mah-jongg. Edith dropped in and stayed a while and we talked with Macao Girl. She told Edith she was thirty-two years old. When Mei Ying and I went to the States, she would like to go to work on a sewing machine in a garment factory. Most people didn't like married *amahs* because they didn't like having their husbands about the place. Macao Girl didn't want to give up married life, so it was a factory for her.

Macao Girl said that she and Mei Ying were exact opposite types. That Mei Ying was active and loved to be on the go. Macao Girl was a homebody and didn't know where to go, and if she went out she was anxious to get home. It was certainly true that she seemed perfectly contented sitting by the Rediffusion, hour after hour, knitting sweaters, listening and contemplating. She was so quiet I was scarcely aware of her.

Ah Fat bought a bottle of delicious Portuguese brandy. I had about an inch in a small glass with lunch. Fat offered me more and I accepted, but Mei Ying objected. Since argument was impossible, I was denied another inch of Portugal's sunlight. It was probably just as well. All those "one more inches" were my previous undoing.

I sent Mei Ying to Japan Air Lines with the check to buy her ticket. This really boosted her morale. She danced around the apartment with the ticket in one hand and the other spread like a wing. "Georgie, I go *Mei Gwoh*. Bye bye Ah Fat. Bye bye Macao Girl. I go *Mei Gwoh*."

I had a strong urge to call Edith all day Tuesday. About four o'clock, I yielded to it. I asked Edith please to call Dunnigan, tell him I had tentative airline reservations for March thirteenth, would it be necessary to change them and, if so, would the visa be ready by the twentieth. Dunnigan said it would probably be the first of April, maybe longer. "Several matters came up in the questioning that I'll have to clear up," he said.

This filled me with feelings of apprehension. Were dark secrets from Mei Ying's past coming forward to curse our plans? Quiet desperation seized me. I was so anxious to go home. Enough of this little corner of the world called Hong Kong. I would go see Dunnigan and try and find out what the trouble was. If he really thought it might take beyond April first, I'd go home. I hated to leave Mei Ying, but she was happy in Hong Kong and I wasn't.

Since I could no longer drown my sorrows I tried to stun them with a tranquillity pill. I went to bed and read *Time*. A tranquilizer and a good night's sleep and a long talk with Mei Ying gave me a chance to think things over and get everything in a brighter perspective. I had stuck it out this long—I reckoned I could stand it a while longer.

Mei Ying now seemed almost as anxious to get to America as I was. She summed up Hong Kong from her point of view. "Hong Kong no good. Only three things do. Play mah-jongg. Drink wine. Go movie. Play mah-jongg. Money go, go, go. No good. Drink wine. No good. Money go, go, go. Go movie. Okay. One thing do Hong Kong."

Her story was changing. Now she said it was her mother's idea that she became a dancer. Mei Ying said, "Mao Tse-tung come on. Me mudder's money go, go, go. She cry, cry, cry. Eyes no good. No rice to eat. One room. She talk me go to Hong Kong. Be dancer." It wasn't that I cared all that much what her story was, but she showed a disturbing pattern of telling different versions of the same occurrences. Edith noticed it too. "Can't she remember what she told me before?" Edith asked me with perplexity.

On our first nice day in March, all windows were flung wide open and the cover to Edi's marvelous goose down comforter was washed. Every night noisy cat fights erupted in the courtyard outside our window and the people upstairs tramped about and seemed to rearrange their furniture and fling large boxes on the floor. During waking hours, Rediffusion did competition with the street noise. I think the thing I yearned for most was quiet. Ah, Kentfield . . . where the loudest noise, as Bud used to say, was the stomping of robins on the grass.

When I thought of Kentfield the most beautiful memories to me were the nights when the moonlight was like quicksilver and seemed to flow over the sea of green vegetation. I recalled one night in particular when Bud was visiting me. We had both been tipping the jug and were in a mellow, receptive mood. About one a.m. in October or November, we sat out on the back walk under the canopy of the big bay tree and soaked in the beauty. It was dead quiet and we spoke in hushed monosyllables.

Warm and oppressively humid weather added impetus to my wish to get out of Hong Kong. Mr. Dunnigan said my presence was not necessary and did not tend to speed things up. I decided to take the first available plane home. Edith was going to lunch downtown so she went to the JAL office and made the necessary arrangements for me.

That last week in Hong Kong was a study in rush and frustration. We went all over the city, doing bits of last minute shopping. We went to the thieves' market called "Cat's Alley" for a last look and I attracted my usual large following of ragged urchins and curiosity seekers.

Two nights before I left, Dr. and Mrs. Sun had us to a dinner of chicken with walnuts and grass carp soup at the Waldorf Hotel on the corner. Mei Ying, Macao Girl, her husband and Ah Fat threw a little farewell party for me the night before I left, complete with soy chicken and Chinese brandy. Each of the Li children brought me a small gift, kissed me on the cheek and told me, "Go with the wind, Uncle Joy."

Edith drove us to Kai Tak. I asked permission for Mei Ying to accompany me aboard the plane, so she could see what such a plane was like inside. We said a few final words and she had to leave. The engines roared, the plane took off and 44 hours later I was saying, "Hi Mama," at the San Francisco airport.

Mama at San Francisco College for Women in the early 1960's.

Back at Barker Manor

Chapter 7

The pure and simple truth is rarely pure and never simple.

- Oscar Wilde

When I awoke in the old oak bed in my bedroom in Kentfield my first morning back home, it took me a second or two to realize where I was. I turned over half expecting to see Mei Ying and realized with a pang that she was eight thousand miles away.

I spent my time relaxing, enjoying the comforts of America, reading and catching up on the neighborhood news until my typewriter arrived. It came in my foot lockers along with my clothes and books.

With my typewriter, I went to work on the visa trail once more. I wrote the Consulate. I wrote Congressman Scudder. And I wrote Edith and Mei Ying begging each of them to inquire at the Consulate. I received a long letter from Edith and several short notes Mei Ying had dictated to the clerk at the St. Francis Hotel.

I once more fell into my routine of reviewing books for the *Examiner*. It felt good to be back in the familiar surroundings and to be back with Mama. But feelings between us were not the same. I think she felt the only way to convince a fool he was wrong was to let him have his own way.

Having tasted independence, I was less willing to accept Mama's ideas as the last word. I am sure she tried, but she could never quite quit thinking of me as her little boy. I felt like the Hemingway character, back from the war as an ambulance driver, whose mother refused to let him borrow her car. My situation was different, however, being so dependent on her to help me do everything. Having to assist me in feeding, dressing and bathing had to affect her attitude, but she never acted grudging about helping me nor was anything but kind about doing so. We both had love and respect for each other, and an appreciation for each other's feelings.

Rather than have a confrontation, I would sometimes bite my lip and go along with her. This troubled me. A part of me felt like Mohandas Gandhi: "A 'No' uttered from deepest conviction is better and greater than a 'Yes' merely uttered to please, or what is worse, to avoid trouble." Most of the time, I was painfully honest and direct. But sometimes being honest resulted in more emotional turmoil than it was worth.

I have always been an incurable optimist. Delusions are as necessary to my happiness as realities. I'm not happy without a delusion of some kind. Maybe Mei Ying's love for me was a large dream built on my wishful thinking.

I still felt passionately for Mei Ying, but now I had questions. What was the difference between love and infatuation? Each of us sees mostly what he carries in his own heart. Why had she lied so much? Did she really love me? Perhaps I was oversensitive, but I resented the hours she spent playing mah-jongg, though I don't know what I expected her to do while I was writing. And now she seemed to be taking her time about coming to the States.

Ah Fat wrote me that Mei Ying was all right and going to the movies and on picnics with Macao Girl. Mei Ying wrote me a loving letter in which she said that she had been to the Consulate several times and thought it would not be long before she had her visa.

A week or so later Mei Ying wrote me with the help of an English-speaking friend, "In the past few days, about twenty per cent out of three million were suffering of influenza in this colony, and I was one of the sufferers. Now I am getting better after the medical doctors' care."

On May sixth Edith wrote me, "Your letter of March 31st has not yet been read to Mei Ying. She's the most difficult person to find—I've called several times a day at all hours and haven't gotten in touch with her. When she called back I was out—damn! Mr. Dunnigan asked me to have her go to see him tomorrow. I told him I'd have to find her first. I'll have a note for her this morning—hoping she'll get it—and as Mr. Dunnigan said, 'Hope she hasn't gone back to Canton.'"

Five days later Edith wrote:

Dear Uncle Joy,

Spent the whole morning Thursday with your wife—picked her up at the hotel at 10 a.m.—went to exchange $25.00 U.S. (you owe me) required by the Consulate—then went to the Consulate for the 10:30 a.m. appointment and found she needed a reentry permit and a certificate of identification from the Immigration Office. So we dashed down there—got the necessary forms and came home with Mei Ying to fill the forms and also type for her a letter of affidavit—dashed down to the Immigration with everything—then called the Consulate for an appointment for Tuesday because the papers from the Immigration won't be out until Monday.

Before I went with her, she waited in the Consulate office one morning on Tuesday and four hours on Wednesday afternoon, and was pretty upset.

She told me to tell you everything is going along well—and that she's been taking vitamin injections from Dr. Li as she's gotten terribly thin after a bout with the flu and asked that you send money to cover her treatment. (I'll find out how much and let you know).

She also said to tell you that she wanted to write and send her regards to your mother—but since you won't be able to read Chinese, she didn't do it.

But don't worry, I'll help her all I can and see that everything runs smoothly without her being too upset again.

Then three days later:

Dear George,

Mei Ying got her visa today!

When you said she was just a kid, you knew your wife better than I thought. After spending the whole morning at the Immigration yesterday rushing all the forms we had put in last Thursday and getting them signed, stamped—we rushed to the Consulate to make another appointment notifying them we have all the necessary papers and getting the earliest appointment for this morning by pleading stress—that she wants to leave as soon as possible. Then I spent the whole morning with her helping with the questionnaire, etc., and booking her passage by JAL for Monday, 20th, arranging everything with the agent to have her taken care of etc. After all the rush, lies and effort to get her going as soon as possible, Mei Ying decided to wait a few weeks before leaving!

She said she had asked her mother to come down from Canton. I asked her why didn't she tell me before all this and she said it had slipped her mind. Sorry I have to explode on you, George, but really! She asked me to write you and tell you she won't come till June. I said "No!" because I understood you want her as soon as possible and all our combined efforts rushed things for her, and she said to ask you for $300.00 HK to throw a farewell party, and I said "No!" because

George stressed that you must be economical as he's having a difficult time as is—I told her to write to you herself. Your guess is as good as mine when she'll feel like coming over—as she knows (the Consulate people told her) that her visa won't expire until middle of September. Sorry to say George—if you want her over right away—just stop sending her allowance. I know you might never forgive me for advising you on this, but I think you really want her with you and are anxious to have your mother meet her too, without the anxiety dragging out; also financially I know it's difficult on you, too. So why don't you write and say you know she has her visa and can come now. (If you're angry at me don't write me—but write Mr. Dunnigan to thank him.)

All is well except my nerves—all the luck.

Edith.

Now I was angry and sent Mei Ying a cable: YOU HAVE VISA COME NOW OR NEVER. Then, almost immediately, I began to regret my rash action.

Two days later I received a letter from Mei Ying in Chinese which my mother took to a Chinese friend in San Francisco to have translated:

George, my husband,

Ever since we parted I think of you all the time. My going to America procedures have been completed and the passport was issued to me on the 14th of this month. I will soon come to America to join you. Mrs. Li was kind enough to make reservations for me for the 20th.

When my mother heard I was going to America she wanted to come to Hong Kong to pay me a visit. Because of this I have delayed my departure. I estimate mother will be here in the next one or two days. Because of this long journey the mother-daughter relationship cannot be looked on lightly. I wish to see her for the last time.

My mother has an eye ailment and she will come and have it tended to here. I estimate that she will be here half a month having her medical needs tended to. Being a daughter, how can I not take care of these things?

For all these reasons I have postponed my trip to America. I am sure you will forgive me and that your love for me is so deep that you will think of my mother in the same way. That is why I told you to return to America first—so you could see your own mother.

Mrs. Li did not see my point of view and there is a little misunderstanding. However, I am grateful to Mrs. Li for helping me and for many other things.

Because of this little misunderstanding Mrs. Li was quite angry with me. I want to apologize but she is still very angry and I cannot readily explain the situation to her. Mrs. Li has been a great help to me and I have great respect toward her. When the opportunity presents itself I will express my thanks and also apologize to her.

For this postponement I have not received her approval nor your consent. I just go ahead doing this. I hope you will forgive me.

You and I are man and wife. We are one. Please do not be too skeptical of me.

Many of my friends have heard that I am going to America and they are happy for me and have given me many parties. I cannot just sit and sponge on people by not inviting them in return. I must do so. Please send me some more money because I'm leaving the 5th of next month for Japan and then America.

I wanted to come earlier but our friend in Japan Air Lines decided I should leave June 5th. His friend is also on this flight and she is also Cantonese. It was very nice of Mr. Leong to ask his friend to take care of me on the trip. Since the plane will be in Japan two days, I will also need some expense money.

My best wishes to my mother-in-law,

> *Your wife,*
> *Mei Ying*

By that time I was sincerely regretful of my hasty action and sent another cable. JUNE 8TH OKAY ENJOY VISIT WITH YOUR MOTHER. Then I scraped the bottom of my bank account and sold my tape recorder to raise some cash, part of which I sent to Mei Ying.

The two and a half weeks until the eighth seemed interminable, but at last we were at the airport. With quickened pulse I saw the big plane land and saw the tiny figure of my wife step hesitantly down the steps.

Then she spotted me. She ran to us and kissed me and my mother.

"Hi baby!" I said grabbing her hand.

"Georgie," she smiled, "I come *Mei Gwoh*."

"Welcome to America," said my mother.

"Thank you, Mudder," said Mei Ying.

Mei Ying started life in Kentfield in grand style. The moment she stepped into Barker Manor, she indicated to Mama by gestures that she wanted some boiling water with which to make tea, and she insisted Mama sit down and let her perform a ceremony. Mama showed her where everything was. Mei Ying made the tea, then with one cup in both hands she gently dropped to her knees before Papa's portrait and bowed three times and gracefully placed the steaming cup on the buffet in front of the oil painting. She performed the same ritual with another cup of tea which she presented to Mama. Then she did the same for me.

This greatly impressed Mama who was strong on customs and traditions. If Mei Ying lost points by procrastinating in coming, she regained them with this tea ceremony. I do not think Mei Ying had that as her goal, however. I believe she came from a traditional family where such things were done as a matter of course.

I hoped Mama would take Mei Ying into her heart and give her the feeling of being a member of the family. She had written me in Hong Kong that she would try to like and accept Mei Ying, but pointed out that she had never met her and could not guarantee her feelings. I figured I could not ask more than that.

Mama thought Mei Ying attractive and liked her manners. But she felt frustrated because Mei Ying had not tried to learn English when she was in Hong Kong. Even the simplest things had to be acted out for them to communicate. Bella had offered to let Mei Ying attend English classes in her school. It was on the other side of the Harbor and I tried to encourage her to go. I don't know what Mei Ying thought, but she didn't attend.

Mei Ying must have felt quite isolated. The quiet of Kentfield was something alien. I had not given it enough thought. About ninety-nine percent of Chinese live their lives within shouting distance of someone. It is a form of security. I had told Mei Ying our home was very quiet but I did not realize that quiet might be menacing.

At that time, there were not many Chinese in Marin County. I did know that a Chinese family owned a grocery in Fairfax. We took Mei Ying to talk to them. She was very happy to meet them. They told her of a Chinese laundry in Sausalito that was owned by a Mr. Lee. They introduced her to him and he offered her a job working on the shirt press. It was hard, sweaty work. The wage was minimal. She enjoyed it though. Once she got a little of her lipstick on the collar of one of the shirts and the owner of the shirt came and complained vigorously. His wife discovered it and he had to do some careful explaining. Mr. Lee asked her please not to wear lipstick at work. We had a laugh together.

One of Edith's Chinese friends, a former student of Mama's at San Francisco College for Women, an older woman, needed a babysitter for her newborn granddaughter. She wondered if Mei Ying would like the temporary job. Mei Ying jumped at the opportunity to go to San Francisco.

From there she found her way into a restaurant job on Grant Avenue. She was coming and going to Chinatown partly with Mama and partly by bus. After a short while, she said that she would like to stay in the city and come out only on her day off. This did not make me happy. I needed and wanted a full time wife, not a weekend visitor. Mama was adamant that Mei Ying come home every night.

Mei Ying said she required more money to send to her mother. Chinese friends of Mama's told her we were sending an adequate amount. I would later learn that not only was her mother dependent upon her, but her young daughter whose existence she had denied and concealed from me. I felt guilty because I could not afford the kind of money that she said her mother needed.

One of Mama's best friends in Marin was married to a lawyer. Mama asked him for advice. He was a rather hard-hearted guy and he wanted me to get an annulment which would mean Mei Ying and I were never married, therefore she would be subject to immediate deportation. Even though Mama didn't want her as a member of the family, she did not wish to be so mean. I felt strongly that Mei Ying was not the only one at fault and opposed the idea that she would have to pay so dearly.

In those days there was no such thing as a no-fault divorce. If Mei Ying divorced me, she would be subject to immediate deportation. If I divorced her, I had to have grounds. Only a few grounds were available—infidelity, desertion and mental cruelty. The lawyer we went to recommended mental cruelty. When I explained it to Mei Ying, she shed a few tears. I had to tell her that I didn't think she had been cruel, but that was the only way to get divorced and let her stay in the States.

For awhile I blamed the divorce on Mama. She had predicted even before I got back to the States that Mei Ying would leave me. I regarded this as self-fulfilling prophecy. I think it was something she wished for and was in a position to help it come true. Mei Ying pointed out to me that every time she mentioned leaving me and going back to Hong Kong Mama was happy and friendly.

However, the more I thought about it, the more I realized that I could not pin the blame on Mama. If anyone was to blame, I was the guilty party. I had pushed forward with all the delicacy of a bulldozer, obsessed with thoughts of making love to Mei Ying, enraptured by her smooth skin, perfect sexy body and charming manner.

"You can't do it all the time," warned Thea.

I had given little credence to all who tried to tell me that our different temperaments, interests and backgrounds might cause us to become tired of one another. Yet, I was becoming bored with Mei Ying because we had almost nothing in common to talk about. And she was bored with me for the same reason and probably several dozen others.

After the divorce, she sometimes took a bus and came to see me while Mama was teaching in San Francisco. I saw her irregularly for a number of years. She came to the house or I accidentally bumped into her in Chinatown on the rare occasions I was able to go there with Mama or a man I hired to take me out now and then. Mei Ying kept me advised of the restaurants where she was working as a waitress and Mama and I had some great meals with her. She remembered Mama's birthday, sometimes with a big Chinese dinner.

Not long after the divorce, Mei Ying got her mother to the U.S. She took her to one of the best eye clinics in the Bay Area and arranged for surgery on her cataracts. Mei Ying left her overnight in the hospital. When she returned in the morning her mother had died of a heart attack. Mei Ying was devastated.

Later when she brought her daughter to live with her in San Francisco, I asked her why she had denied having a child. She said I had been so insistent that we practice birth control, she thought I did not like children.

After she told me of her daughter, I wondered if maybe she did not have a husband in Canton as her aunt had written in the note to Ah Lee. When I asked her who the father was, she grinned and spread her hands and said, "Oh Georgie, you know I don't know. Same plenty Americans don't know. I was working in the business."

Mei Ying helped her daughter go through City College in San Francisco and saw her make a good marriage. The last I heard the daughter was working for the Bank of America in Oakland.

Marrying Mei Ying probably wasn't the most intelligent and logical thing to do. But it had been a good experience and left me many happy memories along with a little heartbreak. I didn't feel I made a mistake. People have told me that Mei Ying took advantage of me and used me as a bridge to get to the States. They may be right. But I used her too.

Mama often quoted Tennyson: " 'Tis better to have loved and lost than never to have loved at all." I didn't feel defeated, just educated. Now I could look forward to something better—what, I did not know.

In October, Ah Lee wrote me, saying he had been sick and had gone to a doctor but had not been helped. I replied, telling him to go see Doctor Henry Li and I would pay for it. Edith wrote me that Ah Lee had been given some tests by Doctor Li and his problem was leprosy. Ah Lee had become almost hysterical when he heard the news. He told Doctor Li that I had given him the leprosy and he was going to sue me. Doctor Li told him that I did not have leprosy, that he couldn't have gotten it from me and that Doctor Li would testify to that fact. I recalled Ah Lee had told Mei Ying I had the disease and she would get it from me if we made love too much. What an ironic twist of fate that of all the people I knew, he should be the only one to contract this rare disease.

I needed more work. Luther Nichols had quit as book review editor at the *Examiner* to accept the position of West Coast Editor for Doubleday. He'd been a very thoughtful, nice person to work for. I quit too. Mama was having more and more trouble finding parking in the vicinity of the *Examiner* offices.

I asked Mama to go to the San Rafael *Independent Journal* office and talk to the managing editor and see if I could write some book reviews for them. She went and talked to Jack Craemer and he told her that they didn't expect to do much book reviewing, but he wondered if I would be able to write some short Nature pieces to "spice up the editorial page." Mama told him she thought I would like that and probably could do a good job. For the next nineteen years I wrote three short editorials a week about the Nature scene in Marin county.

A new reporter started working for the *I-J*, Randall Gould, the same man who had been the editor of the *Shanghai Evening Post* and had come to see me the first year we moved to Marin. With my next bunch of editorials I sent a note asking Randall if he remembered me. When Randall got my note he came right over to see me.

For a short while after the Communists took over in Shanghai, they had left Randall alone to run the paper as he wanted. Then they began trying to tell him what he could and couldn't publish. Randall had a stubborn streak and would not be swayed from his ideal of journalistic freedom of expression.

The Communists, acting through the newspaper union, finally locked Randall in his office and made a commotion day and night clanging improvised drums, gongs and cymbals to deprive him of sleep. He held out for a while until he became ill.

He decided to give the whole thing up and return to the U.S. For a time he and his wife wandered the highways and back roads of this country in their Porsche. Eventually they settled down in Colorado and he became automobile editor for the *Denver Post*. When his wife died rather suddenly after a brief bout with cancer, Randall once more took to the road and wound up in Mill Valley where he stayed with an old friend, Agnes. They had worked together on a newspaper in Honolulu in the twenties and she had known all his several wives. They married and lived in her house looking across a valley to Mt. Tamalpais. Randall and Agnes became close friends to Mama and me, and for several years we had lunch out together about once a week.

Randall fascinated me. He helped me get book reviewing assignments from the *Asian Student*, a small newspaper started by the CIA to which he sometimes contributed. I was disappointed to learn he had not mingled much with the Chinese. Perhaps he felt that being involved with Chinese on a human level would affect his journalistic integrity; that he had to remain aloof in order not to be biased in reporting their political tangles. He was almost a white Sahib, going to parties with other Americans, eating American food and not having much contact with Chinese outside his office. In a way, I felt more Chinese after only nine months in Hong Kong than he did after twenty years in Shanghai. Being confined to his office by his own employees left a mental scar which bothered him the rest of his life. He suffered bouts of depression which he tried to treat with Martinis. He wrote me many notes when he was depressed. I did my best to try and cheer him up without seeming asinine.

The summer of 1960, Mama, Uncle Kim, his woman friend and I flew to Paris and picked up a new Mercedes, which cost us the same as an inexpensive Chevrolet at that time, and drove to the Riviera, around Italy, up through the Alps to Switzerland, Austria, Germany and Holland. Then across the channel to England, where Mama and I stayed for a month in Kent with some friends we had met on Barbados.

The highlight and low point of the trip came in the same night in Paris. Kim wanted to take me and his woman friend to a sexy night club show. We took a taxi around the night club district stopping at several while Kim asked whether their shows were really dirty. After a time Kim found one that claimed its show was really filthy so we went in.

One act struck me as being very beautiful and erotic. A slender, attractive young Egyptian woman performed a belly dance. She controlled magic abdominal muscles, which she moved separately and in groups, and with amazing precision. A genuine athlete, she stood quietly for a moment with arms uplifted and rippled the muscles up and down one side of her belly, then the other. Even with her nudity, the dance seemed to me to be a completely acceptable work of art. It was like watching a beautiful Olympian compete.

Kim bought me several glasses of Armagnac brandy to drink and I was quite moved by her performance. I couldn't get her out of my mind. Back at the hotel, I lay on the bed, the Armagnac burning in my stomach and the Egyptian woman dancing in my mind. I was sorely frustrated and began to feel sick in my stomach. Kim had taken his woman friend back to Mama's room, or so I thought. I got down on my knees and crawled to the bathroom to throw up. As I reached for the door knob, I heard Kim and his woman friend having a good time inside. I quietly withdrew and suffered the night out silently.

Kim borrowed a wheelchair from the U.S. Embassy in Paris so I could enjoy the Louvre and go out on the boulevards. When we went to Grasse and I had to walk around the perfume factory, I realized how much easier life would be for me with a wheelchair. Kim and Mama realized it too because they had to help me around on their arms and after awhile I began to tire and lean heavily on them.

When we got to Rome, Kim again borrowed a wheelchair from the Embassy and I toured Vatican City and even ventured into the Catacombs. In Venice, we once more borrowed a wheelchair from the U.S. Consulate. With all the bridges over the canals, Mama or Kim would push me along the narrow alleys until we came to a bridge, then they would each grab an elbow and walk me over. More often than not, a couple would grab the wheelchair and bring it over the bridge behind us and set it down for me.

I was about thirty-five years old and had been walking on the arm of someone almost everywhere I went. Now I realized I had been missing some things and subjecting myself to a degree of exercise bordering on mild torture. Even in cool weather, the exercise would soak my clothes with perspiration.

When we got back home, I watched the classified ads in the *Independent Journal* and bought a second hand wheelchair. It was collapsible and fairly light weight for that time. Mama kept it in the trunk of our car and we used it when we went out for lunch or when I wanted to go shopping. It made life easier for us. Before we got it, I was sometimes embarrassed because people would see me staggering about on Mama's arm, sometimes perspiring and gasping for air, and could not figure out what was going on. They must have thought I was having some kind of seizure or heart attack. Not infrequently, kindhearted people would solicitously inquire, seeking to be helpful. When I was in a wheelchair, they didn't have to guess. I was obviously disabled.

Ah Wah, me, and Paulina at the Royal Botanical Garden,
Hong Kong, 1961.

Hakka Woman

Chapter 8

If you would be powerful, pretend to be powerful.

- Horne Took

On warm September evenings we sat on the long porch of Barker Manor looking across the little valley. Kentfield seemed quiet and lonely after Europe. I talked with Mama to try and convince her that I should go to Hong Kong and find a girl to marry. She instinctively opposed the notion, but after much debating and drama finally agreed. "If that's what it takes to make you happy, then go to it."

I wrote Ah Fat who arranged to get a room for me at the St. Francis Hotel. I wrote to Bella's sister and asked if she could find a man to take care of me. She had connections with Catholic Social Services. I got a round trip ticket to Hong Kong on Japan Air Lines from a small travel agency in Marin. With some consternation, the airline personnel at San Francisco Airport allowed me to be placed aboard the plane without anyone to accompany me.

Before a long flight, I deprive myself of liquid, so I will not have to bother the flight attendants to help me to the toilet. I did not realize that the days when attendants had time to give everyone lots of attention were on the way out. They neglected to help me with several meals and simply skipped me when distributing one food tray. When I got to Hong Kong, I wrote Mama and told her to raise hell. She did.

I had asked Bella's sister and Ah Fat not to tell the Suns or Edith I was coming, as I wanted to surprise them. Ah Fat met me at the airport with a hotel Vauxhall to save the fuss and bother of changing taxis and pushing the wheelchair on and off the ferry.

It was warm and I was tense, tired and hungry, so we hurried to the hotel and had a drink. My "boy" arrived while I was eating. He introduced himself as Mak Wah. On the spindly side with a rather receding chin, he seemed clean, willing and intelligent, and spoke and read English much better than Lee. Forty-two years old, he had been to school thirteen years, seven studying English. He had worked for a grocery store that went bankrupt. His wife worked as an amah at a Sacred Heart Convent and they had eight children.

My room had one five-foot-square aluminum window with Venetian blinds, looking out on a busy alley. I could see into the shops and apartments across the way. An ancient overhead fan predated air-conditioning. Shoddy, cigarette-burned woodwork and furniture irritated the eyes, but the sheets and bedding were sparkling clean. A sign on the door said "Prostitutes absolutely forbidden in the rooms of this hotel."

The next afternoon Wah pushed me in my wheelchair past the Cathay Hotel, my old home. Formerly a moldy cream stucco, it now had a shining new brick-red and white facade. Only the Man Kee grocery store in the old block remained the same. The store boy immediately recognized me and grinned broadly.

The second night, Bella's sister invited the Suns to dinner, promising a surprise. Bella thought her sister's husband, who was living and working in Borneo, had returned. When she saw me, she looked disappointed. She asked me, "What brings you to Hong Kong?"

I said, "I've come to get married."

She tried to conceal her shock. "What does Mrs. Barker think of the idea?"

I said simply, "She thinks it's okay, if that's what I want."

I explained my reasoning. Writers and teachers are highly respected in Chinese culture. I felt that when I had married Mei Ying, I had gone about it in the wrong way. Instead of consulting friends for help and taking my time to find someone more my type, I had grabbed the first attractive women I met. I thought it would not be too hard for me to find a suitable wife. Many intellectual women had fled penniless from China to Hong Kong. Despite my handicaps, I hoped to find a tender, educated Chinese woman.

She said, "Yes, I suppose it's possible," which I took to be a less than ringing endorsement.

When Dr. Sun phoned the next day, he said, "George, are you married yet?" Then he laughed.

That deflated me. He thought I was half kidding with my marriage idea. But I had been feeding thoughts and dreams for too long to be put off. After my marriage to Mei Ying had broken up, Mama had inadvertently fed my fantasy by telling me that the right sort of Chinese girl might have been perfect for me. I did not know how a Chinese woman would feel about my cerebral palsy or lack of money but I was an optimist. I thought being an American would be an asset.

The turmoil of my thoughts was exacerbated by the cacophony from the street. The traffic on Hennessey Road was a minor irritant compared to the hundreds of voices like the roar of a busy cafeteria in New York. Hawkers shouted their wares above the madhouse. To add to the din, a new facade was being put on the building across the narrow way. The people there had children by the dozens and slept about four hours a night. I could hear the crying of the babies.

Cantonese opera blared forth from Radio Hong Kong until twelve or one in the morning, when the majestic "God Save The Queen" killed it for the rest of the night. Roosters started crowing at the crack of dawn.

If I had not been too proud to accept defeat, I would have gladly chucked the whole venture. I tried to get rest, eat well and go easy on alcohol—because I knew in that noisy atmosphere it would be easy to crack up. I took my vitamins too.

The second morning Wah came to work he confessed he had one bad habit. Every morning he must drink four taels of rice wine, about six ounces, with a bowl of congee. He took his little bottle of wine to a Chinese tea house, read the newspaper and drank his breakfast with congee and dim sum. Wah was always a perfect gentleman, though he said, "I'm afraid sometimes when I drink too much I might lose my manner."

His wine was called "Kowloon," triple distilled, and about the price of milk in the U.S. Wah said it was not as strong as most—but I found it pleasant and plenty strong for my tastes, about like a good martini, with a yeasty flavor.

Several notches above the servant class, Wah did everything I asked without any argument and then thought of things on his own initiative. He was always on time and when I sent him on an errand, he returned quickly. His clothes were spotless and he brought his own towel from home to wash his hands. He kept my face shining by mopping it with a steaming washrag whenever I sweated, which was often. He waited at the bathroom door to wipe my hands as I walked out on my knees. He bathed me thoroughly, while Ah Fat helped me in and out of the tub.

Despite our totally different backgrounds, we enjoyed many of the same things, such as the time a plump, grey-haired Chinese millionaire hobbled in on a stick and told a hotel boy he wanted a pretty, young woman just to look at and feel. About sixty-five, he wore a faded blue Chinese dress and had one wife and four concubines! He set the price at thirty dollars and received private peeking and feeling privileges from an attractive young Taiwanese. We laughed at him, but not without a touch of envy.

I gave up hope of help from the Suns in finding a bride. Edith was a bit more encouraging and spoke to a teenage girl whom she knew through the Anglican church. The girl was not from a rich background or even highly educated, but Edith thought she would be a good wife with a placid temperament, useful in dealing with my mother. The girl had told her she wouldn't mind taking care of me, that lots of women did for their husbands who were disabled after marriage. Edith said she thought the girl was quite nice-looking, but not beautiful, and wanted to arrange a meeting between me and the girl and her family.

Then Edith phoned something about "terms." There was too much noise for me to hear it all correctly. What I did hear was like a bucket of cold water in the face. The girl wanted me to buy a little one or two room flat for her mother. It sounded all too familiar. I didn't have that kind of money and I knew Mama wouldn't go for the idea.

I asked Edith to consider someone nearer my own age. She suggested I ask Wah and Ah Fat to help. She was the only one trying, and she kept talking about sixteen and eighteen year old girls. Ah Fat thought he could find a factory girl near thirty who would "stay with you forever."

I met Paulina on the Hong Kong waterfront, at the Cactus Bar of the Luk Kwok Hotel. Edith had suggested I go there to see the real life setting for a late Fifties novel, *The World of Suzie Wong*. Art deco murals, good lighting and a few girls, some of them pretty, sitting at tables knitting.

Ah Wah and I asked Paulina to have a drink at our table. She joined us for a brandy. She was tall, lean, about thirty, and, I thought, good looking. Her skin was darker than most urban Chinese, her posture proud and erect. She spoke fluent American-sailor's English.

I asked her to come back to the hotel and made arrangements for her to stay all night. She seemed surprised because she said she thought I was "an over man." I figured she meant that I was not capable of having sex.

She stayed on. I learned she had been a *mui jai* in a Hakka farming village in the New Territories. The mui jai system, selling little girls to be household slaves, had been outlawed in Hong Kong since the turn of the century and in China since the late 1920's, but it persisted. Even as late as 1967, my instructor in Hong Kong Social Problems at the University of Hong Kong told us that the system was still providing prostitutes for the bars and brothels of the Colony. At the time I met Paulina, it surprised me to think of little girls being sold into slavery.

Although their name means "guest people," the Hakka are descendants of the original settlers of the area. When the Tang dynasty was pushed south, they "civilized" the Hakka and taught them to read and write Chinese. They are South China's equivalent of the American Indian, except they held onto some of their farm land.

Her mother had sold Paulina's older sister before her. When Paulina's brother was born, it was only a matter of time before they would sell her and concentrate their meager resources on him. Paulina was not given to crying, but she sometimes wept when she talked about being sold and how she kept looking for her mother, expecting her to return and take her back home. "I didn't think we were that poor," she said.

She was resold several times, tried to run away and developed a reputation for bad karma. Finally, she was settled in a farming village in the New Territories in Hong Kong from the age of ten until nineteen. The woman who owned her took good care of her. Paulina worked in the rice paddies, rode the water buffalo and cared for them. She grew into a long-striding young woman. She wanted to be free, but *mui jais* were not released until their first menstrual period. In her case, that didn't come until she was nineteen.

She found her way into a Mama-san's hooker's nest in Kowloon, became interested in American movies and learned enough Americanese to freelance at sailor bars in the Wanchai District. She did not have a day of formal education, but had native intelligence and peasant shrewdness.

She liked the Luk Kwok Cactus Bar. The owners didn't employ the common practice of asking girls to get the customers to buy them many drinks of tea disguised as whiskey to run up a big bar bill. She had to pay the manager a set bar fee every week, and everything she made above that was hers.

"Sometimes you met a sailor who was real mean and made you cry. And sometimes a sailor was a real gentleman and treated you like a lady and took you out for dinner, and was polite, and you laughed a lot and had a good time."

Paulina's little group was intensely loyal to the U.S. Navy. They treasured letters, clothing and souvenirs given them by sailor customers. The sailors were not Johns, they were boyfriends.

The girls didn't play mah-jongg, they played poker. Paulina's favorite song wasn't from Cantonese opera, it was "The Tennessee Waltz." They knew all the Hollywood stars of the day. She thought of herself as working for the Navy, comforting the boys a long way from home.

"I been working for the Navy for ten years," she told me. "I know I'll never have to sleep in the streets and beg for food 'cause I got a cash register in my pussy."

I wrote Mama telling her a lot of Paulina's story and that I liked her a lot and was thinking of marrying her. I said I thought she was good looking and enclosed several pictures. She replied, saying that she was surprised and disappointed that I was considering marrying another prostitute. She thought I had lost my good sense. She said I must have a cog missing if I thought Paulina was pretty, pointing out that she was cross-eyed. I took a good look. It was true. I swear I had not noticed it.

In the meantime, Paulina got Ah Wah to write Mama:

Dear Mrs. Barker,

Hello to you. I want to tell you that everything is all right in Hong Kong with George and don't sweat. I like him very much. I'm thinking you're pretty sure real good mother. I like very much to meet you. I like you to send me one photograph.

Are the two dogs still okay? Do they eat when George is gone? I would like to have their picture. Please let me know what you like in Hong Kong. We got to close now. Good-bye and good luck to you.

Paulina Woo

I still liked Paulina's looks. She was clean, domestically inclined; not frugal, but neither was she a spendthrift. Her perfume was Ivory soap. She spoke good English for a girl who virtually taught herself. She loved animals, especially dogs. She sniffed my clothes, and if there was a hint of odor she washed them. Beyond a small poker debt, there was nothing that she wanted me to pay. She had no strong ties to anyone, but she wanted someone. I was pretty sure she liked me.

Wah concurred. He said nothing doing to a girl who wanted a lot of money. Dr. Sun strongly advised me not to give anyone money. This time I was trying harder to not kid myself.

Despite her disconcerting habit of saying exactly what she felt at the moment without regard for the consequences, Paulina and I got along well together. She had a quick temper, but it all went phhhtt. Ah Wah said, "Wait one minute and it's forgotten."

To find out whether I would be able to take Paulina to the States, I got her and Wah to take me by taxi and wheelchair to the U.S. Consulate. Some of the Americans I had known before were still there. They seemed surprised to see me again, particularly when they found I was there with another girl to marry. A white-haired fellow named Kelly had taken Mr. Dunnigan's place. He jokingly told me two Chinese wives was my limit.

There was no way of hiding Paulina's profession under a nice name, as I had with Mei Ying. Paulina, as a prostitute, was an "excludable alien." The only thing to do was go through all the screening required of other visa applicants, then petition the U.S. Attorney General for a Waiver of Excludability. Again, they told me no guarantee, but if I decided to go through with it they would help me as much as possible.

I thought that first Paulina should go to Dr. Li for a preliminary physical exam. I remembered that Mr. Dunnigan had told me prior to my marrying Mei

Ying that ninety percent of their refusals to grant a visa were due to tuberculosis.

Dr. Li told me I was looking wonderfully fit, much better than when he last saw me four years previously. He gave Paulina a complete exam and said she had a problem, latent syphilis. He explained that it was beyond the infectious stage and probably in her brain. After he gave her a course of penicillin, he would give her a spinal tap to make sure her brain was free of disease.

This new development did not alarm me. My biology professor at Greeley had believed everyone should be aware of venereal disease and what to do about it. As a result, Paulina said every time I made love to a woman I went to the doctor—a slight exaggeration, but I was careful by the standards of the time.

Once more I went through the depressing civil marriage ritual at the old stone-columned Supreme Court Building. Our witnesses were Dr. Sun and Daisy Ho, Paulina's best friend from the Luk Kwok Bar. This time I wasn't shaking with spastic tension.

Dr. Li started Paulina's penicillin injections. One day she went into shock and fainted in his office. She had become allergic to penicillin and still had a way to go. Her syphilis turned out to be a penicillin-resistant strain. Dr. Li suggested he treat her with calcium injections, an old-time remedy. We said all right.

Paulina regularly brewed a number of barks and flowers for her skin. She also made broths out of dried sea horses and the swim bladders of fish with a little chicken. She said she wished she had time to cook some Chinese medicine before the doctor took her "bonejuice."

The spinal tap was encouraging, but there might be a few spirochetes sleeping in her liver or kidneys which could push up her serum count and require more injections. We would have to wait. If the count was down, we could relax. If it was up, Paulina would become a pincushion again.

I told Paulina that the Consular officials would try to trip her up if she lied. She said it would be much simpler to tell the truth. On the first day of her screening, the Foreign Service Officer emphasized that she must give honest answers. She replied, "I've been a business woman at Wanchai bars for ten years. How's that?" He had to say that was good.

Life on the lower floors of the St. Francis resembled that of a tenement. Everyone on our floor cooked on a hot plate in his room and "those spicy, garlic smells" grew stale in the corridor. But I was happy enough with our smells, noises and neighbors. I enjoyed the chaos.

Paulina squatted on the bathroom floor before her hot plate cooking lunches of cashews and kidney, dinners of prawns fried in batter, all with lots of steaming long grain white rice which stayed hot for a long time in the clay vessel.

I thought Wah might feel abused with the advent of salt-fish. Far from it. He would rather eat the familiar foods than venture quite so often into "foreign" cooking.

In the room next to ours lived a darkly handsome East Indian, Mr. Madar, his Russian wife and their four blond children. The two small girls called Paulina Auntie and she delighted in playing with them. Mrs. Madar cooked cabbage, exotic and spicy with garlic, which she shared with me.

Doctor Sun teased, "George, Ah Wah isn't your servant, he's your drinking companion." Between us each day we killed a couple of catties of Kowloon brand *shum ching*. A catty is roughly a pint and a third. I enjoyed drinking with Wah.

My Chinese doctors had no objection to *shum ching* except to recommend moderation. Dr. Ling, Dr. Li's vacation stand-in, had studied cerebral palsy in England and tried many drugs on 300 selected patients. He concluded there wasn't anything better for relaxation at that time than the "time-tested one, alcohol."

Ah Wah had one of his older sons come to the hotel and help him get me into a cab and take me to see where he lived. Wah's wife said it was very dirty and noisy and small. But Wah had told her, "Mr. George never looks down on people." He told me that he and his wife and seven of his eight children lived in a room about thirteen feet square. He told me many children were his security for their old age. Paulina told him he liked to make love too much, but he said it couldn't be helped.

Father and son walked me, one on each arm, up a narrow wooden staircase to the upper floor of a large two-story building. The ceiling was ten or twelve feet high and the floor was divided into small cubicles, each housing a family. Walls were of cardboard, old lumber and sacking. One had cotton sacks printed with red, white and blue ink, "Cornmeal—A gift of U.S.A." The building teemed with children. Little outside light penetrated the gloomy interior and the extraordinary crowding imprinted a very dreary picture in my mind.

Wah brought his wife and littlest girl to visit me at the hotel. Paulina told me that it was only ten days till Chinese New Year's and that I knew they were "poor like'n Hell" and this was a visit with a purpose—lucky money. She wanted me to give Mrs. Wah forty dollars.

Sometimes when Wah visited with his family, Paulina asked me in whispered tones if it was okay for her to give the children movie money or candy money. What could I say? They were "poor like'n Hell."

Once Wah's wife brought us some pastries called *"dan saan"* made of flour, egg, a kind of red bean curd called *"naam yee,"* minced onion, a little salt, and very little sugar. Fried in strips or twists in lard, it tasted like pie pastry, only better. "Very good with wine," said Wah.

The expense of New Year's was greater than expected. Living in a hotel where the Manager had issued special orders for everyone to take care of me had a price. All were my servants and every one came around for *"Lycee"* or "Lucky Money." *"Gung hay fat choy,"* they said, "Happy New Year." A few added a phrase which rhymed with it and meant—"Where is the Lucky Money?" This was supposed to be a joke.

Paulina had her heart set on two hundred dollars worth of clothes. Everyone told her how much more expensive everything would be in America. Ah Baat and the boys told her that American Chinese who came to Hong Kong to marry really bought the clothes. I told her I doubted Mama would send an extra two hundred dollars.

She suspected me of telling Mama not to send so much. That made her resentful. She packed her bag and prepared to walk out.

I did not take her seriously and gave her money for a taxi and went out in front of the hotel to wave good-bye. I was chuckling to myself, saying she would back out at the last minute. Instead, she went out the back way.

The following evening, Ah Wah and I took a cab to her former digs and talked to her landlady, called *"Fei Po,"* Fat Woman. The street where she lived, Lockhart Road, must have had more bars per linear foot than any other street on earth. Fat Woman said she had not seen her, but I learned later that Paulina was hiding under the bed. We went to the Luk Kwok Hotel Cactus Bar. No one had seen her or could tell us where she might be.

The next day she still hadn't come back and I was getting desperate. Finally she phoned to say she was coming home. It was a relief to know she was all right.

Paulina had great respect for Dr. Sun. He acted as sort of godfather and advisor to our marriage. When the Suns invited us to dinner at their new home in Kowloon, we gladly accepted. I hoped we could settle the question of Paulina's clothes.

Tall, thick concrete walls topped with jagged shards of glass enclosed a large compound. Gates of solid embossed metal opened onto an expanse of lawn, broadleafed shade trees, and their Colonial-style stucco house.

Dr. Sun said that according to the Chinese way of thinking, two hundred dollars for clothes for Paulina was a must. Wah added that when he was married twenty-two years before, he gave his wife five hundred dollars for clothing and cakes. Bella's sister agreed that two hundred dollars was a necessity. Bella offered to write Mama and explain.

I hoped Paulina could return with me by mid-April. If not, I had better go home anyway. Wah would help her at the Consulate. "Sure, definitely! Why not? We've all been friends together!"

One evening when I had been drinking we unloaded a number of unkind things. She told me she was happier before she married me, that she'd never love me and to cancel the visa application. I told her to get the hell out. She said, "Right now?" I said, "Yes, right now!" So she left. She returned, however, and we went to see Dr. Sun together to talk it over. Dr. Sun told us life's road was never completely smooth and we must learn to take the bitter with the sweet.

I could see I was headed down the "go to hell road," as Paulina expressed it. Nervous, sleepless, with money and Consulate worries, I feared I might crack up again with the burden of alcohol on my nervous system.

I asked Dr. Li for drugs to tide me over the first dry days, and something to help me sleep. He said that if I quit suddenly I would have to go to the hospital and be under sedatives or run the risk of having the DT's again. He told me to water my wine by an eighth a day so that at the end of eight days I would be drinking all water. He gave me a pill to relax and impart a glow to the spirits. Still, it was not easy.

Ah Wah and I went to the Consulate. The long, lean, sour-faced Immigration and Naturalization Service man, Mr. Glasgow, had told me not to come back to his office but to send Wah. I felt I should go, and did. Glasgow glared at me, averted his eyes and looked like he was getting ready to spit. But he did that every time he saw me. He wore cowboy boots and brought to mind a mean-spirited sheriff. He told us he was busy. I hated the thought of facing him on my first day of straight water, but it had to be done.

He wouldn't see me, but called Wah into his office and told him we needed a birthday for Paulina. Paulina had said that if she could choose a birthday, she would take the end of September when the countryside was green from summer rains and the weather had started to cool. Wah consulted with me in the hall and I had him say she was born the thirtieth of September.

Dr. Sun wanted a watchdog. Paulina told him she would look around the squatter huts of North Point and buy a native chow for him. One of the room boys knew of a litter of puppies and had the owner bring them in a basket for Paulina to make a choice. The lady's pigtailed, pajama-clad daughter smiled broadly as Paulina cuddled one of them. Her mother said the little girl had been afraid we wanted a puppy to eat.

Paulina bathed the roly-poly forty-day-old bag of fur and fat, then wanted to keep it till we left Hong Kong. It ate a small sprinkling of beef with lots of rice. The sandy mutt shared our bed and slept under the covers while we went to a movie. When we got back she found it on top and awake, so she put it on the floor. Instant puddle.

I thought we should take him to the Sun's for the children to enjoy while he was small. She phoned Dr. Sun to tell him we had the puppy and asked him to let her know when he wanted it so she could take it to his office. But I had the distinct impression she told him not to hurry.

Paulina and the "dog baby" played on the bed while wind pelted the windows with cold rain. The little fellow pulled and shook her hair. "George, I love this little dog. He's such a good dog. Do you love him, George? I don't mind cleaning up after him."

We called it *Lo Yeh*, meaning Old Grandfather, until we discovered it was really a girl. I couldn't believe I hadn't noticed. Thank heavens Dr. Sun didn't specify gender. Paulina renamed her Jane, "liken Tarzan's wife." I could scarcely type for her calling "Look, George, look!"

Chinese New Year's Eve was coolish. Many fireworks. Wah, Paulina and I went to the Fair. From my wheelchair, the view was mostly of people's backsides. We saw a pretty red peony chrysanthemum which Paulina bargained down from nine dollars to six. She placed candy and two tangerines on a plate with an envelope of lucky money at our open window, her acknowledgment of tradition.

New Year's day was family time. While Wah enjoyed it in the bosom of his brood, Paulina took care of me alone. She cooked the traditional vegetarian dish which is supposed to impart wisdom, good luck and all the virtues.

Soon after came Wah's day to sweep the tombs of his ancestors. He and his brother would visit their father's cemetery site in Kowloon. Paulina offered to fill in for Wah, since she seldom left my side anyway. "I want to take care you, darling. I don't mind being your *amah,* so long as you love me and are good to me."

One night about three a.m. I was awakened by wild sobbing from the bathroom. Paulina, no drinker, had finished off a bottle of Chinese wine. She sobbed on my chest for about an hour telling me how much she loved her father, mother and baby brother, how they might be still alive and how much she'd like to see them; how the dogs followed her when her mother took her away to be sold; how lonely she had been and how much she cried at first; how she had been afraid to eat in the kitchen of the family of her master, so she would steal lard at night and eat it, until she was caught in the act and forced to eat so much lard she became sick.

After I fell asleep again, she took four Seconal sleeping pills, so potent that Dr. Li warned me not to take more than one at a time. I knew she wasn't suicidal, but was still glad there hadn't been more pills available. I had Ah Wah phone Dr. Li and he asked some questions and said to let her sleep it off. She slept through the next day and into the late evening.

Observing the hotel boys feverishly preparing their bets for the day's horse races, she smiled and said, "They rush out to the races like tigers, and come back like sick cats."

Although she said, "I'm real stupid," her mastery of English led me to believe she had a high I.Q. But she was not good at managing money. She was a soft touch and a pushover for a hard luck story. "I'm always wishin' that just once I had $700 or $800 that I could give to all the poor children."

I worried that my mother was disappointed in me. I figured I either had low tastes or was a true democrat in the tradition of Robert Burns. I preferred the latter.

The hot season was coming and I knew I had to get out of Hong Kong. The U.S. Consulate said it might be months before Paulina got her visa. Paulina agreed I should go. She would take back her old room on Lockhart Road until she could follow.

Ah Wah and I got my return ticket from the hotel safe and took the hotel car downtown to the JAL office. When the clerk saw the name on my ticket, he lost all pretense of politeness. Because I had complained about the service on the flight to Hong Kong, Japan Airlines refused to take me back unless I hired an attendant to accompany me. I asked to talk to the manager. He stonily confirmed what the clerk had told me. I was stunned. I couldn't afford to buy another ticket for an attendant. I left the JAL office in a mood of anger and seething frustration.

I thought JAL was crazy to think they could just abandon me in Hong Kong. Desperate, that night as we lay in bed, I had an idea. I knew in that instant I could redefine the game and win. "I'll screw JAL if it's the last thing I do," I told Paulina. I was so relieved I laughed myself to sleep.

The next morning when Ah Wah came to work with a bottle of *shum ching* in his hand, I sent him out for poster paper and a black marking pen and had him make a picket sign, saying "JAPAN AIRLINES UNFAIR TO ME—They Brought Me To Hong Kong But Won't Take Me Home." Meanwhile I typed several statements giving my version of the situation.

We were done by noon. It was Saturday and I wanted to hit the Sunday papers. I had Ah Wah call the three English-language newspapers and tell them in an excited tone that there was a big commotion in front of the Saint Francis Hotel and hang up quickly. Then we hurried down to the front door, me in my wheelchair and Wah with the picket sign. Picketing was a novelty in Hong Kong. Within five minutes a large crowd gathered. Then came the reporters and photographers, then the police who threatened to arrest me for obstructing the sidewalk. Pictures and my story were on the front page of the English papers, as well as inside their Chinese affiliates.

Now that I was in a battle, I put aside my resolve to quit drinking. I wanted to roar like a lion. To hell with being reasonable. During this time, I was making almost daily visits to Dr. Sun's office. He seemed to think I was doing the only thing I could. Some of his relatives worked for Pan American Airways in Hong Kong and he knew all the inter-airline scuttlebutt about my case. He laughed and shook his head. My other Chinese friends, like Edith, were polite, but asked, "Do you think this is a wise procedure?"

Monday morning at 8:30 a couple of men from the American Consulate knocked on my door and told me the Japanese Consulate had called them saying JAL was going to sue me for libel. They wanted me to stop picketing. They said I was giving America a bad name, and if I wanted to come to Hong Kong again, I'd better not cause trouble or Hong Kong Immigration wouldn't let me return.

They caught me at my weakest time of day: half-awake, without coffee, without wine. I didn't believe I was causing trouble to anyone but JAL. But without my spirit of resolve I crawled on my belly like a snake before those asses and promised I would picket no more.

Within an hour, another knock. A refined Englishman, the Superintendent of Hong Kong Immigration, said he was there to collect data and see if he could assist me. I told him what the Consular officials had told me. He said, "It's not true. No one can keep you from coming back." He indicated that my surmise was correct, that JAL had an obligation to take me back since I had a valid ticket and they had brought me over unescorted.

Now I seethed at the U.S. Consulate. I typed a note to Mr. Kelly telling him about my conversation with the Superintendent of Immigration. I said I would take the Consulate's advice on Paulina's visa, but in other things I would go my own way, and added, "I am going to screw JAL if it's the last thing I do." I took several swigs of *shum ching* and went with Ah Wah by taxi to the Consulate, delivered the note in person and left without a word.

The Consulate contacted me by phone and wanted to know what they could do to help me. I expressed surprise. They told me I hadn't asked for their help. But they had tried to force me to capitulate, by hiring an attendant and paying for his flight. That kind of help I didn't need. But I said sure, just help me get home without losing any more money. They said they would try, but I felt they were hand in glove with JAL.

Several days later, Wah parked me and my wheelchair outside the JAL office in downtown Central. Wah raised our picket sign. Immediately, a big crowd formed and within ten minutes we were arrested for obstructing the sidewalk.

I hadn't made any arrangements with the reporters because I wasn't sure it would work out as planned. This was sort of a trial run. Police carried me in my chair up the steps of the station to the office of the inspector, a blue-eyed English fellow about my age. He asked Ah Wah, "Why are you helping him break the law? Why don't you stop him?" Wah replied that I was his boss and he had to follow me—even to jail. The policeman and I joked while he waited for instructions. I said I rather hoped he would put me in jail. He said it was not comfortable and I wouldn't like it, but he knew his Superintendent would tell him to let me go free.

He smiled and said he could see he was going to have trouble with me. He told me there was no sense in demonstrating on Sunday because the Central District was almost empty. As we left he said, "At this point I am supposed to warn you of the law's dire penalties. See you on Monday!"

The police had taken my sign but I had another ready. JAL and the U.S. Consulate begged me to quit picketing, saying they were working on getting me home. I didn't trust them and kept the pressure on. Doctor Sun told me that JAL executive board in Tokyo had held three meetings about their Hong Kong problem. *Shum ching* added to my feeling of tremendous power.

One fine afternoon I received a phone call from JAL asking me whether I wanted to leave the following day. I was, of course, delighted. They told me to be at the airport at 8:30 the next morning, my plane would leave at 9:40. Wah and Paulina worked like hell, packing, taking me to the barber for a quick shave, all the knotty little details. That night we accepted an invitation from Dr. Sun and Bella to be their guests at dinner again. Back at the hotel we talked till one o'clock, got up at six, settled the bills, and took the hotel car to the airport.

When we got to Kai Tak, we discovered that a clerk in the Kowloon office of JAL had made a mistake and wasn't aware that Tokyo had refused to fly me. Hong Kong's JAL people were very apologetic and tried to get Tokyo to let me go anyway, but to no avail.

Dr. Sun told me to be patient, that if all else failed his brother-in-law with Pan Am would find a passenger willing to be responsible for me. He said the other airlines were pulling for me, except for some young women in the Pan Am office who were frightened by my distorted spastic movements as I produced the noises that constitute my speech. I tend to forget that not everyone instantly recognizes me as a noble spirit.

JAL was under pressure from San Francisco to accept me, which I attributed to Mama, who had consulted an attorney. JAL Hong Kong office was trying to get Tokyo headquarters to let them take me. I had Wah call the local people and propose they fly Mama out at the end of May to be my attendant, for which I would call off my picketing.

Mr. Tanaka, a handsome, dignified and soft-spoken member of the Japanese Royal Family, came to see me that afternoon. I had met him in the JAL office and been told he was learning the airline business. He asked me please to be patient and cease picketing, that JAL would have news for me very soon. I trusted him and knew he was embarrassed by Tokyo's attitude. I agreed to stop for a week. Mr. Tanaka smiled slightly and said I was a naughty man. I replied that JAL was a naughty airline. We both smiled.

People stopped Wah on the street and asked him, "Any news yet?" When the news dealer at the newsstand across the street asked him, a man spoke up: "Is your boss the crippled American writer who has had two Chinese wives? Tell him I've got a friend working for JAL who told me they are going to take him home."

Two days later JAL let me know I would be flown to San Francisco with a personal flight attendant. They said the Japanese union wouldn't permit the regular cabin attendants to give me the help I needed. I would have to sign documents to protect JAL from litigation. They wouldn't be ready for several days because they were consulting with their attorney. At that point, I would have signed anything that would take me out of the humid heat and noise. I agreed not to sue or publicize the outcome for seven years. The agreement was signed three days later before a Notary in the American Consulate.

That night as we were getting ready for bed, a knock came at the door. My old helpers Ah Lee and Ah Chiang stood beaming on the threshold. A friend from MacDonnell Road had spotted me at the American Consulate and found where I was staying. Ah Lee was his same contagiously enthusiastic self. He'd had nine children, after which his wife had "the operation." Ah Chiang was a taxi driver in Kowloon, married with three sons.

I was pleased to see Lee, the old rascal. Edith had suggested I avoid him because he had threatened to sue me over his leprosy. Far from giving me trouble, Lee promised Paulina and me that we would have many boys, then whipped out a picture of himself and signed it for me. I told him Ah Wah and I had been to Welsby House looking for him, and were told he and his brother and Ah Chiang no longer worked for the company.

We laughed like old times. He looked well. I asked him if he had any more trouble with his leprosy. He said he received many injections from fifteen various doctors, and it had been arrested. He was all right except for paralysis in the last two fingers of his left hand.

The time had come for me to depart. Paulina, Dr. Sun and Ah Wah saw me off at the airport in Kowloon. JAL took me home in style, assigning a neat, young male flight attendant as my personal aide. In Tokyo, where the flight spent the night, I was met by several junior executives of JAL and escorted to the hotel where they told stories, helped me with my dinner, and bought a large bottle of brandy for us to share. The next morning the flight was delayed, so they took me on a guided tour of the Meiji Shrine and wherever else I wanted to go. Before I knew it I was once more greeting Mama at San Francisco Airport.

Paulina, Barker Manor in 1962
and visiting her New Territories village in 1973.

A Fit of Temper

Chapter 9

Men are admitted into Heaven not because they have curbed and governed their Passions or have No Passions, but because they have Cultivated their Understandings.

- William Blake

Back in Kentfield, I learned that the Immigration Service had sent an agent around our neighborhood asking if I was a moral man. This irritated me and embarrassed my mother. I felt that they were maligning me by innuendo, and smearing Paulina before she even arrived.

They also interviewed Mei Ying to find out if I was capable of sexual intercourse. One of the consuls in Hong Kong seemed obsessed with the idea that I was having, as he put it, "hanky panky" with Paulina. I don't know what he thought we did in bed, but he knew a pervert when he saw one, despite my repeated assurances we were having ordinary sex. The agent who interviewed Mei Ying told me with a smile that she said I was very good.

After several months without a word, I wrote an indignant letter to the U.S. Attorney General. He replied that Paulina's record of prostitution required them to proceed with caution. They might have thought I was a white slaver.

When Paulina finally got her visa, Mama and I met her at San Francisco Airport. Paulina got off the plane wearing a black Chinese dress and high heeled shoes. In the terminal she fell and sprawled on the floor. She skinned her knee a little, but her pride was hurt more.

Paulina got through Customs and we went outside, where she and Mama had their first personality clash. Paulina was shivering in the cold fog of a South San Francisco August evening. Mama ordered her to put on a sweater. She refused. We rode home with Paulina in the back seat looking very cold and holding back tears.

Despite their different backgrounds, Mama and Paulina had much in common. Both were super clean. Mama joked that Paulina wanted to wash everything. They both loved to garden. Gardening was their life. Paulina was a good Chinese home-style cook, but when she cooked salt fish it drove Mama up the wall because, although it tasted good, it smelled to high heaven. Mama was afraid it would permeate the furniture. Rather grudgingly, each admitted the other was good at heart.

Paulina did not regard sex as a big thing. She had anesthetized that part of her life. She said she thought she would learn to come after she had been out of the business for a while. Paulina performed her marital duty laughing most of the time, but she was not exciting in bed.

She felt more at ease with dogs and birds than with people. She felt that animals were more honest in their emotions. Many times she told me, "A dog will never cheat you." When she first arrived in Marin, Mama and I took her to the Humane Society and let her pick a puppy. She chose a small brown dachshund mix, which she loved and bathed daily and fed the choicest meat in the house mixed with rice.

Sometimes she would fly into brief rages. One afternoon, Mama, failing to realize how poor Paulina's eyesight was, kept telling her how to set the oven. Paulina was trying and they both became exasperated until Mama finally said curtly, "Here, let me do it." Paulina turned and kicked the dog across the kitchen and fled out the door crying.

This episode helped convince Mama that Paulina was utterly unreasonable, and also that she would have to take her to an eye doctor and get her a pair of reading glasses. Paulina told Mama she went to an eye doctor in Hong Kong and he had said he couldn't help her. Mama consulted her friends and took Paulina to the best. They left the house like would-be conquerors and returned like Napoleon's army retreating from Russia. The doctor said Paulina suffered from a deformity of her eyeballs caused by a childhood trauma or disease and was almost legally blind, and nothing could be done to help her, not even glasses.

Paulina knew she had a bad temper, and told me she wished she could see a psychiatrist for help. At the time, I did not know how to get help for her and Mama was not about to put up big bucks for a fancy head doctor with weird Freudian notions, when in her view all the world's troubles could he resolved by applying common sense. But Paulina knew something was missing, and told me, "I don't know how to love."

She stayed at Barker Manor only three months, then begged me to let her go back to Hong Kong. She said she was not happy and that I didn't need her. I said no, to wait until spring when Kentfield would be beautiful with all kinds of blossoms and flowering trees, then decide. I was unusually adamant. I had worked too hard to get her over here.

That night Paulina and I were watching TV together in our bedroom and drinking a little wine. Mama had retired to her room for her ultimate luxury, reading in bed. Paulina and I were engrossed in a psychological mystery. At the climax, someone smothered someone to death with a pillow. Paulina picked up a pillow and advanced toward the chair in which I was sitting, with a half smiling face. She threw the pillow on my face and leaned on me with all her weight. I could not breathe and after about a half a minute, I became frightened. We had been drinking some light wine and my bladder was full. The more she leaned on me the more scared I became. I lost control and peed on her. She recoiled and let up on the pillow. I yelled out and Mama came running and pulled her away.

"What is going on here?" Mama demanded.

"Georgie peed on me. He won't let me go to Hong Kong. I'll kill him," she sobbed.

"She tried to smother me," I yelled.

Mama held Paulina by one arm, pulled her out into the living room and tried to calm her down. Paulina pulled away from Mama and started crying. She bawled, "Georgie won't let me go back to Hong Kong. I have a no good mother, Georgie has a real good mother."

Mama said, "Now, now, calm down. I could be your mother too. Let me try to be your mother."

After a while, Paulina calmed down and I wanted to talk to her. But Mama said we could talk in the morning. She told Paulina to go sleep downstairs. Mama cleaned up the mess I had made and put me to bed. Paulina said the next day that she didn't mean to hurt me. I don't believe she wanted to kill me, but Mama thought she was in earnest.

Edith appeared in San Francisco to visit her brother and his family, and wanted to come to visit me the next day. I was embarrassed about Paulina, especially since I had declined Edith's choice of a wife in favor of her. Paulina felt terrible about the previous night, and stayed hidden downstairs. Mama was too chagrined by the goings-on to tell Edith that Paulina had tried to smother me. We managed to get through the visit and even had a few laughs. It was an awkward meeting with my good friend. I think she could feel the trouble in the air.

The upshot of the unhappy episode was that I agreed to let Paulina go back to Hong Kong. But before she left, Mama took us to a lawyer and we agreed to have him file for an uncontested divorce.

The first day after she was back in Hong Kong, she wrote me a letter begging me to take her back, saying that the moment she got on the plane she realized she had made a mistake. The divorce was already in the courts and I thought everything was settled. I wrote her and told her, as I had before she left, that when she left me things were over between us. I honestly didn't think Immigration would let her return. After several more letters, I told her to go to the Consulate and see if she could come back. She found she could return anytime within a year.

I was no longer interested in Paulina as a wife or lover, but she had a quality of spirit that I found unique. The heart has its own unfathomable logic. Mama did not want her back and stalled for eleven months. As we awaited the final divorce decree, I pestered Mama to let her return. We would have to buy the ticket for her.

At the last moment, Mama relented and Paulina returned. Mama imposed the stipulations that Paulina would find live-in work and pay Mama back for her return airplane ticket; we would go ahead with the divorce, and Paulina would have to be independent. Until then, she could sleep downstairs and take her meals with us.

We helped her find a job as a live-in housekeeper for a kind and loving elderly couple in the neighboring town of Greenbrae. Her peasant love of the soil soon manifested itself in gardening. She had a green thumb and grew enough vegetables for half the people on the road. She saw her role in life as that of peasant farmer. When she got a chance, that was where she turned—back to the land, growing vegetables and flowers.

Mama said my interest in Paulina was part of a "Pygmalion Complex." I didn't believe it, but I was glad that I had not turned my back on her. Determined that no one in this country should know anything about her past, I said, when queried, that we had met at a restaurant where she was a waitress. Only Randall, with his long experience in the Far East, expressed some doubts about where such an uneducated young woman learned such fluent English.

I helped Paulina to the limit of my capability in an effort to get her happily situated. Mama had the notion that Paulina was waiting for her to pass away, so I would take her back and she could be Queen of the Manor. Paulina and I were fond of each other, it's true, but I had found her to be such a strong personality that I preferred her in small doses. When Paulina was recovering from surgery, she was so depressed and lonely I bought her a small TV to help distract her. That proved to Mama I was hopelessly smitten.

Uncle Kim worked for the Social Security Administration's adjudication division in Baltimore. He wanted me to apply for Social Security under Mama. A veteran himself, he felt that I was as deserving as many of the vets who were drawing big disability checks. Since I had been permanently disabled before I was nineteen, I was eligible for a monthly sum equal to half her benefit while she lived and three-quarters after she died.

Mama opposed the idea of my being on any kind of welfare, which taking any money from the government represented to her. She felt her marriage contract included taking care of me, and further it was her duty as a parent. To involve the state in family business seemed to her akin to communism. Some of her friends told her it was foolish not to take the money because she had paid for it through her taxes. She remained proud and conservative, but she let me apply.

Once I got on the government gravy train, I rode it full throttle ahead. I found it provided a veritable cornucopia of goodies. By the mid-Sixties there was SSI which gave me more cash, and Medicare and MediCal which took care of my doctor and dental bills. About that time I found out about IHSS, In Home Support Services, which would pay a person to take care of me. I figured Mama could get that money because she was not my real mother, had never legally adopted me and was not legally responsible for me.

Mama didn't want to take money for caring for me. At the same time she felt that was a lot of money to let go down the drain. Torn between her conservative political principles and a waste-not-want-not nature, she agreed to sign for it but let me keep the money.

Eventually, I got her to accept some of it to buy stocks and help pay for trips to Hawaii every winter, a big trip to Mexico and several to Canada and eventually trips to England, New Zealand and two more to Hong Kong. The regulations at that time were very lax. I arranged with my social worker to get all this money in Hong Kong for a year. It went directly to my bank and I used it over there. It was all legal. Mama never felt good about my taking so much money from the government. Not proud of it myself, I just closed my eyes and mind and plunged onward, grabbing the money as I went.

Once Paulina had returned and settled down, I had an opportunity that I hoped would change my life. A lady working for Social Security came to talk to me. She told me about a new kind of experimental brain surgery developed for persons with Parkinson's disease, but it was thought that it would probably be beneficial for relaxing the muscles of people like me who had tension athetosis. It was educated medical roulette and I was desperate enough for relief from my personal devil, physical tension, that I was ready to gamble.

The surgeon would be Dr. Bertram Feinstein, a well-known San Francisco neurosurgeon who had studied the technique in Sweden. (He had a wife named Dianne who was on the verge of entering politics at the time.) Mama took me to San Francisco to be examined. There was a momentary crisis when the Social Security lady told me their quota had been filled. But when Dr. Feinstein read my medical record from Stanford, he volunteered to perform my surgery free of charge because he said I had done so much for myself. Mama and I arranged for a local foundation to pick up the cost of my hospital stay.

The first operation required a general anesthetic and involved screwing pins in my skull to hold a stereotaxic frame. The other, the actual brain surgery, would be performed with an electric needle, one hemisphere at a time, under a local anesthetic to numb only the scalp, since the brain feels no pain.

Doctor Feinstein wanted to be able to question me and watch my muscles move as he probed various parts of the motor cortex with an electric needle. It was scary and uncomfortable, as I could hear the electric drill going through my skull and it sounded like it was tearing up big splinters and grinding away. There was no pain during the surgery, but I felt uncomfortable, as though my brain was under intense pressure.

The surgery did relax my right side, but it was not an unqualified success. Along with the tension went a good deal of my limited dexterity. My right hand, which was always grasping and refusing to let go, became as limp as a dishrag. Now I could hardly grasp at all. But my left hand became more useful because of a sympathetic idiosyncrasy of the nervous system.

I felt relieved of the terrible tension that had plagued me since I got out of the hospital when I was thirteen. But I was unwilling to have the other side of my brain operated on because if I lost any more dexterity, I felt I would become totally useless. I learned to sign my name with my left hand and it became my dominant side.

The surgery also affected my speech adversely. I became even harder to understand. The left side of the brain controls speech and I slurred my words worse than ever. On balance I was glad I had gone ahead and had one side done. The world is never as perfect as it might have been in hindsight.

Mama, who had not favored the surgery as much as I, did not hide her feeling that I had made a mistake. When fresh from the hospital, I felt so weak on my right side I had to lie on my bed and rest while Mama taught in San Francisco. When I slid to the floor to go to the bathroom I took about two steps on my knees and fell. My muscles would not hold me up. And I could not get to my knees. Mama returned from work about five o'clock to find me on the bedroom floor in a puddle. Somehow, I felt guilty for pushing forward with the surgery. But I gradually regained my strength, and Mama came to agree with me that it had not been a bad thing.

For several years during this period, I subscribed to several learned journals on China and received a number of propaganda magazines direct from Beijing. I also subscribed to the *Far Eastern Economic Review* from Hong Kong and *The Economist* from London, and took *Newsweek*, *Forbes* and *The New Republic*. Mama subscribed to *U.S. News and World Report* and the *Wall Street Journal*. Reading most of these from cover to cover was almost a full-time job.

I began to fancy myself as a China specialist and wrote a weekly column for the *Independent-Journal* which I modestly called "Barker on China." This ran for about a year and a half. I was also still writing my three little Nature editorials every week. And Randall got me a little job writing occasional book reviews for *The Asian Student.*

Randall had worked for the OSS, the agency that preceded the CIA during World War II and he made the life sound fascinating. I read Allen Dulles' book, *The Craft of Intelligence*, and dreamed of working for the CIA. I wrote to Sherman Kent, one of the Kentfield Kents, who I read was very high in the CIA and proposed that they send me to Kwangtung Province and let me settle down there, renounce the U.S., integrate myself into the life of some rural village, learn to read Chinese and understand Cantonese better, and become an observer. I told him I did not think anyone would suspect such a severely disabled person of being a spy. He took me seriously enough to send an agent around to the house to talk to me.

The agent was a retired Old China Hand and pre-Revolutionary rug manufacturer in Tientsin. A very alert, heavyset man with a mild wheeze and ruddy complexion, he seated himself in the kitchen which also served as my office and regaled me with stories of his adventures. He told me he lived in San Rafael and read my column on China, and thought I showed a good ability to analyze situations.

Alone and unable to speak so he could understand me, I felt frustrated by my inability to communicate better and knew that he was not impressed. He did tell me that I was right in thinking no one would suspect me. That was the last I heard from the CIA. My wildest dream went out the door that day.

Following my discovery of a gold mine in the government, I occasionally hired men to drive me places in their cars while Mama taught in the City. I remember one in particular, Mickey, a jazz musician, a talented classical pianist and student of radical politics. He and I were about the same age and kindred spirits in many ways. He was proud of his Irish ancestry as I was of my Scottish blood and we both felt the U.S. should not be fighting in Vietnam.

We had a number of small adventures together. We planned an overnight camping trip to the redwoods of nearby Samuel P. Taylor Park on Chinese Moon Festival. The huge autumn moon silhouetted the fernlike branches of the majestic redwoods. I woke up once looking directly in the face of a curious coatimundi, a relative of the raccoon.

Mickey and I went to Chinatown, sometimes taking Paulina. We also looked up Mei Ying now and then. Together we tried to learn to read and write Chinese, with the help of the husband of one of Mama's former students, a retired bank executive who had been a friend of Edith's father. Mickey was good at Cantonese because of his understanding of tones.

One night he took me to his San Anselmo home for dinner with his wife and daughter. He and I had been reading about a new drug that was supposed to cause instant enlightenment. The drug was called LSD and Mickey had gotten hold of some and we tried it that night. After dinner he gave me a tiny bit and I sat in the living room while he played Bach and Liszt on the piano. It was a warm summer night, but I sat entranced and uplifted by the beautiful snow scene outside his picture window.

Mickey was a kind and generous guy but he lived under a dark cloud of foreboding. He told me his father had committed suicide and that he thought about it often. I asked him to explain his reasoning to me, but a look of such anguish crossed his face that I let the matter drop. When I was in Hong Kong the next time, Mama sent me a clipping from the *Independent Journal* that Mickey had leaped to his death off the Golden Gate Bridge.

Not long after my surgery, I found myself at a Baha'i Fireside, one of the cozy coffee and cookie meetings by which Baha'is spread their faith. I was under no pressure to join, but it seemed to embody some of the best features of Buddhism, Christianity and Islam, as I knew them. I liked the absence of clergy, the quality of the people, and the warmth with which they welcomed me and everyone. I loved the poetic quality of the Baha'i prayers: "I am a broken-winged bird and my flight is very slow." Thus, I became a Baha'i for social, psychological and literary reasons, not because of a great spiritual awakening.

Mama decided in 1966 to retire after twenty years teaching at San Francisco College for Women. We decided that she would go around the world on a big last trip and I would go back to Hong Kong and stay for a year or maybe longer. She would fly as far as Hong Kong with me and on our way we would visit the Fujia Hotel in the mountains near Lake Hakone in Japan. Set in gorgeous gardens in a hot springs area, the Fujia was a uniquely beautiful old hotel that Mama and I had enjoyed on two earlier occasions.

I would be going to Hong Kong as a Baha'i pioneer which in the jargon of the Baha'i Faith meant spare-time missionary. I had initially been under the impression that it was a blending of Buddhist and Christian principles, which was true to a point. I was slow in realizing that these teachings were unimportant compared to those of Baha'u'llah, the prophet of the Baha'i faith. By the time I was ready to go I had begun to have a few doubts. But the people were good and I thought I could do as good a job making converts as the next fellow.

The entryway and Johnny Chee and me at my apartment.

Tsimshatsui Editor, 1966-69

Chapter 10

You can't go home again.

- Thomas Wolfe

I considered moving to Hong Kong and living out the rest of my days there, if Mama should die before me. I thought I would be able to live more economically, have good Chinese help, and a variety of cuisines and lead a more interesting, production-oriented life. During the day, my Chinese helper would be in constant attendance. All my attention could be devoted to writing. No more struggling to put another sheet of paper in the typewriter. No more laborious crawling on my knees to the bathroom.

But Hong Kong was changing. Rents had soared, wages were rising and Chinese were turning away from jobs as household help in favor of factory work.

Before I returned to Hong Kong, an American Baha'i lady in Kowloon had found a Chinese man to be my helper. He took one look at me and decided taking physical care of a severely disabled person was not the kind of work he wanted. Mama thought it was an ill omen and wanted me to give up the idea of remaining in Hong Kong and continue on around the world with her. But I hated giving up.

Going against the advice of my Chinese friends, who depended on word of mouth recommendations to find good help, I ran a classified advertisement in the newspaper for a helper. On the morning after the ad appeared, about thirty men crowded the hall outside our hotel room.

One young man had been waiting since seven. His name was Johnny Chee and he had left China with his parents as an infant. He had been raised in tiny Belize in Central America and his Caribbean English was better than his Cantonese. Lean and muscular, he had studied first aid and done weight lifting at the YMCA to improve his strength. I liked Johnny's initiative, attitude and direct manner, and hired him without interviewing the rest.

When Johnny had returned to Hong Kong in his early teens with his parents, he was an alien in a strange country. He couldn't read or write Chinese and according to his best friend, Sherman Hui, his Cantonese was not perfect either. He had recently graduated from middle school in Tsimshatsui,

Kowloon's big hotel and tourist shopping district next to the Star Ferry. He lived with his parents in the heart of Tsimshatsui on Cornwall Road among the bars and shops.

When I was sure I was returning to the Colony I wrote Ah Wah. He had a good job working as a switchboard operator at Canossa Hospital on the island. However, he told me he would like to work for me on Saturdays, which was his day off. This would give Johnny a break and me a chance to renew my acquaintance with my loyal friend Ah Wah.

This time I wanted to live on the Kowloon side of the Harbor. Dr. Sun knew that I liked living downtown where anything I needed was easily available and there was plenty of human drama. He arranged with the manager of the Grand Hotel to give me a good deal on a very small single room. Johnny lived only three blocks away. But alone in that tiny room most evenings, I began to feel jailed and cut off from human contact. I did not know any of the hotel boys, and they did not appear eager to become my buddies.

Johnny suggested I try to get an apartment nearby. We watched advertisements in the papers and found a place directly across the street from the Grand. Dr. Sun agreed it was a good move and thought, because the apartment was located above the Tsimshatsui police substation, I would be safer than at other places.

The entry on Carnarvon Road was through a long art gallery lined with oil paintings of Hong Kong. The owner, Ricky Leung, a gifted painter of Chinese junks, became an acquaintance. His gallery contained a number of delicate portraits of beautiful young Chinese women by C.K. Chien, as well as several luscious nudes. The gallery faced Hanoi Road, with huge, shady banyan trees in the middle, and along both sides French, Malayan and several styles of Chinese restaurants, not expensive but with good food. Johnny and I usually ate at the New Marseilles.

Strong and willing to take me anywhere in my wheelchair, Johnny demonstrated his dexterity and stamina by bumping my chair up and down high curbs, pushing me up steep hills, running and dodging through traffic, and threading me in and out of the crowds on Kowloon's densely packed sidewalks. I relished the sense of danger, the speed and excitement of going places with him. He loved taking my chair up and down escalators. We never took a taxi, unless our destination was miles and miles away.

About twice a week, he pushed me past the elegant old Peninsula Hotel to the Star Ferry Pier and up or down the gangplank, depending on the tide, then across the harbor on the ferry to the Central District to visit Dr. Sun at his office. We enjoyed the gentle splashing and smell of the sea, the city skyline with the backdrop of Victoria Peak, the monotonous, strangely soothing sound of the engine—an interlude of tranquillity.

Through Johnny, I discovered the extramural classes offered by the University of Hong Kong and the Chinese University. He and I signed up for a number of them, including History of Hong Kong, Some Hong Kong Social Problems and Hong Kong Today, which included field trips to the Po Leung Kuk, a famous Chinese orphanage; a government housing estate; one of the most efficient cotton mills in the world; a village in the New Territories. Several wives of U.S. Consulate and business people were enrolled. We also took Birds of Hong Kong, taught by a tweedy English government nurse.

If we had an evening class on the Hong Kong side, we would often cross the harbor twice in a day. After class, about ten at night, we bumped down the steep, empty cobblestone streets above deserted Central District offices and shops, Johnny's feet off the ground, holding onto my wheelchair for dear life as we gained momentum down the hill. I clutched the armrests with all my might and held my feet straight out in front of me, as I bounced around, my butt seeming to float above the seat between impacts. The ride made a roller-coaster seem mundane.

When Johnny took me to renew my visa, the Hong Kong Immigration officials told me that I had entered the Colony under the pretense of being a tourist, and here I was enrolling in classes at Hong Kong University. I was obviously a student. The officials were as obnoxious as anyone it has ever been my misfortune to meet. They gave me thirty days to leave the Colony.

Taken by surprise, I didn't know what to do. Edith told me to write the Superintendent of Immigration. Dr. Sun said if I could become an accredited correspondent for the *Independent Journal*, the government could not kick me out. I appealed by letter to the Superintendent of Immigration. I also wrote Jack Craemer who had hired me at the *I.J.* and asked if he would be willing to make me the newspaper's official Hong Kong correspondent. He replied he did not approve of giving the credential willy-nilly but would help me out in view of my long service for the paper. He included a letter appointing me to the job.

At the same time, Randall Gould had a friend who was starting a new monthly magazine called *Business Digest*. Randall told Harlan Trott about me and my problem and suggested I write to him and offer my services, which I did. Mr. Trott replied: "Your qualifications are exactly what we are looking for in Hong Kong. Your employment as Hong Kong Correspondent of *Business Digest* will commence upon receipt of this letter. I plan to run your contributions under the tentative heading: 'Hong Kong News Letter' with your by-line. I would like about an 800-word piece each month. Fragmentary items as well as a substantive interpretive articles will be welcome."

I was now an accredited Foreign Correspondent. Hong Kong Immigration sent me a note requesting that I come to the office for a visa extension. Johnny and I crossed the Harbor, got a key to my Government Information Services box which gave its point of view and local news to correspondents in daily handouts, saw Dr. Sun, visited the exhibitions at City Hall and attended a lecture on the "Economic Scene," and I studied most of the night. This was my idea of living!

As a correspondent, I thought I needed a cable address. I sent Johnny down to the cable office and he returned with three choices: "BARKER," "GEO-BAR," and "GEOKER." I chose GEOKER because Dr. Sun said I took life as a joke. He said I should have the title, "Geoker, Duke of Tsimshatsui," since the people treated me like royalty. It was true, the Chinese in my neighborhood were unusually kind and deferential to me.

After I got my apartment, Johnny's friend, Sherman, was with me most of the time on weekends and evenings. He was a tall, thin, smiling fellow, with long, slick hair and large black-rimmed glasses. I had a small cot beneath the living room window and Sherman liked to stay the night rather than go home to a tiny one-room apartment and a stepmother. He was interested in world affairs and I enjoyed talking to him, typing things out when he couldn't understand me. Sherman was completely helpful, sweet and loyal.

Johnny and Sherman were kindred spirits. Outgoing. Warm-hearted. Not judgmental. Just great guys. I decided I should take them one evening a week to a different nightclub. In those days Hong Kong had reasonable nightclubs and good acts, such as acrobats, singers and dancers. The nearby Golden Crown Nightclub and Restaurant had some of the best Chinese food in the colony and was usually crowded. We called it the Boys' Night Out, and I was one of the boys.

Sherman had a tiny, devoted girlfriend named Betty who usually visited us on Sundays and cooked a big meal for us, or we all went out for morning tea and *dim sum* together at the Golden Crown. I was kept busy writing and going to classes and studying my magazines.

In the evening, I would read the newspaper while kneeling on the floor. Then I would crawl to my bedroom, where a few pieces of chocolate and a big glass of strong red tea waited beside my typewriter.

There were about twenty Baha'is in Hong Kong. We were a mixed bag: Americans, English, an Indian family from Bombay and a wide assortment of Chinese. One evening a week, we met in my apartment and everyone talked about religion. Johnny made strong red tea and bought some cookies. Most of the Baha'is were strongly spiritual, some so sincere and earnest they made me think again. Maybe this Baha'i business wasn't really meant for me.

Among the Baha'is living on the Hong Kong side of the harbor were a Pan American Airlines steward and his wife and several children. They had a large house on the beach at Shekko and invited all the Baha'is and their friends to come for a Sunday beach party. This is where I met Celinda.

Celinda worked as a governess for the steward and his wife in exchange for their teaching her English. A conscientious young woman, she was small and dark, with the high cheek bones and smiling personality of the Malay people. From the Lesser Sunda Islands, she became a Communist early in life and went to Red China under false documents to study medicine in Shanghai.

After about a year, the Indonesian government broke with China and began persecuting its large Chinese minority. In return, Beijing made life miserable for students from Indonesia. Several of Celinda's classmates committed suicide and she was disillusioned with Communism. She went to Canton and mingled with a family that was going to Hong Kong and managed to slide through, eluding Hong Kong Immigration.

The steward's wife loved Celinda because she brought her knowledge of medicine to the children. Celinda's large brown eyes and animated personality quickly drew my attention. With an open invitation to visit my Baha'i friend's place and enjoy the beach, I went to see her as often as I could, considering the distance, my busy schedule and the problem of getting someone to go with me and help me.

Christmas Day, I had Johnny buy several pounds of turkey and dressing from the Russian bakery and restaurant on Carnarvon Road and open the can of Ocean Spray cranberry sauce I had bought several months earlier at the Dairy Lane. Johnny's shapely thirteen-year-old family servant brought us a big kettle of congee—rice and greens and just a little pork liver cooked together a long time to make a delicious thick soup.

Most Friday afternoons, Dr. Sun would call and tell Johnny and me to wait for him by the curb outside the apartment, that he would be by about six o'clock and take us to dinner. I had my first beggar's chicken, Korean barbecue, Mongolian hot pot and Indonesian *gadugadu* with him.

Doctor Sun was direct and outspoken, but his background remained something of a mystery to me and to his children as well. He was born in the city of Hue, the royal capital of Vietnam. He grew up among scholarly people. I suspect they had some connection with the royal family. He was educated in France and some of his schoolmates were high government officials during Prime Minister De Gaulle's long term in office.

His manner was charming but commanding. He was fast-moving, impatient but cool about it. He seemed to take charge of every situation without thinking about it. He had several intellectual hobbies and one of them was tracing the migrations of people around the world. When he got started on that subject he could go on for an hour and hold me spellbound.

Once he phoned about six in the evening and told me to be home, he had a surprise. He arrived more quickly than usual. He rushed to the window and closed all my Venetian blinds and picked up the phone, said a few words in French and told me to wait for one minute. My doorbell rang and Dr. Sun escorted a tall, slender man who moved with catlike grace into the room. After a few words in French, Dr. Sun introduced me to General Nguyen-Huu Co. The General wore khakis devoid of insignia and had a relaxed military bearing.

As quickly as Dr. Sun spoke his name I recognized the General. His picture had been all over the newspapers and magazines that week. He had been one of the ruling triumvirate in South Vietnam along with Generals Ky and Thieu. That week the other two sent him to Taiwan to represent South Vietnam at Chiang Kai Shek's birthday. Then the other two Generals refused to let him back in the country. Dr. Sun laughed and told General Co he was stupid to go. He told me General Co was an uncomplicated man and had trusted Ky and Thieu.

The only place Co could go was Hong Kong. North Vietnamese and South Vietnamese intelligence were after him. British intelligence put him in the apartment above mine because it was above the police substation. For several weeks I could look out my window and see British soldiers with Tommy guns on the roof of the Grand Hotel across the street, always looking at the General's apartment. I would wave and they would smile and wave back.

General Co liked to eat at the New Marseilles and the old Marseilles, so we saw him quite often. He came down to visit with me several times in the evening but my speech problem kept us from becoming friends. I tried to talk to him, but the harder I tried, the stiffer my tongue became and the more involuntary movements plagued my arms and legs. The situation made us both uncomfortable. It was too bad. A great story had fallen in my lap but I could not dig it out and write it because I couldn't communicate properly.

I regarded sleep as something of a bad habit. In high school I had read about the life of Nikola Tesla. He had been able to get along on very little sleep. A pure deductive scientist, he promoted use of alternating current for lighting. Compared to him, Edison was an enthusiastic tinker. I thought Tesla was great and tried to follow his example as far as sleep went. It was too extreme, but I found it easy to get along with four or five hours. Alone at night, I invariably wrote or studied until one or two in the morning, then dragged myself to bed.

In March, I had trouble filling out my income tax forms on my typewriter and didn't get to bed till five or six in the morning. Later that week, Sherman and Johnny asked me if they could have a Chinese New Year party and dance at my place. They rolled up my rug and waxed my floors and invited their girl friends and a few of their buddies to come. I figured they would go home about one in the morning.

About two, I suggested to Sherman that he should tell everyone the party was over. Sherman seemed in a state of mild shock and told me he didn't think anyone was ready to go home yet. They rolled out all my blankets and cuddled up on the floor. Finally they went to sleep and didn't wake up until seven or eight. I was in my bedroom drinking coffee and trying to write an editorial despite the distraction. By the time I gave up, it was about dawn.

I began thinking my apartment had been bugged. I had gone to the U.S. Consulate and asked that I be given translations of articles from the Chinese mainland press which were published daily and available to China scholars. The alacrity with which they placed my name on their mailing list made me uneasy. They seemed to know all about me.

There was a piece of scrap metal on the table that I thought looked suspicious and I threw it down the toilet. Johnny looked at me rather strangely as he retrieved it. He looked even stranger when I told him I thought it was a bug. Soon thereafter he told me he would have to quit working for me. He said his father wanted him to get a more permanent job. I also thought Johnny was unhappy with me because I did not give him the usual double pay that most Chinese employees receive at Chinese New Year. Instead, I gave him pay and a half, because he had worked for me less than half a year. I felt bad about this, but I was living on a tight budget and didn't think I could afford it. Then I began talking about going across the harbor five nights a week to take intensive Cantonese classes given by the Government.

After Johnny and I agreed to disagree, I ran an advertisement in the *South China Morning Post* for a man to cook, clean the apartment and run errands for me. I must have worded the ad very poorly because it attracted a very motley crew, out of which I selected Henry. He was taller than most Cantonese, darkly handsome and very neat, with a narrow black tie, a dark maroon velvet jacket and black trousers. He had never worked as household help, but he had several good references and letters of recommendation as a waiter and he was sure he could handle the job, which really wasn't difficult. I asked him if he was married and he replied, "No, not yet."

I was sitting abstractedly at the typewriter, thinking about the plastics industry in Hong Kong. He had said good-night and I had said good-night, when he kissed me and left the flat quickly. True, it was a discreet kiss, tenderly and on the forehead, but I was stunned. It just hadn't occurred to me that this might be the reason for Henry's rather strange, reserved manner. The next morning I asked him if he was gay and he replied yes.

Inwardly, I groaned. My problems with Johnny, the increased awareness of the street noise now that spring had come and the windows were opened wide, and a heavy writing schedule combined with the pressure of the unfamiliar job of promoting a new magazine in a poor country on a limited budget, all were taking their toll on my emotional stability. I felt once more close to the brink.

Tall, slow-moving, with large, soulful eyes, Henry had been orphaned early in life and raised by an *amah*. He had been in Switzerland, working as a waiter in an exclusive boarding school on Lake Geneva. He had a Swiss lover and showed me beautifully written love letters the guy sent him from Lucerne. He would have still been there but his uncle died in Hong Kong and he flew back to attend the funeral. He thought it would be easy to return, but Switzerland had tightened its visa restrictions. Henry dreamed and lived for the day he would be back in Switzerland. But it became more painfully apparent with each passing month that it was only a dream.

He loved to be out partying at night and come to work around eleven, which drove me nuts because I needed to get up at eight and start working. He preferred to walk slowly and observe the scenery when pushing my chair.

There were streets he did not like to walk because he said the girls in the bars there called him names. My attitude was, to hell with what people said—full speed ahead. But it was important to him. He did not like to push the chair. It exhausted him. He always suggested we take a taxi if our destination was more than a few blocks distant. He wanted me to get a TV so we could watch it together.

I began hearing voices again, and I had been drinking only a little with Ah Wah on Saturdays. I had Henry push me to visit Doctor Sun at his office. When I told Dr. Sun I was hearing voices again and it frightened me, he advised me that I had been working too hard and getting too little sleep. When the Japanese bombed Shanghai during World War II, Doctor Sun was awake at the hospital helping with surgery for two days and nights, and he began seeing things that weren't there.

Doctor Sun said it was common, nothing to worry about. He suggested I let him book a room at the Carleton Hotel on the hill overlooking Kowloon for the weekend. He told me with a smile, "Zheorge, it is very simple. You worked too hard, trying to live up to the undeserved praise piled on your articles." He gave me a sexy novel that one of his patients had given him and told me to go and have a good time, forget my work and I would be all right.

At the Carleton Hotel, Henry went into a snit because he wanted me to nap all the time and I declined. He persisted and I told him I was the boss. My remark turned an ordinary snit into a raging royal purple snit. One of the waiters at dinner that night told him the job of caring for me was more suitable for an old woman. That had been Henry's attitude all along. He felt ashamed and degraded having to care for an adult like he would a baby.

Following Dr. Sun's advice, I recovered quickly. If I could get the equivalent of the DT's from hard work, I would relax and have a little fun. When Wah came the next weekend, I had him take me to the nearest bar. I drank seven shots of whiskey that day and met Connie, who went to school mornings and worked in the bar on Hanoi Road afternoons.

That was the week that everybody told me how well I looked. Connie brought me flowers a couple of times. She was a sweet, pretty, sixteen year old. Her family was very poor. Her mother and elder sister were *amahs,* her father was an elevator operator at Jardine's. She was trying to push a younger brother through middle school but he did not want to study. Connie and I became friends.

Doctor Sun was worried about his son. Michael had a skin condition that made living in Hong Kong's climate impossible. I asked Mama to let Michael live with her in Kentfield. She was sympathetic but cautious, and concerned about how Michael would fit into the completely different world of Marin County. I was unsure myself, but felt I owed a tremendous debt of friendship to Dr. Sun. Mama agreed and Michael became a part of Barker Manor household for three years.

My first inkling of trouble in Hong Kong came from Daisy, an old friend of Paulina, who phoned the apartment and told Henry not to take me out because there was big trouble in Kowloon. That night Wah had to sleep at the hospital because his area of Kowloon was under curfew. He called to ask Henry please to come and get me up, that he'd be a little late coming to work, that he wanted to go home and check on everything and get a shower.

Johnny came to visit me that afternoon and we talked and as soon as he got home he phoned to tell Wah to put in a big supply of candles and water, that the water works employees and the power workers were expected to strike that night. Then Marcello, my landlord, came to the flat and advised me, in addition, to buy a ten days' supply of tinned food.

Wah began to worry about his children, who would be frightened if there was no light. So I told him to go on and I could get Connie to come and get my dinner. When she left, I sat around listening to the riot reports on my radio, about how rumors of a power and water strike had spread, and that they were without foundation.

Radio Hong Kong never indicated that the trouble was a spilling over of the Red Guard Movement from China, where militant school children were terrorizing everyone in the name of Communist purism with the approval of the government.

For me, it was exciting. Tsimshatsui was out of the riots at first. I was staying close to home. As Henry pushed my chair along Hanoi Road for dinner that night, the road and the restaurants were virtually deserted, and the shops were shuttered tight. I finally rented a TV. While watching "The FBI in Peace and War," I could hear the exploding tear gas shells dispersing mobs on Nathan Road.

The radio stations kept going all night with riot reports every hour. I kept my little transistor radio by my pillow that night and heard that mobs were stoning the Fortuna Hotel. Bands of hooligans were roaming Tsimshatsui. They were coming closer, but I felt safe in my flat above the police station. All bus service in Kowloon had been suspended. The radio "advised" people to stay off the streets.

About two days later things were pretty quiet so I decided to have Henry push me across the Harbor to visit Dr. Sun and then go to the Government Information Service, which had some really beautiful photographs for correspondents to send to their newspapers. While we were waiting for the boy to get the copies of the pictures I had selected, we heard shouts of "Mao Tse-tung! Mao Tse-tung!" from the street below. It was a group of about two hundred young communists, waving their little red books on their way to present a petition to the Government. They were well disciplined and the way they chanted Mao Tse-tung was like a hammer striking an anvil.

On our way home, we ate at the coffee shop of the Hilton Hotel. The next day a mob of two thousand Maoists in downtown Central chased a European into the lobby of the Hilton. The manner in which the Hong Kong government handled these half-crazy crowds was a miracle of restraint, and their courage in standing up to Beijing was great. Everyone seemed to be taking the disturbances with remarkable calm.

My air conditioners kept the flat at a blessed eighty while it soared to ninety-four outside. Everybody warned me to stay in, so I read my magazines and the local newspapers, watched the riots on TV and bought a pair of beautiful parakeets from a friend of Henry's.

I would sometimes take Ah Wah out to dinner at a good restaurant. On several occasions he brought his fourteen-year-old son, Tom, a tall skinny youngster who was his father's favorite. Tom spoke excellent English and had the effortless manners and social skill of an older, more experienced person. He could drink a liter of beer with a thick steak without apparent effect and Ah Wah was proud of it. Tom exhibited a lively interest in young women and had a steady girl friend.

I'd had enough of Henry's complaining about my wanting to go across the harbor so often, his disdain for speed, and his disregard for my time. Ah Wah said Tom would like to work for me. Johnny had indicated he would like to return to work for me too. I gave Henry a month's severance pay and let him go. He seemed more sad than angry, and I felt unhappy for him, but he was not my kind of helper. I could see my stay in Hong Kong would soon come to an end and that Mama would probably have to come over and go back with me. I decided to hire both Tom and Johnny to work for me for the remainder of my visit. In my year in Hong Kong, I had carved out a place for myself. I could never be a true China specialist, but with all my experience and classes at Hong Kong University and the Chinese University of Hong Kong, I had inadvertently become a minor expert on the colony.

Following the advice of my social workers, I had been careful to do what I could to maintain my residence in Marin County although I was living in Hong Kong. I voted by absentee ballot and gave my Barker Manor address as my home on all official papers. But as September rolled around and I had been in Hong Kong for a whole year, the Marin Social Services Department wrote me a letter and called Mama and told her I would have to move back to the county quickly or lose my helper income.

I invited Mama to come over and enjoy a few weeks as my guest in my apartment before I had to leave. With both Johnny and Tom working for me and Dr. Sun and his wife entertaining us, Mama had a wonderful time.

One day after she came, someone dropped what appeared to be a bomb under the gas tank of a car parked in front of our apartment. Mama and Tom had just taken me down the elevator to the ground floor going out. We had to hide behind some big concrete columns in Ricky's art gallery while the bomb squad examined, sandbagged and detonated the device. The bomb had been a fake. Mama took it calmly, relished the excitement and was glad no one was hurt.

Then a ten-year-old girl had her hand blown off. This galvanized public opinion against The Red Guards. People began boycotting the Red Chinese Department stores. Not long after the bloody incident, life returned to normal.

I felt badly about leaving the *Business Digest* without a Hong Kong writer. Mr. Trott liked my work and had elevated me to Hong Kong Editor. I arranged to cover the whole area as Far Eastern Correspondent by intensive reading until I could return the following year. Mr. Trott repeatedly had great difficulty getting the magazine printed on time and I feared it was heading for oblivion.

It seemed dishonest taking money from the Baha'is, even though it was a pittance. They were good people, but I was not convinced that Baha'u'llah was of the same stature as Jesus, Buddha and Mohammed. I made a mistake involving myself in an organized religion. My belief is that each of us contains the essence of an individual religion which can be developed and sculpted by exposure to religious philosophy and the world in general. When I got back to Marin, I formally withdrew from the Baha'i Faith.

I returned to Kentfield and a quiet ten months reading and writing and getting caught up on the local news. Michael Sun had been living at Barker Manor for several months when I returned. In Hong Kong I did not really know him except to exchange greetings, but back in Marin we became good friends. Mike was a smiling, happy, witty person and a joy to be with.

Many an evening at my "office table" in the kitchen we laughed ourselves silly. He called me the "dread *hom sop gwai lo*," which means filthy-minded foreign devil. And I kidded him about not showing proper respect for members of the superior race. I helped him with his English and we went to the movies together, and in warm weather we would go to the little park in San Anselmo for a barbecue with Paulina.

Not long after, Paulina married a well-to-do retired salesman and he told me that he had arranged matters so she would never have to worry about money. They had a mobile home in a retirement community and took trips and went fishing. Paulina had her own garden and loved to cook. A mynah, two cockatiels and a mutt she had rescued rounded out her life. She cleaned up her language a bit and was playing the part of American middle-aged homemaker. She was even a bit prim. Mama was relieved that I would not be able to remarry her, but surprised that such a nice man would be attracted to her. I was happy for Paulina and also relieved that this bone of contention between me and Mama had been removed.

Tom and I kept in touch. For a while he studied at the Columbia Television School, then dropped out to work for the Dairy Lane, heaving big cartons around. During this time he had unlimited access to ice cream and when I next saw him he was no longer a skinny kid, but a well built young man.

Johnny had moved with his parents back to Belize and was managing his father's cookie factory. Cookies were not one of Johnny's favorite foods and he was not too keen on the job. He had visited me in Kentfield on his way to Belize and we had relived our months together.

By the next fall, I was eager to get back to Hong Kong. Returning, Mama and I were met at the airport by the Suns and Ah Wah's entire clan. For a few days, we stayed at the Ambassador Hotel where I had booked a room through Sherman, who was working there as an account clerk.

Dr. Sun and Bella took us to their home and made us welcome. Mama slept upstairs and I was given a small room on the ground floor just off the kitchen, containing my cot from the old apartment. It was not far from Tom's home in

Wong Tai Sin, a Government Resettlement Estate. But being way out in a residential district, cut off from the hustle and bustle of Chinese life, I was not happy.

I had kept in touch with Celinda and asked her if she could work for me, as she had written me she had parted company with the Pan Am steward's family. She was willing to help me when she could but did not have a big amount of time as she was studying bookkeeping, English and German. She lived not far from Dr. Sun's house, on Boundary Street, the boundary between Kowloon and the New Territories. She helped me find a room in a Shanghai couple's apartment on Hankow Road in Tsimshatsui, right across the street from the Pink Pussy Cat Bar. My landlord was a tourist guide and his wife was even more devoted to mah-jongg than Mei Ying. They had a nicely decorated modern apartment.

Celinda proved to be a true friend. Although deeply involved in her studies, she managed to be available to help me evenings and some weekends when Tom had his time off. My speech was still quite poor, but we managed to converse by my writing on my electric typewriter. She had a million questions and I don't think I ever typed so hard in my life. Sometimes I almost felt she was brainwashing me but we really got well acquainted in a short time. She made it clear that she was not interested in becoming my lover. I felt disappointed at first, but accepted the fact.

As far as sex went, I talked to my young friend Connie who had worked at the bar on Hanoi Road. I asked her if she knew a woman who was not a professional bar girl whom I could hire on a regular basis. She knew a young lady from Shanghai married to a Filipino musician who had returned to the Philippines, leaving her with a baby girl. "She doesn't work in a bar but she is a butterfly," said Connie.

After meeting her and Connie over lunch at the New Marseilles, I hired her to flutter by my place once a week. A well-built, attractive Chinese, she was pleasant and practical, and had lovely smooth, milk white skin. It was a good arrangement for me at the time.

One evening Tom pushed me in my chair way out Nathan Road to the new Nathan Hotel. Everyone had told us how good their *dim sum* was and we wanted to try it. I ran into Mei Ying there. She was having *dim sum* with a famous Cantonese opera star, a woman they called the Big One. We recognized each other at the same time and she was as surprised as I was. We exchanged phone numbers and not long afterward we got together with Macao Girl and her husband and Ah Fat for a reunion. Mei Ying was in Hong Kong visiting her relatives. Everyone was well and Macao Girl was even plumper than before.

Mei Ying looked the same. It felt good to see that she was happy and prospering.

Before I returned to Kowloon, *Business Digest* folded and I had to think of something else to do. I noticed there were no restaurant guides in a colony where everyone loved to eat. I talked it over with Dr. Sun and he introduced me to the Director of the Hong Kong Tourist Bureau. I had written reviews for about thirty Hong Kong and Kowloon restaurants. I showed them to the Director and he offered to have the Tourist Bureau promote the finished book if I would pay for its publication. It was a good offer, but I was too embarrassed to tell him I was broke and living off the generosity of the American taxpayer.

Tom and I were eating out twice a day to try to cover as many restaurants as we could. One day we sat down with the classified section of the Hong Kong phone directory and counted eight hundred restaurants. At the same time I was beginning to feel a little nauseous at the mere thought of eating out so many times. Restaurant food is purposely rich and not suited as a daily diet for a small man who didn't get a lot of exercise. I decided I would not borrow to invest in the project, even though I felt it was a grand idea and wished I had the money and the guts to see it through properly.

Without a job or purpose in Hong Kong, I thought I'd do better to leave this exciting life behind me and really settle down back in the States. When I finally returned to Kentfield, I wanted Mama to think of a place where she would like to go. The only place that really attracted her was the English countryside, so the following spring we flew to London and rented a car which Mama, in her seventies, managed to drive on the left side of the road down to West Farleigh, near Maidstone in Kent, where her friend Winnie lived. For a month, we roamed the floral paradise of springtime England.

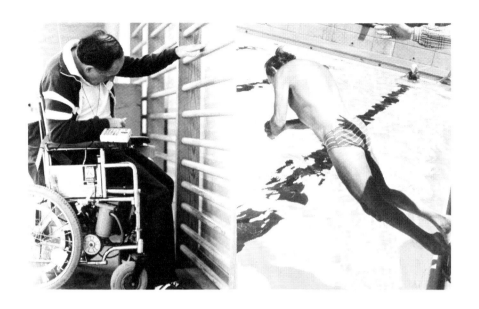

At the college in Marin.

*Mama helping me down the back stone steps and into motorized chair
for my daily drive to the Physical Education Complex.*

Exercise and Ecstasy, 1976-85

Chapter 11

True enjoyment comes from activity of the mind
and exercise of the body; the two are ever united.

- Humboldt

Mama and I settled down to a pattern of Januarys in Hawaii and little car trips to Carmel, Yosemite, Mendocino, and the Napa Valley. I began kissing my Maori Tiki charm in June of 1976, wishing for a little luck to break me out of the rut into which my daily life had fallen.

After nineteen years of writing three little Nature editorials a week for the San Rafael *Independent-Journal*, the paper's management decided to revamp the editorial page and my work was no longer wanted. My acquaintance with Marin County's Nature was limited by my inability to hike and observe first hand. But I had a small library of Nature books and magazines, and was blessed by a wide variety of flora and fauna which I could watch from our spacious screened porch by day and in our floodlit backyard at night. Mama and I supported generations of California quail and other wild birds on generous servings of seed. And we supplied dozens of raccoons with dog kibble and knew them as individuals. We fenced the property to keep the deer from eating Mama's roses, and squirrels played tag in the bay tree above the porch.

I produced three editorials a week regardless how I felt or where I lived. One of my greatest writing challenges was imagining myself in quiet, woodsy, loosely populated Marin and writing about Nature while living in a tiny room amidst the babble of human noise and big city traffic in the concrete canyons of Causeway Bay and Tsimshatsui. Sometimes I would write a charming, witty little editorial which I thought compensated for the equal number of dull, mundane ones I wrote.

I had no by-line, but I received occasional fan mail. Some of it was addressed to the Raccoon Editor. In Kowloon in 1966, I was surprised to receive a postcard forwarded by the *I-J* from Royce Brier, the most intellectual columnist on the San Francisco *Chronicle's* daily editorial page. He said he always enjoyed my little Nature editorials and suggested I write about the Oregon Junco, his favorite Marin bird, which I promptly did. The paper also received letters from people who didn't like my editorials or didn't like raccoons or felt I had written something derogatory about their favorite bird. At least I had readers.

When I started doing editorials, the *I-J* was a competent small town newspaper, covering mostly news of Marin. A fire on Fourth Street got more prominent coverage than the overthrow of a foreign government. By 1976, the part of the county around San Rafael was becoming one big urban area and the paper was becoming more and more metropolitan. I think my Nature editorials were out of place.

After 2,500 pieces, it became almost torture to come up with fresh ideas. All but two of our raccoons disappeared, probably victims of distemper and poisoning. An influx of cats drove away our quail. My friend Bud, my botany expert, no longer visited me and kept me up to date on the wildflower situation. When the paper wrote me that my services were no longer needed, disappointment was tempered by relief.

I knew I should exercise more. After dinner every evening, I would walk around the living room rug on my knees about a dozen times. We kept my wheelchair in the trunk of the little Mercedes and I moved about the house mostly on Mama's arm. The world of books, television and news magazines held me in dream more interesting than my own life.

When I lived in Hong Kong, most evenings my helper would go home about seven and I would study or type until one or two in the morning. I got around my small apartment on my knees. When I returned to California, the habit of midnight work persisted. I did a large part of my writing at night when everything was quiet and there were no distractions.

Mama did the gardening, shopped and cooked, took care of me, kept the house spotless, and enjoyed books, *U.S. News* and the *Wall Street Journal*. At seventy-seven, she could still outwork most of the occasional help she hired for heavy house and garden work, but, although she seldom complained, it was becoming obvious that her strength was starting to decline. Lifting me up out of a chair to help me walk, helping me down the rustic stone steps outside on the way to the car, and helping me up out of the bathtub were becoming increasingly difficult.

One June day I asked the high school boy who mowed our lawn to push me down to the College of Marin Campus in my wheelchair, just to get out of the house and look around. While on campus, I had him push me to the physical education building and asked the only coach around if there was any way I could use the weight training equipment.

He told me I should see Laurie Lanham. "She has just started a class for people with disabilities."

I wrote Laurie a letter explaining my situation and got an appointment to meet her at the College. Laurie turned out to be a genial Comanche, with the sturdiness of that people, who had received most of her graduate training in Veterans' Administration hospitals. She was a Certified Rehabilitation Therapist and knew disability firsthand, having been disabled with multiple sclerosis and made an almost full recovery. I felt Laurie was developing something that would be great for me and was probably unique.

When the Adaptive P.E. class was in its infancy, we had the use of the college pool, one Universal gym and some mats. I was one of just six students. One of my favorite exercises was working out on the Universal gym leg press. I used to fantasize that I was a small Arnold Schwarzenegger because I had strong legs and could push more than twice my own weight. The secret of strength lies in concentration and I was experienced in that art. In the next ten years the program grew to ninety students, ranging in age from eighteen to ninety-two.

After the weights came yoga. Supple Malini Shuyten started as a volunteer and stayed on as an instructor, teaching us the joys of belly-breathing and the benefits of a midday meditation mini-vacation, along with more rigorous yogic discipline.

By concentrating all my thoughts on deep belly breathing, I found I could escape into a goose-down-lined nest inside my head whenever I felt life was painful. I found this nest more useful as a daily resting place for half an hour to calm the nervous system than as an emergency escape. With calm there are no big emergencies, just some problems to solve. Malini was a living advertisement for yoga, radiating joy and good health. I felt genuinely fond of her and enjoyed the things she taught us.

Before encephalitis, I loved the water, was a good swimmer, knew all the strokes and had earned a certificate as a Junior Red Cross Life Guard. When Laurie spoke with her contagious enthusiasm about getting me in the college pool, I looked forward to it with eagerness. To my chagrin, I found I swam like a rock. As a swimmer, I was the Mark Spitz of drowning. I lacked the necessary coordination and breath control that I had forty years before, and I had too much rigid muscle and too little fat just to float.

Nevertheless, the pool held a singular attraction for me, in addition to appealing women in bathing suits. My disability made it impossible for me to walk on land without a strong person holding me on one arm, but the weight of the water helped hold me up so I could walk around the entire pool unaided, except for an alert companion to retrieve me on my way to the bottom should I lose my balance and fall.

Moving against the resistance of the water, the exercise was considerable. When I worked out in the pool, I didn't hesitate to exert myself. After getting my footing, I took off and didn't stop until I was ready to get out about forty minutes later. We laughed and teased and had a good time. I was one of the four or five members of our class to go in the pool the year round, regardless of the weather. Laurie called us The Polar Bear Club.

I had wanted a motorized wheelchair since I first read about them in the early Fifties, but my experiences trying to drive those early dinosaurs were disastrous to my ego. They were bulky and had controls very difficult for me to handle.

I had begged Mama to take me to an orthopedic supply store on Mission Street in San Francisco. I sat in the unwieldy chair and everyone stood back as I pushed the button control forward. The chair, with me frozen to the seat, shot out the door, across the sidewalk, over the curb and into the busy street, amid the shrieks of Mama, the squealing of auto brakes, the blaring of horns and the horrified yells of the salesman, "Let go of the goddamn control!" The salesman saved me and the chair, but the experience made me abandon thoughts of owning a motorized wheelchair.

Now Laurie asked me what I thought about getting one. She said it would be great for me and she was sure I could learn to manage one of the newer models. By that time, I had acquired great respect for her opinion on anything concerning physical rehabilitation, having witnessed wonderful gains by others in the program. If Laurie thought I could master the art of driving a motorized wheelchair, I knew I could.

After an inauspicious start, during which I knocked over a lamp and practically wiped out a nurse's station in the Kentfield Medical Hospital, I gradually gained control of the peppy little chair. Laurie had it delivered to the College and I practiced maneuvering on the asphalt area in back of the Physical Education Complex for several weeks until I felt competent and comfortable driving it. I drove it from the College to home and back, accompanied by Martha, a pretty blond aide. Then I was on my own.

Initially, some of Mama's elderly friends were against the idea of my venturing forth upon the roads of the part of Kentfield where we lived. Without a hint of sidewalks, bikes and pedestrians shared the narrow asphalt roads with autos. Mama was seriously concerned that I would be severely injured or killed and asked me to give up the crazy idea, that it would only bring us grief. She later had a complete reversal of opinion and told everyone about my motorized wheelchair exploits.

Randall Gould was most fiercely opposed to the idea. He said that it was a motor vehicle and I couldn't drive it out on the road without a driver's license!

He practically dared me to get a legal opinion. I declined out of suspicion he might be correct.

Despite its small and dainty appearance, my new wheelchair was a solid, rugged, outdoor heavyweight. Without me in it, it still weighed 150 pounds, most of which could be accounted for by the two automobile batteries. Every night it had to be plugged into a recharger which operated on regular house current. Two batteries lasted me from six months to a year, depending on how far I went.

When I first got my chair, I drove to college for evening classes in Real Estate Principles and Sociology and Japanese Literature, besides my four days a week in P.E., and a pair of batteries lasted me a scant six months. With new batteries, I could go a little over ten miles on a single recharge, so I went exploring on my own to all the nearby towns, Larkspur, Ross, San Anselmo and Greenbrae, making generous use of the bike paths.

A joy stick on a control box connected to a simple computer board commanded the chair and made it possible for me to operate it. The control was quite sensitive. During the first two years, I had a number of accidents, mostly caused by one wheel going off a sidewalk, flipping me over a high curb and onto my side. The Kentfield Fire and Emergency Services got to know me pretty well as I learned to avoid narrow sidewalks and high curbs. I delighted in tearing along at full speed, which was only about ten miles an hour, but I never ran into anyone hard enough to cause serious injury. I was exuberant, but not reckless.

It was ecstasy for me to be free to come and go on my own, out in the open air, driving along the tree-lined streets, roads and bike paths in sun, rain and wind. Going to the College the year round for almost a decade to knock myself out exercising was a kind of heaven for me. I would leave at 8:30 in the morning and get back home about four o'clock, absolutely exhausted, but exhilarated.

I received a pamphlet from U. C. Med. School's Department of Human Sexuality intended for Michael Sun who was a Pharmacist in Detroit, announcing a one-day minicourse on "Sex and Disability" for Pharmacists. Using three film projectors and three giant screens at once, a class of twenty-four hours had been compressed into eight hours of lectures and movies. I asked Martha, the tender-hearted, divorced nurse in her mid-thirties who had helped me learn to drive the wheelchair, to go with me.

For eight hours, our heads were turning from screen to screen as Martha and I and 400 pharmacists watched attractive and ordinary elderly and disabled people engaging in a sexual tour-de-force in living color. This was accompanied by three sound tracks going at once and broken by lectures and explanations. It was a grand exposition of the glory of sex, beautifully done with only a hint of sleaze.

Fascinated by women and their bodies, just as I was when zapped by encephalitis, I sometimes wondered if I was caught up in some kind of baffling adolescent time warp, but exposure to the great minds of the sexuality world solidified my notion that I was quite normal.

Martha invited me and a small group of disabled people and aides to a party at her tiny cottage in Mill Valley. Following a few drinks and prolonged eye contact, Martha and I were in each other's arms. After the others went home, we made love on the wide couch, on her oriental rug and in her bed until we were both several times satisfied and wasted and fell asleep.

Mama had to be aware of our sexual alliance because whenever we went out, we always stayed all night and came home looking like we'd just run a marathon together. However, she never said anything and seemed to like Martha. When Mama expressed a desire to make one last visit to her childhood home in the Shenandoah Valley and to visit her two brothers nearby, I encouraged her to go, saying Martha would stay at the house and take care of me, which she did.

For me, Martha was Aphrodite incarnate. She had the graceful and pleasing figure that Francis Bacon called a perpetual letter of recommendation. I liked her, loved and respected her, and enjoyed every moment we were together.

She loved me too, I am sure. It required a very loving, nurturing nature to come to the house, help me to the car and into it, load the wheelchair in the trunk; then at a restaurant, take the wheelchair out of the trunk, help me out of the car and put me in the chair, push me into the restaurant, help feed me, push the chair back to the car, help me into the car, put the chair in the trunk; then at her home or a motel to take the chair out of the trunk, help me out of the car and into the chair, push me inside; the bedroom scene required her to help me to bed and undress me. It was the least romantic scenario one could imagine but she carried it off with verve and style.

The end came not long after we returned from a delightful weekend trip to Carmel. Her car broke down and she was unable to come to the house and pick me up for ten days. After that, she worked double shifts at Marin General for two weeks and disappeared.

Two months later, she suddenly appeared at the College during lunch break and told me that she had been on holiday in Hawaii, had become pregnant and was getting married. We wished each other the best of luck and our paths parted. I am surprised, looking back, that I felt so little emotion at the news, but my life was so full at that time. Now, I wish I had been more expressive of my appreciation to Martha for her kindness and generous spirit.

I was in my element at the College of Marin, having practically grown up on the campus of the college at Greeley. College campuses have a lot in common and I felt as though I had returned home.

Knowing how a college is run and how to get publicity, I tried to help Laurie and the Program. Laurie was a rehabilitation genius. A student's gait—the way he held his head or picked up a pencil, little things that other people had missed—became valuable clues for her to devise a comprehensive exercise program that got results. Beyond adaptive physical education, she talked at length with all her students and became involved in their lives.

For Laurie, heedful concern for her disabled charges was almost a religious vocation. Most of her off-work days and evenings were spent taking one after another of her students out to dinner, to a movie, to a lecture or a concert. Her keen mind, innovative ideas and sense of humor made her fun to be with. She helped many students who had practically given up to realize their potential, get moving and back into life.

No genius is without a touch of madness. Laurie so loved her work, she came to regard the Program as her personal dominion. When she felt something was amiss, she acted quickly with passion and conviction. Her unvarnished manner antagonized some people. She was not a campus politician.

She felt that her disabled students with their crutches, wheelchairs, artificial limbs and deformities were resented by the physique-conscious physical education jocks. And she resisted every hint that we were not just as important to the College as the football team.

Just before the end of my first semester at the College, I wrote a note to the *Independent-Journal*, saying there was a good story in the Adaptive P.E. Program and suggesting they might want to cover it. They ran a flattering article on the front page with a photo of me and a pretty girl in the pool. After that the Program grew by leaps and bounds.

With my motorized wheelchair, most people in the Kentfield neighborhood knew me by sight. The campus was quite accessible, but going against the traffic on Sir Francis Drake Boulevard to get there from our house took some ingenuity and risk. The County, at the urging of Barbara Boxer, the attractive Supervisor from our district, put in some curb cuts for me. I was appointed to the County commission that monitors local Comprehensive Education and Training Act (CETA) programs.

I learned that Laurie did not have any kind of tenure and was paid on an hourly basis, and that the College Administration intended to limit class size to less than thirty by refusing to let her hire more student aides. This seemed to me unfair to her and to all the disabled people in Marin who were becoming aware of the Program.

The Program, receiving funds from several sources, was a financial bonus for the College. Many of the older students had been property taxpayers for decades. But some of the guys who taught classes in the Physical Education Complex felt they had given up enough space for the disabled already. Due to a shortage of students at that time, some of their jobs were in jeopardy—and they had the sympathy of the College President, himself a former football coach.

I knew in my gut the College could be compelled to enlarge the Adaptive P.E. Program and give Laurie the money and job security she deserved. I wrote and circulated a petition on the campus, asking that Laurie's job be upgraded to a full time, salaried position and that the Adaptive P.E. Program be enlarged, including more aides. In two days, I had about 300 signatures—enough, I thought, to give the petition credibility. A hotly contested Board of Trustees election was coming soon and the *I-J* was full of it. After doing a little research into the background and views of each Board member, I wrote individually tailored letters to each and enclosed a copy of the petition.

Then, I sent a letter to the *Independent-Journal*, saying that the Adaptive P.E. students were going to picket the meeting of the College Board. The paper ran an article about the dispute and the plan to protest.

The students and aides made picket signs. Some of the more conservative students were uncomfortable with the idea of being part of a raucous, pushy demonstration. All I intended was a quiet, dignified show of force. In my worst nightmare, I would not want to be part of a howling mob of unruly disabled fist shakers. We had to make the signs to show we were serious in our feeling that the College was being unfair to the Program and Laurie. I doubted we would have to use them, but the word that we were hard at work would quickly get back to the President and the Board and be unsettling.

The President started to worry a little and sent an intermediary to ask me not to demonstrate, that things could be worked out without it. If I stopped everything now, I would never be able to start it again. Events have a psychological momentum that has to be nourished. We would have had a weak compromise and lost all credibility. I had to say I could not promise.

The morning of the evening Board meeting, I had Mama get me up early, feed me a quick breakfast and was off to the campus in my motorized wheelchair, clutching a letter to the President, which I hand-delivered to his office. It was bold, restating what we wanted and saying that making Laurie a salaried teacher was non-negotiable.

I thought it would probably make him angry to have this pipsqueak cerebral palsied guy, who couldn't even talk so anyone could understand him, telling him what was negotiable. However, we both smiled when we saw each other and I certainly felt no animosity towards him. I regarded the contention more in terms of a chess game than a fight. He was just trying to do his job and shepherd the College's limited resources.

The Board meeting room overflowed. People sat in the aisles and stood along the sides. We leaned our signs in a corner.

I had tossed a pebble and created an avalanche. One after another, disabled students stood up, leaned on crutches and canes and walkers and sat in wheelchairs, pouring their feelings straight from the heart, telling the Board what the Adaptive P.E. Program and Laurie meant to them. The obvious sincerity of their feelings would have melted granite. We got everything we wanted.

Not long afterwards, the College Engineer, citing the national energy shortage, recommended that the gas heat to the open-air pool in the P.E. Complex be turned off, which would mean an end to all swimming. I suspected he had grabbed an exaggerated cost figure off the top of his head.

I asked Paul Ngai, one of the young Chinese men from Hong Kong who had lived with us for a summer while attending College of Marin and was now a solar heating engineer, if he could give me a more precise figure. He labored far into the night over several weekends and produced a perfectly detailed paper in which he factored in the monthly temperatures and hours of sunlight, the exact volume of water, the height of the walls, the effects of the wind, the color of the pool's interior, heat loss by day and by night. He concluded it would cost half the Engineer's figure, and if the pool was covered at night about a fourth as much. I took it to the President and he recommended that the heat be continued and the pool covered at night. The Board agreed and it was done. The Engineer resigned.

The pool temperature was a source of contention between the Adaptive P.E. Program and the swimming coaches. In general, most disabled people do their best when the water is warm and swim teams do their best when the water is on the cool side. Laurie and the coaches reached a *modus vivendi* and the pool temperature was kept at about eighty degrees.

Then the pool walls and bottom began to crumble. One of the swimming coaches complained the problem was black algae, caused by keeping the water too warm. It was true that there were patches of black-looking algae on the pool walls. No one in Adaptive P.E. knew much about algae and this coach made it sound like Black Death for swimming pools. We felt guilty and helpless until Laurie and Yvonne, our swimming instructor, began questioning why only our pool, out of dozens of warm pools in the area, was so afflicted.

I suggested Laurie ask Dr. Gordon Chan about black algae. Chan was a well known marine biologist on the College faculty. He asked Laurie to bring him a jar with wall scrapings from the deepest, warmest part of the pool. He examined them under a microscope and sent her a beautifully informative one-page report. The sample revealed the presence of relatively benign blue-green algae, nematodes and worms, but no black algae. He stated that the pool should be relined with fiberglass and epoxy resin, which was done.

I became Laurie's unofficial secretary. She had grown up on Oahu, speaking Hawaiian English with her friends and had a complex about writing, though her spoken English was flawless by then. She was at her best handling the Program's business in person or by phone. When she had to write a letter, she would scribble a few notes and ask me to write it for her on College stationery she supplied.

When the summer Program appeared threatened by budget cuts, I asked the Associated Students to buy video tapes and wrote a video screenplay about the Program. I had to read first how a screenplay was done, and then with my spastic fingers type it so slowly it was a pain in the butt. The cameraman and editor told me I had done a professional job. I wrote and helped direct two little videos which were shown at special assemblies, on local cable TV and to civic groups to increase support for the Program.

About the middle of my decade at the college, Laurie injured her back while stopping the fall of an elderly student with ALS from a bench on the Universal Gym. Since it was an on-the-job accident, she followed protocol and went to the college-recommended physician. He ordered a CAT scan of her spine and declared it showed no damage. Ten years later, a specialist at University of California Medical School in San Francisco examined the same CAT scan and said it clearly showed a ruptured disk.

Laurie was in almost constant, sometimes excruciating pain, getting nerve blocks and trying to handle the ever-expanding program at the College. She was desperate, being passed from doctor to doctor, not able to pin down the exact cause of the pain which was spreading to her hips and legs. She endured hints of malingering. Her face clearly showed the strain. She became more abrupt and outspoken.

Laurie was forced to curtail her social life and contact with most students outside class. She did drop by now and then to visit Mama and me. Mama liked Laurie and admired her dedication.

By 1985, Laurie began experiencing pain so severe that she missed several weeks teaching. Less experienced therapists were ready to take over her job, but Laurie was loath to relinquish leadership of the Program she had built from scratch.

When the College hired Jean Hall as a Counselor for the Disabled, I learned that she was a licensed speech pathologist and arranged for her to give me an hour of "speech counseling" each week. When I asked if she could help me, she said we would be pioneers in an uncharted wilderness. We were kindred spirits and filled her little office with laughter.

Jean made me realize that my speech problem was one of emotion as well as mechanics. One day she didn't smile or joke for ten minutes. My speech slowly strangled to death. When she pointed out the connection between what she had done and what had happened to my speech, it was a moment of truth. I had been crushed by a missing smile. I was working too hard to please others. Half-joking, I said she was my psychoanalyst because of her habit of probing my psyche and making me dig out the answers myself.

She asked, "What would you do differently if your speech improved?" I tried to think of something, anything, but I couldn't. I was doing exactly what I wanted. I had spent so many decades not being understood half the time that I had adapted. I could repeat, repeat, repeat and still repeat again. If that didn't work, what the hell. It wasn't going to ruin my day. I had no burning messages. I could type anything important.

Perhaps I am not properly sensitive to the way others perceive me, but I cannot get excited about names given to disabled, handicapped, or whatever people. I know what I can do and no label will change that. Not long ago the Easter Seal Society was called the Society for Crippled Children and Adults. Then it became forbidden to say crippled. We became handicapped. The handicapped took offense at that. They wanted to be called disabled. Now disabled is under fire. The latest I've heard is physically challenged. I did object once when a friend said, "George's disease is cerebral palsy." I have a condition, not a disease, and it is not contagious.

Some of my disabled friends are very sensitive about people they perceive as condescending. Because I don't articulate properly, people frequently speak very loudly to me, probably thinking I am hard of hearing. Other people sometimes think I am mentally deficient. I don't take offense. How are they to know? It is just one of those things that I have adjusted to without thinking much about it.

My motor neurons play involuntary wrestling games, pitting opposing sets of muscles against one another, moving and straining them back and forth. I had practiced progressive relaxation exercises for most of my life and, in the yoga part of the Adaptive P.E. Program, the relaxing and belly breathing meditation. They work well while I am doing them, but I've never been able to incorporate relaxation into my everyday life.

I changed the focus of my writing from Nature and the Far East to disability. I doubted that writing about disability would interest many people, but I'd had nearly fifty years experience and thought I'd give it a try. I wrote a long article about what it feels like to live with cerebral palsy, and sent it to the *I J*. To my surprise, I received more response to that article than to anything I had written previously. For almost a month, the mail brought me two or three notes or letters each day commenting favorably on the piece.

Encouraged, I sold two similar articles to *Disability Today*, an attractive magazine put out by the federal government. I got a contract from Penthouse's little *Forum* magazine to write an article on sex and disability for more money per word than I'd ever received. Despite the pay, I was disappointed. It was edited so poorly it made me seem angry. As one friend said, they seem to believe that disabled people can't be sexy and that they have no sense of humor.

Johnny Chee and me in Belize, 1996.

January 1997, Mary and I returned to Belize. Johnny gave me this ten acre orange farm in the rain forest and is building my house here.

At left: Greenbrae, California, 1996.

At right: with Mary at Stone Cottages in the Cayo, Belize, 1996.

And Now Belize, 1985-96

Chapter 12

Grow old with me.
The best is yet to be,
The last of life
For which the first was made.

- Robert Browning

Mama's health began declining about 1978. Her weight dropped from a robust 140 pounds to a skinny eighty-five. As spring of 1985 approached, I learned that she had about a month to live. X-rays showed her liver so swollen with cancer that it was nearly pressing her rib cage on both sides.

She told me she just wanted to go quickly. I knew Mama did not want to die in a hospital among strangers, her body invaded by tubes and hooked up to respirators, beeping monitors and flashing lights. With the help of Laurie, a few friends, Hospice and a nursing agency, I arranged for her to receive around-the-clock home care.

Outside her bedroom window, a cloud of deep pink flowers on the hawthorn tree opened. Bright red roses bloomed. Creamy citrus blossoms dispensed their fragrance. Mama said she'd had a good life, seen a lot of the world and had outlived most of her relatives and friends. Now she felt like the last leaf on the tree.

She asked me to figure out some way to speed her death without getting myself in trouble. She was practically bedridden, getting out of bed only to walk with assistance to the bathroom. Food no longer tasted good and she had trouble keeping more than a tiny amount down. She had to take Brompton's Solution, a mixture of morphine, alcohol and cherry syrup, to assuage the constant pain.

I could think of only one thing to do: have her take plenty of Brompton's to depress her already weakened heart. She went along with the idea. Hospice provided a logbook for nurses and aides to keep track of her medications, but when her friends were around and her care people were out of the room, I would ask her if she needed more Brompton's. She always did and people were glad to be unwitting help.

Mama answered the phone on her bedside stand to learn that her brother, Kim, had passed away. I felt I owed Uncle Kim a great debt for teaching me things like playing ball and cards, and for financing my first trip to Hong Kong. Mama had an agreement with Kim that he would help take care of me when she passed on, but his wife, after first agreeing, had changed her mind. I was certain I did not want to be dependent on him or anyone. I didn't want to move to Maryland and Kim's wife and I were not congenial.

One midnight that same week, an agency home health care aide, whose unsmiling visage and excessively padded body assaulted my jaundiced eye, helped Mama walk to the bathroom, supporting her on one arm. Mama slumped to the floor beside the toilet. The aide, realizing that she had had a heart attack, panicked, became hysterical and, despite explicit, repeated instructions that she was to call the hospice nurse in any emergency, dialed 911.

I was in bed, heard Mama call me, got on my knees and crawled frantically to the bathroom, saw what had happened, and crawled back to the kitchen where the phone was, banging my knees on the hard linoleum floor in my effort to go as fast as I could. With my spastic fingers I slowly punched the memorized number of the hospice nurse, who said hold everything, that she would drive from her home in Forest Knolls, normally a twenty-minute drive, as fast as she could.

The paramedics looked gigantic and spoke with an aura of authority and well-meant earnestness. They wanted to take Mama to Marin General immediately and said they would not be responsible if her condition worsened. I asked Mama if she wanted to go. Wearily, as though she wanted to wash her hands of the whole situation, she said for me to decide. I found myself in the strange position of saying that I would be responsible if she died that night, while being a co-conspirator in her death.

As the ambulance eased down our long driveway, the hospice nurse's car whipped into position at the end of the drive and blocked it. The tiny nurse jumped out and raised her hands and shouted "Stop! Do you have Ella Barker?" After the driver assured her that they didn't, she came to Mama's bedside.

Mama brightened when she saw her. The nurse did nursely things, like taking her pulse, making sure she was positioned comfortably in bed, and chatting about inconsequential matters until she fell asleep. She waited half an hour more to be sure Mama was secure for the time being, and took her leave.

Mama lived several more days. The last two days, she woke in the small hours of the morning and called my name because she thought she was slipping away and wanted me to be there to hold her hand. I stayed with her for two or three hours, not saying much, letting her know by the pressure of my fingers I was there. I told her, "I love you, Mama," and she told me, "I love you too, dear."

As the rising sun bathed the bedroom with a pink glow, she said, "I thought for sure I was going this time. I never thought it would be so hard to die. You go get some sleep now."

She died about five in the afternoon where she could see her beloved flower garden and photos of her family, after a day of short conversations, being read to by friends and dozing while her favorite music eased her spirit. I had gone out of the room for a bit, leaving her to talk to Laurie. Passing away in familiar surroundings with a trusted friend is not a terribly traumatic ending.

The following morning I called Paulina. She and her husband divorced after five years of marriage. She developed a severe case of asthma and had to keep oxygen by her bed. She told me she was scared and fear was in her voice. I told her I would try to get up to Rohnert Park to see her soon, but that I was busy and couldn't say when. I thought I sounded unnecessarily cold. She died that night. I felt guilty.

I did not grieve openly for Mama. But a great void suddenly loomed. I would think, "I must tell her what happened today." Then I would realize with a start, there was no more Mama to talk to. This pattern slowly faded. God knows I loved her, but at the same time I must admit I felt good about being able to make my own decisions. They were not always wise, but they were my own.

Mama did not want a funeral nor a memorial service. She felt undertaking had become a blatant commercial enterprise and asked me to have her body cremated and to take her ashes back to Greeley and place them next to my father's and her mother's grave.

One of the aides, a shapely blond named April, who had helped take care of Mama during her final three weeks volunteered to help me fly to Colorado. In Denver, we rented a car and she put my manual wheelchair in the trunk for the trip to Greeley. On the back seat rested the plain brown wrapped cardboard box the mortician supplied for Mama's ashes. April and I looked back to see ashes sifting out of the box. We were taken aback but could not repress laughter at the ridiculous situation. In accordance with Mama's wishes, I had a pink peony planted above her ashes so she could return as nourishment for a flowering plant.

Two weeks after Mama passed away, I purchased an early model Macintosh 512k personal computer. I was enthralled by it. Early that year, Jean Hall had taken me to her home in Sausalito and had let me dabble about with her new Macintosh.

I told Mama about it and said I'd like to get one. She said she was sure it was an interesting machine, but she did not share my enthusiasm for computers and other electronic gadgets. She suggested that I think it over until she passed away, then if I still wanted it, buy it. "Learning to use it will give you something to do after I'm gone."

Until I got my Mac, I was at a great disadvantage as a writer: my typing was painfully slow and I had to get everything right the first time. I fumbled around, trying to put paper in the typewriter with my hard-to-control spastic fingers. I couldn't make notes in the margin and then add them when it was retyped. The computer enabled me to cut and paste and move paragraphs around and reorder sentences, and do the things necessary to good writing, just by working at the keyboard. Printing was simpler than typing my name.

Computer technology seems to roll over every two years, so I am currently on my fifth Macintosh. I keep my brokerage account on-line, and all my writing, some recipes, indeed, everything that is put to paper resides within my computer. More recently, I have found vast libraries of information on-line and on the Internet. I find I can scan photographs and print them often better than the original. Each morning I hurry to get to my Mac to see if I have any e-mail.

I planned to live in the old house until my death. I imagined myself continuing Adaptive Physical Education at the College, going down the road in my motorized wheelchair four days a week until I was old and feeble. I found the expense of taking care of the garden was eating me up, as was all the help I required. Because Mama had left me with some stocks, I felt I would never run out of money. Now I found I would have to be very careful and not blow my money. With Mama's death, I lost all my government benefits except a little Social Security.

Mama created a great cosmetic illusion that the house was substantial and sound by keeping it well-painted. I was shocked when a contractor inspected it and said, "Well, parts of it are salvageable." When I read his written report a week later, I knew I had to sell and accept a much lower price than I had dreamed. I thought I had a sale for $400,000, and now I was told the fair market value was closer to $260,000. The property itself was valuable and in an affluent neighborhood, but the foundation was crumbling, the electric wiring was rotten, the water pipes were narrowed from decades of sedimentation, the roof was sway-backed from too many layers of shingles. About the only thing holding it up was the termites. More Scotch tape and baling wire would not save it.

When people told me they thought I was foolish to sell such a lovely old home, I would swallow my feelings and integrity and say I needed more money for help and travel. I thought it might affect the sale if I told everyone the house was a disaster waiting to happen. Leaving the quaint old garden wrenched my gut.

At the college, I had made friends with several people who played a lot of country music. I invited several of them to move in with me. They were old-time hippie type people, brilliant but uninhibited, with long hair, beards and old clothes. They parked their jalopies in my front yard and made the Manor ring with happy music.

When it came time to move, I received a lesson in the triviality of "things." Dishes, furniture, paintings, lamps, jewelry, clothing, and travel memorabilia sold at give-away prices. Antiques that fit in well with Mama's Lady of the Manor lifestyle were not of much use to a disabled bachelor with sturdier needs.

My friends managed a yard sale for me. The seventy foot long porch sagged with cartons of books, dozens of oil paintings, furniture, antique glassware, china, dishes of all kinds, garden tools. A clothesline hung heavy with my garments, from triple knit nylon shirts to all wool sweaters to tailor made shirts of Indonesian batik. I sold most of it, gave the Hospice Thrift shop its pick of the remainder and sent the rest to the dump.

I bought a condominium in the Spyglass Hill complex in the town of Greenbrae, next to Kentfield. I no longer spent my days exercising at the College. Instead, most of my waking hours were spent glued to my Macintosh, writing, writing, writing. I did go in the condominium pool now and then, when I could get help, and some evenings were spent watching a marathon of videos. My magazines went unread.

My new abode suited me. I lived in a large sunny study, where books, a computer, desk and plants, files and birds resided. My days and evenings were spent amidst a chorus of parakeet, cockatiel and finch chatter. If I didn't spend time with them every day and say a few words to them now and then, I felt I was being uncaring. A few Monterey pine trees grew close to the windows on two sides. Sometimes a doe and a fawn browsed under them. Occasionally, a scared skunk loosed its fragrance on the hillside.

For a time, I subscribed to the local paper primarily to find out what the specials were at nearby stores. In short, I was spending money for the paper, so I could pay somebody to drive me to the store to save a few cents on "bargains." I think in the back of my mind was the fear that I would be lonely if I stayed home alone and didn't go out a lot. Gradually, I tightened my budget and hired less help and tried to do more writing.

One April day, three years after I moved, I drove my chair down the hill and on the bike path to the College, then continued on to where Barker Manor had stood. I felt as if I were visiting a profaned temple. The yard had started to lure rubbish—discolored newspapers, discarded bits of building material and old automobile tires. Deep bulldozer ruts scarred the red clay soil from the two day orgy of demolition when the house was razed immediately after my departure. The garden was overgrown with tangled weeds, blackberries and wild roses past their peak. The periwinkle and the deep reddish pink wild valerian were also blooming, as were red roses on the ruins of the redwood rail fence. The house site itself was devoid of vegetation, being clay hardpan.

I found the redwood seedling Mama had given me the last Christmas before her death, smothered in a clutter of weeds and blackberry vines. For my birthday that year, she presented me with a forty foot flagpole implanted in a block of concrete so I could run up Old Glory on my birthday and whenever I felt like it. That too was gone.

I had made a number of friends while working out at the college. The first years after Mama died, I drew on them for my helpers. Among them were two aerobic dance teachers, a private investigator, several musician-composers, several nurses, a book store clerk, a Bible scholar, a cocktail waitress, several students, a Vietnamese refugee lawyer and a couple others I have forgotten. Most worked for me only a few hours a week. All seemed to have a nurturing spirit and to be genuinely interested in my welfare.

One of my helpers frequently caught my eyes covertly observing her superbly sculpted equatorial regions especially when she wore tight jeans or other form fitting pants, and said I had a crotch fixation. Not so nice was the one person who ripped me off, a young woman, borrowing $1,800 with a hard luck story about her infant son. She promised to repay me the next month. I never saw her again. I had liked her a lot and felt betrayed and disappointed, but let it go, thinking it was probably better to be cheated occasionally than not to trust at all.

Luckily, most were like Susan, a high school student, working in the Adaptive Physical Education Program as a summer volunteer aide. She was nicely proportioned, mellow, athletic and to my eye very pretty. I asked her if she could come to my house and get me out of bed and dressed and fix me a simple breakfast on weekend mornings after Mama became too frail to help me. Then, after I moved to Spyglass Hill, I needed her to help me walk in the condominium pool.

Two summers, she helped me exercise a lot. An hour a day in the pool and an hour of stretching exercise on the living room floor. We went a number of places in my van together and had fun. When she left in August to go to physical therapy school at UC Long Beach, I found myself thinking: Susan, I am going to miss you! I love your outgoing, tolerant spirit; your sly sense of humor; your soft voice; your beautiful muscular legs and all the rest of you. What is a mere forty years difference in age? Let's run away together to some tropical isle. It was a lovely dream.

One of my first helpers after I moved was Stanley, a new neighbor, who got me up, showered, shaved and dressed me, and gave me breakfast. A garbage man in Chinatown and a huge bear of a man, Stanley started using drugs in junior high and was hooked on narcotics until he hit bottom with hepatitis. He'd been clean for a decade. He was kind, generous, outgoing and loud. Stanley came again in the early evening to feed me dinner and get me ready for bed, then I was on my own. He loaned me some movie videos, among them *The Last Emperor* and *The Color Purple*. He also encouraged me to economize and scavenged two pairs of athletic shoes for me.

Mary entered my life before Mama died. A pretty, Shanghai Chinese, a mother of three girls, with beautiful white skin, laughing eyes and a glorious smile, she has a quiet nature that spreads itself like oil on troubled waters.

At the time Mary began working for Mama Saturday mornings cleaning house, she had just come to this country by way of Hong Kong and knew only a few words of English. Mama was in the early stages of a partial loss of hearing. Mary's daughter, May, brought her to the house and introduced her. Mama caught only May's name and thought she said her mother's name was Mary. It was not until several years after my mother's death that she told me that I was the only one who called her Mary.

Mama told me, "This woman is a high-class Chinese. It is written in her manner and bearing." After Mama died, I learned Mary's father had been a teacher at a university in Shanghai and Mary had a degree in architectural design from a university in China.

Three months after Mama died, Mary returned to Hong Kong for a year. I liked her and we kept in touch with occasional letters. When she returned, I had moved to Spyglass Hill. I hired her to take care of me on weekends, while she worked weekdays as a baker. Gradually, we have become very close. Now she is my only regular helper and my best friend.

Wall to wall carpeting throughout my new home made getting around on my knees easier. The hardwood floors at Barker Manor gave me recurring bouts of 'housemaid's knee' or chronic bursitis.

Being unable to open and close the door, and come and go at will, was like being a prisoner in my own home. I had a remote control installed that operates on the same principle as a garage door opener.

I bought a new wheelchair with plenty of power, one that tackled tough hills without flinching. I get the same exhilaration from zooming down the steep hills of Spyglass that some men get from skiing down a great slope. I receive a shot of adrenaline and am given cautionary advice about breaking my leg. I need to get out in the wide open spaces and practice my chair driving skills now and then, ventilate my lungs, absorb a little sunshine and say 'Hi' to friendly neighbors.

My first year at Spyglass, I bought a Ford van equipped with a hydraulic wheelchair lift. It had been customized for a fellow student in Laurie's class. He had multiple sclerosis and passed away about the same time as Mama. It was meant to be driven by his father who took meticulous care of it. Mary drives me in the van to do my shopping.

Because I am usually alone at night, I keep a phone on the floor to call 911 and tell the Larkspur Fire Department when I need help. One night I had to call at three in the morning because I was sick at my stomach and slipped down to the floor getting out of bed to go to the bathroom on my knees. When I am flat on the floor, I can roll around and wriggle from one room to the next, but am unable to regain my knees.

I am usually a happy person full of adventurous thoughts, but to be sick and cold and alone and disabled in the middle of the night is not my idea of fun. Several times I suffered from such severe diarrhea and vomiting I decided the end was nigh and had appropriately morbid thoughts.

One Friday night I began sniffling and my throat was scratchy. Saturday, I felt mediocre all day and struggled to bed about ten. About eleven I felt quite ill and got up on my knees, but not before I threw up a little on my bed and my shirt.

I crawled to the study and phoned Mary. She came, gave me a shower, cleaned everything up and put me back in bed about one. By two, I was burning with fever and nauseous again. I knew I had to sit up or lose it again. Instead of getting out of bed onto my knees, I felt myself slipping, so I turned over and was half sitting on the floor with my back to the bed. I dialed 911 on my little remote phone.

I said, "I'm okay, but I need help." The dispatchers knew me by then, and replied, "Is this George at 732 Via Casitas? Did you fall and need help getting back up? I'll dispatch the Larkspur Fire Department." A moment's pause. "The Fire Department is on its way."

I had the firemen put on my shoes and sit me on the sofa in my living room. After they had been gone about an hour, I still felt feverish and nauseous and unable to nod off. At four, I decided I would feel better if I crawled to the bathroom and completely emptied my stomach in the toilet. I did and felt improved, but still unable to sleep after I regained my seat on the sofa. By six, I thought I might as well crawl back to bed. As I was sliding down to get on my knees, I just kept sliding. There I was! Out flat again, unable to regain my knees, with neck and shoulders leaning against the couch. I was not uncomfortable. I heaved a helpless sigh and dozed off, knowing Mary would arrive in two hours.

Despite my tendency to be a recluse during the cold, rainy windy days of winter, I like to be out going somewhere in my chair when Nature smiles. One of my neighbors calls me "Fair Weather George."

When the lady tellers at Home Savings see me coming, they swing the doors open wide and greet me like an old friend. They help me get out my wallet and zip it into my jacket when the transaction is done.

One day, while the weather was pleasantly hot, I thought I would try to go to Larkspur Landing in my motorized wheelchair. After Stanley gave me a shower and dressed me, I chomped down a big bite of chocolate, gulped a mug of coffee and, clutching a long list of grocery and produce specials, had him belt me into my chair and headed by way of a paved bike path for the supermarket at Larkspur Landing Shopping Mall. I was out the door in my wheelchair at ten till nine. At the store forty-five minutes later, I asked a clerk, "Can you help me?" and handed her my list. She called one of the baggers. It took him about forty minutes to get everything on my list and fit it all in my backpack.

Another day, I bought a nine-pound ham shank for Mary to cook and a dozen eggs, then stopped by the book shop to buy a heavy book of publishers' addresses and requirements. Perhaps, it was the extra weight in my backpack or maybe I pushed back too hard with my feet to keep from going in a gutter. Whatever the reason, coming up an especially steep stretch of hill, my wheelchair tipped over on its back. I felt foolish, on my back, belted in my chair, head downhill, looking at my feet. However, I was neither scratched nor bruised, bumped nor rattled.

I thought: if I am patient, someone will come along soon and help me. Help arrived within a minute. Two distraught young women in separate cars stopped and, after ascertaining I was uninjured, pulled the chair upright. Then a city policeman arrived in time to rehang my battery box. Not only was I unscathed, not one egg in my backpack cracked.

Mary and I went to Red Hill Shopping Center for bird food and a few staples one Saturday. Mary wanted something from Long's and I was driving around in my wheelchair with my mind disconnected while waiting for her. I ran into a parked shining red, sports car and slightly scratched the rubber bumper.

The car's owner, a beefy, red-faced man, was speechless with rage. I felt terrible and tried to apologize. He jumped out of his car and tried to push my wheelchair way back on the sidewalk. My chair weighs about 250 pounds with me in it and does not respond to pushing. The brakes lock when it is not put in motion by my controls. I tried to be cooperative and move it back, but the guy pushing on the chair did not help me.

"Now you just stay there until I get my car out," he scowled.

As he drove away with a pretty blond woman, I felt like Don Quixote, an old guy in a wheelchair attacking a shiny red-metal monster. Just the week before, I had listened to the book, *Don Quixote de La Mancha*, and saw a bit of myself, as well as a lot of Papa, in the imagination and posturing and escape from reality of the Knight of the Rueful Figure. When I was a kid and Papa read it to me, I liked the story of the old guy challenging the windmill to battle. Now I relish the mood and the notion there is a little noble craziness in most of us.

Mike Frush, a tall, strong, super polite fellow with glasses, whose great grandfather was raised by the Chinese in San Francisco after his father died playing the piano in a Barbary Coast saloon, worked for the Spyglass management and was a student of Kempo Karate. He had borrowed a video of a martial arts movie filmed in Hong Kong from one of the guys at work. He didn't have a VCR and wondered if I would like to see it. One might think the lust for mayhem should have been civilized out of me. But my mind and body were engaged that night, even in my wheelchair. Mentally, when I am immersed in any story, I have no physical limitations.

Mike did a great job putting in a solid oak portal to replace the cheap-looking, narrow doorway between my living room and study, giving me room to maneuver in my wheelchair. When he finished, he rubbed the oak with lemon oil, after sanding it smooth. It brought out the grain beautifully. We sat in silence and drank coffee and admired his work and the exquisite wood. Every five minutes, one or the other of us would exclaim, "Jesus! I can't believe it's done!" or "God! That wood is beautiful!"

Through Mike, I made friends with a number of foreign students at the College of Marin. When Alfonso, an exuberant, happy intellectual Colombian, needed a place to stay temporarily, Mike asked me if I would be willing to help him out. I said "Okay, but only for a couple of weeks." Within two weeks, I did not want to see Alfonso go. I almost felt he was my son in spirit.

Mike helped me find a typist, Helga, a strong, bright, good-looking Bavarian, who was in the process of becoming Alfonso's girlfriend. It was obvious they belonged together, but both were in the U.S. on temporary visas. They wanted to get married, but had to leave the country soon. Finally, they decided they would get married here and live in Germany, after consulting the German Consulate and James, a Roman Catholic priest and a mutual friend.

Helga's visa expired. She, Alfonso, Mike, Father James and I drove up to Reno, Nevada, in my van. We promptly found the Marriage License Office, then a Marriage Chapel. Mike was the best man and he and I were both witnesses. After that we went to dinner and did a bit of gambling. It was a wonderfully happy time.

Travel was difficult for me, but I enjoyed it. After Mama died, I made my first big trip abroad with Denise. Statuesque Denise, a young street-wise intellectual, skate shop owner, and long distance mountain bike racer, whom I met when she volunteered as a student aide in Laurie's class, was my helper on a fast trip to Seoul, Hong Kong and Guangzhou (formerly called Canton) in Red China. She had been extra kind to Mama and volunteered to stay up all night and look after her one weekend when everyone else begged off.

I bought a lightweight sports wheelchair to take with us because it would be impossible to take my motorized chair. Most Asian cities are not adapted for disabled people. The curbs are often small cliffs and the side streets and lanes are frequently paved with cobblestone, if not plain dirt, and are bumpily uneven.

Denise and I made all our travel arrangements by phone with an agent in Millbrae. We did not tell her I was disabled because I knew the People's Republic of China discouraged the disabled and elderly from undergoing the rigors of their guided tours. China is so densely populated and poor that disabled people's needs have a low priority. Even in one of Guangzhou's best Western-style hotels, the White Swan, a super-luxurious one in any language, architectural barriers abound in the form of stairs. Denise had to help me stand, walk me up steps, lean me against a wall, run down stairs, drag the chair up and help me sit down.

Our Chinese tour guide lifted and dragged me on and off our minibus, while Denise tried to explain that we could do it, that I could walk with help. The guide told Denise at every stop of the bus, "He doesn't want to get out here. Many steps. Very difficult." She told him firmly that it was up to me. I usually went anyway. We were with a small group of British and they were helpful, assisting me on the other arm going on stairs. I was prepared for the primitive rest rooms and avoided using them by limiting my liquid intake.

That same May, Peter and I went for a three week journey to Greece, Israel and Egypt. Relaxed, plainly dressed, sturdy as a bull, he was a songwriter, amateur geologist, botanist and watercolorist. He had read the Bible through a number of times and in several languages. He worked for me as my gardener at Barker Manor. When I moved to Spyglass Hill, he brought his skill as a carpenter to help me adapt my condo to my needs. For a time, he helped me get up in the morning. As he fed me breakfast, he read to me out of the red leather-bound Bible he gave me. Before we knew it, he had read the entire New Testament.

As I listened, I recognized that my cultural and spiritual roots were as much in Jerusalem and Nazareth as in Yorkshire and Edinburgh. Papa and Mama, though not active church people, lived by religious principles and were well-versed in the Bible. Some of their most interesting expressions were taken from the Old and New Testaments.

My friend Celinda from Tsimshatsui days had married an Israeli shipping executive and moved to Haifa. Several years later he died and she moved to Frankfurt, Germany. We kept up an irregular correspondence. When Celinda wrote me that she was returning to Haifa to sell her apartment, I seized the chance to invite myself and Peter to visit her and the holy places in Israel.

We went first to Greece where Peter pushed, pulled and dragged my wheelchair to the Parthenon atop the Acropolis in Athens. He managed to take me by bus to the mountain village of Delphi, home of the Oracle. In our chalet room overlooking the Sacred Plain, planted with olive trees, I had a tremendous sense of well-being, as if I'd found the "navel of the world," which the ancient Greeks called Delphi. At my suggestion, we stayed an extra day.

Celinda met us at the airport in Tel Aviv. She was the same tiny, lively, indomitable person I had known two decades earlier. We rented a Subaru Justy and drove to her apartment in a working class section of Haifa. It was about forty-five minutes drive from Nazareth and less than two hours from Capernaum on the Sea of Galilee, where Jesus gathered the disciples and did some of his most important teaching.

Peter told an Eastern European Jewish couple, neighbors of Celinda's, we planned to travel through Israel's hill country the following day. The Jewish couple became serious. They said, "You're going through Nablus? Very dangerous. Tomorrow is the twentieth anniversary of the six-day war. We would not go near Nablus! Maybe no rock will be thrown, but I would not guarantee anything."

Against his urgent inner feelings, Peter agreed to follow Celinda's neighbor's advice and take the level, orange-grove-covered coastal road, which we had seen on the ride to Haifa. As we left, we asked directions to the coastal road. Someone made a mistake, and we were headed to Nablus. Peter insisted it was not planned.

The inhabitants of Nablus were kind and helpful. Here, Celinda showed her formidable side. She commandeered help, and at Jacob's Well performed the feat of persuading the lone teenage boy in charge into letting us in wearing shorts. For Celinda, all rules and regulations had an exception, and we were always it.

Peter's insistence on our seeing every significant Biblical site possible in ten days required him to push me in my manual wheelchair for miles through the rough streets of Jerusalem, Nazareth and Bethlehem, up and down hills and steps, many of them quite steep. Often, on the more difficult steps, he helped me walk up and down. He pushed me around the archeological site of the Dead Sea scrolls in the terrible midday heat. And he drove miles through incredible deserts and the lush Jordan River Valley.

I had told Peter my father was fond of quoting Christ's Sermon on the Mount, so he made a point of taking us to the Church of the Beatitudes on the Mount near Capernaum. We arrived in the late afternoon to find it was closed for the day. Celinda employed her persuasive powers to prevail on the kindly Italian nuns in charge to let us have a quick look inside the Church of the Beatitudes just after closing hours.

Peter positioned himself outside the door to get a picture of Celinda wheeling me out of the church. In Old Jerusalem, I'd experienced Celinda's way with a wheelchair, as we charged through crowded streets with abandon, heedless of the feet and ankles of the multitudes. Peter looked through his camera lens to see Celinda wheeling me quickly toward the limestone steps of the church, and, hitting them at an angle, tipping me sideways, over and out. I banged my head on the stone stairs but somehow managed to avoid injury. Several nuns came rushing in alarm. I assured them I was all right.

Peter took me back the next day to visit the place and to reassure the Sisters that I was uninjured. We spent the morning soaking in the feeling of that idyllic spot overlooking the Sea of Galilee.

In 1994, for my sixty-ninth birthday, I realized a lifelong ambition to visit French Polynesia. Mary and I relaxed for two weeks in thatched cottages on lagoons in Moorea and Bora Bora, and the Hyatt on Tahiti, enjoying the tropical beauty and flowers of the islands, the easy warmth of the Polynesian people, and the breezes.

Ten days after Mary and I returned from French Polynesia, Mike and I flew to Munich for a reunion and sightseeing with Alfonso and Helga. The next year, Alfonso called to tell me I was a grandpa, that Helga had just given birth to a baby boy.

Angel, our plump, brown-skinned, middle-aged tour guide on Moorea, called me Papa. I accept the fact that I am getting old. Sometimes it depresses me to think I have done so little with my life. Too many daydreams and not enough focused labor. Then I think—what the Hell! Before another seventy years have passed, most of my generation will have been forgotten anyway. And I've had an interesting life.

On my first visit to Hong Kong in 1956, Edith introduced me to a blind Chinese astrologer who told me my fortune would flourish late in life. I believed him then, and I still have hope.

In 1996, I went to Belize with Mary. I had kept in touch with Johnny Chee, and he had visited me in Kentfield and Greenbrae. I saw him waving as we stepped off the plane at the airport in Belize City. He drove us around town before heading east toward Belmopan, the capital with a population of about four thousand people. By the time we got to Belmopan, the sun was starting to set and there was a gorgeous red moon on the horizon, silhouetting tropical vegetation, the rain forest. We spent the night at his city house. It was only partly finished, and we roughed it.

I'd read on the Internet about Rudy and Margaret's Stone Cottages near Xunantunich ruins near the Guatamalan border. I'd written them I was in a wheelchair, so they built two big ramps for me. We enjoyed Margaret's English-style cooking with a Central American accent, and the laughter of the young village women, Shelley and Flora, coming from the kitchen. Rudy took us somewhere nearly every day—the rain forest, the Medicine Trail where many of the jungle medicine trees of the Maya grow and are marked by signs, a Guatamalan border village, the clinic where Margaret, a nurse from Yorkshire, provides medical care for the villagers, the nearby town of San Ignacio, the Mayan temple on the hill. He introduced me to Elicio Cocun, the elderly Mayan watchman who had been raised in the nearby village and whose first language is Mayan. The old man brought me a corn tamale boiled in a banana leaf. I gave him one of my t-shirts. Like most Mayans, he was small, under five feet. We became friends.

The rain forest, the warmth of the climate, the people and the Mayan mystique of Belize struck a spiritual chord in me. The Belizeans I met are warm and uncomplicated. Johnny has prospered and owns land and a big farm and several small businesses. I asked him how much it would cost for me to buy a house. He said he would build one for me for ten thousand dollars on land he owns. We shook hands on it and grinned. He tells me I can live okay on my limited resources. As I grow older, I require more help, which I can afford there. Johnny is married to an American nurse and she wrote me that she could understand why I would rather go to Belize than risk going into a nursing home, as she had been a supervisor of a large nursing facility in Oregon before she hit the road to Belize.

Living in the U.S. is difficult for elderly disabled people without big bucks. Marin County is lovely, but no longer the semi-rural Paradise that drew me there fifty years ago. Back to nature and bugs and all the rest! I look forward to getting acquainted with Belize and my new neighbors. One more adventure—a Mayan Moon Gate Dream.

The End.